Irish Urban Cultures

Edited by
Chris Curtin
Hastings Donnan
Thomas M Wilson

Institute of Irish Studies
The Queen's University of Belfast

First published 1993
by the Institute of Irish Studies
The Queen's University of Belfast
University Road, Belfast

ISBN 0 85389 502 3

Printed by W. & G. Baird Ltd, Antrim

Contents

Acknowledgements

Grateful acknowledgement for financial assistance is made to the Cultural Traditions programme of the Community Relations Council which aims to encourage acceptance and understanding of cultural diversity. We also thank Anthony Sheehan of the Arts Computing Unit of The Queen's University of Belfast, whose help in the production of a final manuscript was invaluable, and Michael Donnelly of University College Galway, who prepared the index.

Contributors

Marilyn Cohen teaches in the Sociology Department at Montclair State College in New Jersey. Her research on the development of the linen industry in County Down has resulted in numerous articles. She is at present editing a book of interdisciplinary approaches to the Irish linen industry.

Chris Curtin is Professor of Political Science and Sociology at University College, Galway. He is the author and co-editor of many books and articles, including *Gender in Irish Society* (1987, Galway University Press) and *Ireland From Below* (1989, Galway University Press). His current research interests are collective action, social movements, agrarian politics, and state-voluntary relations.

Eoin Devereux lectures in sociology at the University of Limerick. He did his B.A. and M.A. degrees in sociology at University College, Galway. Currently an RTE Research Fellow at Dublin City University, he is writing a doctoral dissertation on the portrayal of poverty on Irish television.

Hastings Donnan is Reader in Social Anthropology at The Queen's University of Belfast. He is the editor of *Man: the Journal of the Royal Anthropological Institute*. He is also the author of *Marriage among Muslims: Preference and Choice in Northern Pakistan* (1988, E. J. Brill) and co-editor of several books including *Social Anthropology and Public Policy in Northern Ireland* (1989, Gower).

Stephen Gaetz studied anthropology at the University of Calgary and York University in Toronto. In addition to his work on youth, public policy, and community development in Ireland, he has carried out research on the punk subculture in Toronto.

Jane Helleiner lectures in anthropology at Brock University, Ontario. Her doctoral thesis (1992, University of Toronto) is entitled *The Travelling People: Cultural Identity in Ireland.*

Richard Jenkins is Reader in Sociology and Anthropology at the University College of Swansea, Wales, and was educated at The Queen's University of Belfast and the University of Cambridge. He has done research in Northern Ireland, England, and South Wales. His most recent book is *Pierre Bourdieu* (1992, Routledge).

Lee Komito is a Newman Research Scholar in the Department of Sociology in University College, Dublin. He received his PhD in anthropology from the University of Pennsylvania. His current research focuses on the implications of new communications technologies on transnational culture, altered definitions of community, and social structure.

Barbara LeMaster teaches anthropology and linguistics at the California State University in Long Beach, and holds a postdoctoral position in the UCLA Medical School. Her research has focused on identity, gender and language variation in the United States and Ireland.

Kay Milton is Lecturer in Social Anthropology at The Queen's University of Belfast. Her doctoral research was on Christianity in rural Kenya, and her current research interest is in environmentalism as a cultural perspective. In 1992 she convened the annual conference of the Association of Social Anthropologists, on the subject of anthropological perspectives on environmentalism, and has edited the conference volume (1993, Routledge).

Liam O'Dowd is Reader in Sociology in The Queen's University of Belfast. He is the author and co-editor of several books and articles, including *Culture and Ideology in Ireland* (1984, Galway University Press) and *Ireland: A Sociological Profile* (1986, Institute of Public Administration). He is chairman of the Royal Irish Academy's National Committee for Economic and Social Sciences.

Eoin O'Sullivan is a graduate of University College Galway and the University of Limerick. He is currently a research and information officer with the Streetwise National Coalition in Dublin, and a teaching assistant in the Department of Sociology, Trinity College Dublin, where he is engaged in post-graduate research.

Marilyn Silverman is Associate Professor of Anthropology at York University, Toronto. She has carried out field research in Guyana, Ecuador, and Ireland, and is the author and editor of numerous books and articles in political and historical anthropology, including *Approaching the Past: Historical Anthropology Through Irish Case Studies* (1992, Columbia University Press).

Hervé Varenne is Professor of Education at Teachers College, Columbia University. Born and raised in France, he received his doctorate in anthropology from the University of Chicago. He is the author of many books and articles on aspects of everyday life and education in the United States, including *Americans Together* (1977, Teachers College Press) and *Ambiguous Harmony* (1992, Ablex).

Thomas M Wilson is Senior Research Fellow in the Institute of European Studies, The Queen's University of Belfast. He is currently conducting research on the impact of the European Community's single market on communities in Ireland. He is the co-editor of *Cultural Change and the New Europe* (1993, Westview) and *Ireland From Below* (1989, Galway University Press).

1   Anthropology and Irish urban settings

**Chris Curtin, Hastings Donnan and
Thomas M. Wilson**

For over fifty years anthropological research in Ireland has focused most of
its efforts on the countryside. This is true both of Northern Ireland and of the
Republic. While some see this as an unhealthy bias which deflects attention
from more pressing issues, many of which are acutely manifest in Ireland's
towns and cities, others see it as perfectly justifiable and even desirable given
the distribution of the island's population. Both positions clearly have merit
and it is not the aim of this volume to argue for either of them, nor indeed
even to suggest that a characteristically different kind of anthropology can be
found in urban areas even if it may be possible to identify distinctively urban
issues. To argue too forcefully for either view would be to risk a crude
compartmentalisation into urban and rural which this book would like to
avoid, its title notwithstanding! It is certainly no insight, even if in practice
it is observed more often in the breach, to insist that city and countryside
must be seen as bound by mutually dependent relationships, a sense of which
is essential if either is to be adequately understood (see Leeds 1988). In this
regard, the present collection of essays, by directing attention to Irish urban
life, is intended to be read as a companion volume to an earlier compendium
which brought together the best of contemporary Irish rural ethnography (see
Curtin and Wilson 1989).

But, ambitiously perhaps, this book tries to do more than provide what
otherwise might seem a parochial overview of Irish urban cultures. By
pointing to the similarities and differences between Irish towns and cities and
those elsewhere, and by suggesting that Ireland might have much to offer
urban ethnographers in general, it raises questions about why Ireland has not
figured more prominently in broadly comparative anthropological overviews
of urban life. With only one or two exceptions, Irish ethnography generally
is barely known beyond the small body of scholars with a professional
interest in the island. In fact, much of the existing ethnographic writing on
Ireland has focused on either the praise or the condemnation of the few
works which have influenced anthropological discourse outside of Ireland, a

theme which we return to later. Such academic insularity, to which ethnographers of Ireland have perhaps too readily acquiesced, and by their projects have arguably helped to perpetuate, may well, of course, turn out to be deserved; however, we suggest below that hitherto the negligible impact of Irish ethnography beyond its own shores has been a consequence of what has been constructed by insiders and outsiders alike as being of interest about the island, both historically and intellectually.

Irish urban life

Seen in the context of the island as a whole, Irish urban growth has developed along two distinct trajectories, each now clearly marked by the fracture of the political border which separates Northern Ireland's six counties in 'the north' from the twenty-six county Republic in 'the south'.[1] Baldly stated, while the bases of modern urban industrial life were established early in the north, alongside the development in the north-east especially of the ship-building and linen industries, urban centres expanded rather more slowly in the south, largely due to the Republic's relatively late industrialisation (O'Malley 1985). Between 1841 and 1911 the rate of urban growth was much faster in the north than anywhere else in Ireland (Clarkson 1985: 139; in fact, the urban population in the south declined during this period, see McKeown 1986: 365). As a consequence, north and south have each been characterised by a set of urban 'problems' distinct in certain but not all respects.

This can be seen in the everyday lives of those who live in urban areas on each side of the border and who to some extent experience a different set of problems associated with urban existence. In the twenty-six counties, as a result of recent urban growth, the problem many people are facing is one of coming to grips with city life as they leave their rural homes for the promise of the Dublin suburbs. In contrast, the north has had a different set of problems because of its longstanding urban character; historically these have involved the cultural, social, political and economic peripheralization and isolation of large chunks of the countryside which, when layered on other differences, particularly religion, configured relatively early relationships which are still being played out today. Thus Protestant Belfast was able to gather to itself the reigns of hegemonic control and to dominate the rest of the province after the country's partition in 1921. In short, while Belfast dominated its rural periphery, the reverse was true for Dublin. Thus Garvin (1974) observes that the Republic provides an example of a polity in which rural ideological concerns and political preferences dominated the urban centre.

This fundamental difference in Irish urban development can also be detected in the kinds of problems which have preoccupied different types of urban researcher on each side of the border. Not surprisingly perhaps, the spatial dimension of urban sectarianism has occupied considerable attention in the north, particularly among urban and social geographers. Of special interest here has been how rising levels of sectarian violence have sharpened territorial boundaries, particularly in working class areas, with sizeable population movements leading to residential segregation in single religion enclaves (Boal 1970; 1976; 1981; 1982; Boal et al. 1976; Darby 1986). Sectarian spatial patterns did not, of course, emerge in isolation but developed in harness with early urban industrial growth which in the north drew skilled labour from like-minded people of similar faith. The linen and ship-building industries, in particular, prompted dramatic urban growth in the north (see, for example, Beckett 1969: xiii; Camblin 1951), with Belfast soon overtaking and quickly outstripping all other major Irish urban centres by the late nineteenth century (its population quadrupled between 1841 and 1911; see Table 1).[2] These developments are now well documented, and economic and social historians have done much to illuminate, *inter alia*, the articulation among sectarianism, industry, and urban expansion (see, for example, Beckett et al. 1983; Geary and Johnson 1989; Hepburn and Collins 1981; and see Clarkson 1985 for a discussion of the different kinds of factors leading to urban growth in the north).

	1841	1851	1861	1871	1881	1891	1901	1911
Dublin	232,726	246,679	246,465	246,326	249,602	245,001	290,638	304,802
Cork	80,720	82,625	79,594	78,642	80,124	75,345	76,122	76,673
Limerick	48,391	48,785	43,924	39,353	38,562	37,155	38,151	38,518
Waterford	23,216	22,979	22,869	23,349	22,457	20,852	26,769	27,464
Galway	17,275	20,055	16,448	15,597	15,471	13,800	13,426	13,255
Belfast	75,308	97,784	119,393	174,412	208,122	255,950	349,180	386,947
Derry	15,196	19,727	20,519	25,242	29,162	33,200	39,892	40,780

Table 1
Urban growth in Ireland 1841 - 1911
Source: Vaughan and Fitzpatrick 1978: 28-41

In the south, studies have focused on a small number of urban themes. These include the expansion or decline of individual towns and cities and the social, economic and political connections and exchanges between urban centres and the rural hinterlands. For example, Clark (1979) emphasises the role of urban groups, in particular merchants and shopkeepers, in the Irish agrarian revolution. A century later the same groups were to the fore in collective efforts to initiate economic development (Curtin and Varley 1986). Since urbanisation has become such an important feature in the dynamics of demographic change in the past three decades, migration patterns and the concentration of population and economic activity in urban areas have received considerable attention (Cawley 1991; Hourihan 1982). Finally, as Dublin contains almost one third of the Republic's population, it is not surprising that it should receive special notice. In the Dublin context attention has focused on subjects such as social area analysis (Hourihan 1978), housing and class relations (Byrne 1984), transport systems (Horner 1988), neighbourhood and community action (Kellegher and Whelan 1992), and uneven economic development (Hourihan 1991; National Economic and Social Council 1979).

Nevertheless, it would be a mistake to over-emphasise the differences between urbanisation in north and south. There are a number of common themes which are in effect composing parallel narratives of urban life throughout Ireland. Violence in the street and in the home has become a common concern for all Irish, and one not confined to working class and inner city life. Conflict in both the domestic and public domains is fast becoming part of Ireland's suburban character. All urban areas are suffering the effects of poor planning policies, and are experiencing policy disputes over transportation, environmentalism, housing, and equal rights for all minorities. All of these developments are reflections of the increasing internationalization of Irish cities, resulting from such disparate forces as tourism, international town-twinning, multinational corporate relocation, the global media, and the supranationalism of the European Community. The commonalities and differences between and among Irish towns and cities are increasingly the focus of a number of disciplines, most of which came to the study of Irish urbanism relatively recently. Irish urban history, for example, was in its infancy only a decade or two ago (Harkness and O'Dowd 1981: 1; MacNiocaill 1981: 7), but it has matured quickly, and more recently has produced some challenging and innovative insights into the origins and subsequent development of Irish urban areas (for a selection of such work, see Graham and Proudfoot 1993).[3] Unfortunately the same cannot be said of anthropology which has arguably still to make its mark. In certain respects this is surprising, given the fact that Ireland was one of the earliest European locations to be studied by anthropologists (Haddon and Browne 1891;

Arensberg and Kimball 1968) and given that what eventually came to be called 'urban anthropology' developed early in the discipline as a whole.

Why this should have been so is more fully considered later in this chapter, but for the moment we might note that in this respect early Irish ethnography was little different to that being carried out contemporaneously throughout Europe and North America, where the study of the social life of cities was largely left to sociologists and historians. Instead, those cities to capture the imagination of the early urban ethnographers were those of the developing world, particularly African and Latin American cities, many of which exhibited novel social, economic and cultural forms generated in the wake of rapidly growing migrant populations. Two broad strands might therefore be said to characterise the early social scientific study of the city: one sociological, based mainly on the study of North American cities and associated with the 'Chicago School', the other anthropological, focused mainly on Africa, and linked to the 'Manchester School', though the value of such labelling must remain chiefly organisational given the many convergences as well as divergences between these two developments.

While it is unnecessary to elaborate at length on the content of these two 'schools', since a number of excellent overviews of each already exist (see, in particular, Hannerz 1980; see also Sanjek 1990), it is perhaps worth remembering that some of the questions asked by each were similar and arose in response to broadly similar circumstances. Cities in pre- and post-war North America and in Africa at the end of the colonial era were in the process of responding to the heterogeneity of immigrant and other ethnic residents, and while there were obvious differences between these places, similar questions could be asked of each: how does urbanisation affect the culture of the new arrivals? How are patterns of sociality transformed by city life? What becomes of people's traditional ties and alignments?

Such questions were of particular concern to the Manchester School and resulted in the famous Copperbelt studies by Wilson, Gluckman, Epstein, Mitchell and Pons, among others. Chicago too was a crossroads for diverse populations (see Hannerz 1980: 19), its sociologists exploring the heterogeneity of city life styles, producing studies not only of immigrant neighbourhoods (for example, Wirth 1928), but also of street gangs, the homeless, and others at the margins of society. Indeed, as Hannerz remarks, the Chicago School pioneered

> virtually all the kinds of topical anthropologies in the city which we are
> used to by now: studies of ethnic enclaves, gang studies, studies of deviant
> occupations, studies of behavior in public places or of public entertainment,
> studies of mixed neighborhoods (1980: 55).

The influence of the Chicago School was not confined to the study of the United States; it also stimulated early ethnographic explorations of urban-rural relationships in Latin America (as begun by Redfield 1941). Latin America later became the focus of what might be considered a third strand in the development of urban anthropology.[4]   This concentrated initially on shanty towns and squatter settlements (see, for example, Epstein 1972; Lloyd 1979; Lomnitz 1977), exposing the state's inability to deliver adequate or efficient public services (see Castells 1983), but it later emphasised how cities are embedded culturally, politically and economically in wider national and international networks which move capital and labour round the globe. Such work has done much to reveal the impact of world economic forces on cities (see, for example, Rollwagen 1980; Wolfe 1980). But though the role of world market forces in shaping cities is now widely recognised, it is only very recently that the historical development of this process has been fully appreciated. At the same time there is occasionally a tendency to treat the historical phenomenon of urbanisation as a 'nationally autonomous process' (King 1990: 130). By documenting the articulation of local and wider regional and international forces in the urbanisation of Gilford and Thomastown respectively, this is a tendency which Cohen and Silverman in their contributions to this volume are careful to avoid.

These three strands arguably combine to differentiate an anthropological perspective on the city from the perspectives of other types of social researcher working there. Sometimes, though, exaggerated claims have been made for the novelty of the former and, at best, a distinctive anthropology of the city remains a promise (Kenny and Kertzer 1983: 5). It certainly seems to have been more elusive than some would claim.[5] It has been argued that anthropology's distinctiveness lies in one or other combination of the following: in a holistic approach which seeks to study the city in its totality, and to demonstrate how the different forces at work interrelate and integrate in particular cases (see, for example, Fox 1972); in avoiding the contextual fragmentation of city sub-cultures (for example, street corner gangs, drunks, ex-convicts) which is allegedly characteristic of other kinds of urban research (Ansari and Nas 1983: 2); in providing the 'micro' side of social life to complement the 'macro' picture painted by other kinds of urban researcher (Eames and Goode 1973), in bridging the gap between microsocial studies of inter-personal relations and macrosocial studies of urban structures (Southall 1973: 7); and in its methods of data collection which provide 'a view of how people's lives are actually lived' (Kenny and Kertzer 1983: 5).[6]

While each of these possibilities does go part way to distinguishing anthropology in cities from other disciplines, counter examples can be adduced for all: other urban researchers sometimes adopt an ethnographic approach, anthropologists sometimes fragment the subject of their study and so on. There is little of intellectual value to be gained by defending disciplinary boundaries in this way; on the contrary, by their very nature, the study of cities demands disciplinary transgression. Yet it would be equally erroneous to suggest that anthropology has no insights of its own to contribute. The value of using anthropological methods and theories, and the benefits of being able to draw on an extensive body of comparative knowledge and experience, have been useful for explaining a number of features of urban life world wide. In short, anthropological theories and methods can produce valuable insights irrespective of the social environment to which they are applied as we hope the essays in this collection demonstrate.

So while anthropologists may have come late to the study of Irish urban cultures, they came with already formed theoretical and methodological assumptions and with a clearly defined set of notions about what was of interest to ethnographers in urban settings (these are listed, with attendant criticisms, in Sanjek 1990: 152). Not surprisingly, most of the chapters in this volume touch on these classic urban anthropology themes -- urban poverty (O'Dowd, Helleiner), rural-urban migration (Cohen), adaptation to urban life (Helleiner, O'Sullivan, Varenne) -- but most of them also address issues which Sanjek (1990: 152) points out were largely ignored by the previous generation of urban ethnographers: the urban middle and lower middle classes (Varenne), the history and geography of urban development (Cohen, O'Dowd, Silverman), public policies, urban protest groups and grassroots politics (Milton, O'Dowd, Komito, Devereux), gender divisions (LeMaster), youth cultures (Gaetz), and the production of culture (Jenkins).

Thus, most of the themes which define the anthropological experience in the world today can be found in Irish towns and cities. This volume's contributors explore contests over space, wealth, and power, in which the symbolic constructions of community appear to be dialectically related to material survival strategies. Minority groups such as Travellers and the Dublin deaf construct and reproduce urban culture in ways which are influencing the future of Irish cities. In some communities violence is becoming as important in everyday life as it is in New York and Rio de Janeiro. In fact, in all ways except perhaps size -- urban spaces are, after all, quite small in Ireland in comparison to just about anywhere else in the world -- the anthropology of Irish towns and cities mirrors the anthropology of urban and rural areas everywhere. 'Urban' is no longer the defining feature of a special or particular sub-discipline. We agree with Sanjek, who suggests that "'urban anthropology' as we knew it in the 1950s-1970s is dead . . . urban anthropology is diffusing into a reintegrated social-cultural anthropology" (1990: 154).

The convergence of urban and other types of social anthropology, or the dissolving of urban anthropology into the wider field, should not be seen to be a suggestion that certain issues are not primarily or even uniquely 'urban'. On the contrary, a 'new' urban anthropology is a recommitment to apply the methods and theories of social anthropology to or among communities of people wherever they are, and in whatever size of community they reside. This anthropology of urban life seeks to remove disciplinary barriers which were constructed in the past in order to validate an anthropology of modernisation, industrialism, and the modern world. This disciplinary claim has been staked. This battle won. Now anthropologists must return to the comparative analysis of society and culture in every 'urban' and 'rural' area, however these are defined by both researchers and inhabitants. For Irish anthropology to achieve this a number of stereotypical images, of internal and external origin, must be overcome.

Urban ethnography and anthropological images of Ireland

We mentioned earlier that while there has been an anthropology of urban issues for many parts of the world, to date there has been very little in Ireland. It is therefore not surprising to find that Sanjek (1990) makes no reference to Ireland in his survey of world urban anthropology in the 1980s. Nevertheless, there are a number of urban ethnographies from both Northern Ireland and the Republic, though in both places these have focused on remarkably few locations.

For example, Dublin has been the most studied urban area in the south. Even so, there have been relatively few anthropological studies there. Indeed, apart from Humphrey's (1966) analysis of the effects of urbanisation on the structure of family and community, anthropological research with a Dublin ethnographic base has been thin on the ground. Komito (1989) has explored the special character of Dublin politics, a theme he returns to in this book; Bennett (1984) has explored the lives of hawkers in Dublin's City Quay; and Gmelch (1977; 1980) and Gmelch (1989) have focused on the Travellers in Dublin. But outside of Dublin there has been very little done. Bax (1976) has documented the political rivalries and tensions between town-based elites in County Cork; Eipper (1986) has explored the relationships between church, business and the state in the context of the intervention of a transnational oil corporation in Bantry; and Harris (1984) and Ruane (1989) have examined the impact of industrialisation on gender divisions and the relations between 'locals' and 'outsiders' in Mayo and Clare respectively. More recently, historical anthropological research in a number of towns and cities has been highlighted by Silverman and Gulliver (1992).

The most intensive and coherent body of urban Irish ethnographic analyses comes from Northern Ireland, where a dichotomy developed between rural village studies and urban ethnographies. The former tended to focus on integrative forces and peaceful co-existence (see Leyton 1974; Buckley 1982; Bufwack 1982; Larsen 1982a; 1982b), while the latter recognised both the pervasiveness of violence and the ability of people to adapt to it in ways which allow them to move in and out of private and public domains in order to get on with their day to day lives (for a discussion of this rural-urban ethnographic divergence, see Donnan and McFarlane 1986). Because of rather than in spite of 'the troubles', as the northern sectarian conflict is locally referred to, ethnographers in Northern Ireland's towns and cities have had to deal with everyday conditions of war (Sluka 1989), and to understand the many ways that 'formations of violence' both construct and deconstruct urban lives (Feldman 1991). One aspect of this, for example, has been to document how urban space is 'ritually' marked out at certain times of the year -- the so-called 'marching season' -- when the opposing sides to the conflict stage their respective commemorative processions (see Cecil 1993; Jarman 1992; in press).

However, not all urban ethnographic research in Northern Ireland has concentrated on violence and war, nor has it all been undertaken by anthropologists. For example, sociologists and political scientists have conducted field research in Belfast neighbourhoods or in the city more generally (Burton 1978; Nelson 1984; Brewer 1990). The clearest and strongest analyses of class in all of Irish anthropology come out of Northern Ireland, especially from its working class housing estates (see Bell 1990; Jenkins 1982; 1983; Howe 1990). With all of this research and writing taking place, much of it in just Derry and Belfast, it is surprising that the interests and research designs of the large number of Irish and visiting ethnographers do not turn away from the few stereotypical models that seem to inform most anthropological research on the island. We shall hazard a description of these models, and proffer some explanations as to why they are so dominant in Irish anthropology, in an effort (another in a series of attempts) to reset the research agenda of Irish anthropology (Wilson 1984; Donnan and McFarlane 1986; Kane et al. 1988; Curtin and Wilson 1989).

In the south the powerful influence of Arensberg and Kimball's (1968) *Family and community in Ireland* stimulated a series of would-be successors to come to Ireland in search of stable small-farm dominated communities. By contrast, the urban dimension to Arensberg and Kimball's study — that is, their work on the town of Ennis — has received much less attention, even though it was based on a much sounder ethnographic footing than their work in rural areas. By the 1970s the search for 'community' had proved futile and even the status of the ethnographic base of the original study was questioned (Gibbon 1973). Attention was subsequently focused on rural decline, anomie and communal demoralisation. The theme of the dying peasant culture of the remote rural west (Brody 1973; Scheper-Hughes 1979) came to dominate anthropological research in the south, almost to the exclusion of everything else. Ironically, it was this theme which filtered from wider scholarly consciousness Arensberg and Kimball's perceptive remarks on the Irish urban process (see Bell and Newby 1971: 131-7).

The anthropology of the Republic of Ireland, then, has caricatured 'Ireland as a dying society, a culture in demise, a social system characterized by pathogenic tendencies' (Peace 1989: 89). Many anthropologists, many of whom are visitors to the island, ethnocentrically reinvent the Irish as a type of non-Western 'other'. In his review of this influential academic literature, Peace (1989: 105) concludes that 'the essential problem lies not with Irish society but with the anthropology of the ethnic Irish'.

The ethnography of Northern Ireland, on the other hand, has scrupulously avoided portraying the province in terms of societies and cultures in decline. This has as much to do with the academic training and intellectual biases of the researchers (most of whom have been trained as social anthropologists, i.e. in the British tradition) as it does with the structures of Northern Irish society itself. The image that has prevailed in the ethnographies of Northern Ireland, however, is that of two diametrically opposed 'communities' or 'cultures' (i.e., those of Catholics and Protestants) who, in spite of a host of reasons which divide them, are able to tolerate each other in most every day situations.

A long series of ethnographic studies has explored the cultural and socio-structural bases for what appears to be an essential contradiction in a Northern Ireland rent by the troubles: how can these two groups with different pasts, values, behavioural patterns, and cultural trajectories, share the same space? This 'tribal' model of Northern Ireland has a long pedigree (ancestral highpoints include Harris 1972; Leyton 1975; Glassie 1982; Larsen 1982a; 1982b; Buckley 1982; Bufwack 1982; for an overview of the 'tribal' image more generally in commentaries on Northern Ireland, see McCann 1987). Most of these works go to great lengths to explain peaceful co-existence in Northern Ireland in spite of both the intrinsic cultural differences between the two groups and the violence that for a quarter of a century has put the province on the world's stage. While there are ethnographic exceptions to this pattern of tribal space and tolerance, some of which have explored the causes and effects of violence in and between communities (see, for example, Sluka 1989; Feldman 1991; Vincent 1989), the totality of Northern Irish anthropology results in an image of sectarianism and traditional cultural incompatibility between disputing clans. It would be outlandish to deny the accuracies of much of this literature - in fact, to us it would seem that most of the anthropology of Northern Ireland has been both more accurate and more relevant than that of the Republic - but we must also point out that much that is true of everyday life in Northern Ireland is being ignored by anthropologists, who seem intent on explaining the 'tribal' relations of the province to each new generation of scholars. Initiatives have begun which seek to address other problems in Northern Ireland besides the troubles (Donnan and McFarlane 1989; see also Jenkins 1989), but the cultures of anthropology in and out of Ireland present formidable barriers to any ethnographic explorations which depart from the models of 'anomie' and 'tribalism'. Such typifications have created 'zones of cultural invisibility' and thus continue to exclude important problems from ethnographic study (Rosaldo 1988: 79).

One of the continuing, if only informal, debates among Irish anthropologists (as opposed to anthropologists of Ireland) is the relative lack of an impact which their research has had on international scholarship. There are exceptions of course (such as the debate on the Irish stem family; cf. Gibbon and Curtin 1978; 1983; Varley 1983; Harris 1988; Shanks 1987), but most 'Irish' anthropological impact outside of the island has been the result of visiting scholars whose analyses have arguably done little to further the intellectual understanding of Irish society, in Ireland, and for the Irish. This is not to say that such works - Arensberg and Kimball (1968), Scheper-Hughes (1979), Messenger (1969), and Brody (1973) are probably the most influential in American and British anthropological circles - are not sound anthropological analyses, but Ireland has become a reservoir for outside researchers who seldom look for much beyond the stereotypical images derived from a very short list of internationally known books. We recognise that there is a culture of anthropological research at play, in which the production of anthropological culture often has as much to do with the pressures of the profession as it does with the salience or accessibility of ideas. In fact, the stereotyped images in the anthropological literature outlined above can be found in anthropological analyses whose sources are internal as well as external to Ireland.

There are a number of reasons why these biases are so entrenched in Ireland's anthropology. There seem to be push and pull factors at work in the Republic of Ireland in terms of ethnographic preference for the rural northwest, west and south. These are the locales associated with Gaelic culture, the Gaelic revival, Irish nationalism, and Hollywood films which privilege traditional culture (O'Connor 1993; Wilson 1987). This anti-urbanism among intellectuals and many others is a powerful force in the Republic (O'Dowd 1987). The extremely influential ethnographic model established by Arensberg and Kimball also set the standards for what Peace (1989: 104) has called, paraphrasing Raymond Williams, the 'dominative mode' of anomic rural change. Such modes create cultural trends, even in anthropology, which tend to reproduce themselves in academic seminars, scholarly publishing, and funding. Rural research in Northern Ireland, on the other hand, appears to owe some of its popularity to the impression that the countryside offers safer research locations. This notion is partly both cause and result of a number of ethnographies of rural Northern Ireland which privilege inter-group tolerance and adaptability, while urban studies often privilege notions of violence (Sluka 1990).

Simply put, there have developed at least two gate-keeping concepts in Ireland, those of the dying peasant community and those of the two tribes of Northern Ireland (see Crozier 1985: 12 who also remarks on the dichotomisation of ethnographic research in Ireland into studies of 'dying community' and 'political and religious schism'). These two regions have thus become exemplars of particular features and problems, just as other parts of the globe have become associated with certain lines of inquiry in the manner eloquently outlined by Fardon (1990). Many scholars -- we suggest more from outside Ireland, but not necessarily so -- need to privilege these concepts to get through the gate, with the keepers being the entrenched arbiters of PhD committees, publishers, and international funding agencies. As a result, Ireland has become a net importer of anthropological theories and methods as, for example, can be found in the structural functionalism of Arensberg and Kimball (1968; see also, Wilson 1984) and the pluralism of Harris (1972). This has been due, in most part, to both the overwhelming numbers of outside anthropologists who visit the island, and because most professionally employed anthropologists in Ireland were trained in Britain or America (there are no more than twenty anthropologists in tenured university posts in Ireland today). One of the arguments we make in this introduction is that if anthropologists are to transform the culture of the discipline, in and about Ireland, they must attend to the problems of Ireland's towns and cities, among the everyday cultures of the majority of the island's people.

Conclusion

This book is an attempt to fill in gaps in the ethnographic record of Ireland. It is an attempt to 'catch up', in an ethnographic sense, with the processes, including the problems, of city and town life and urbanisation in Ireland, north and south. In this attempt, it is patently clear that anthropology has been almost totally unmindful of the growth and impact of the processes of de-urbanisation, ex-urbanisation, and suburbanisation which currently characterise the island (see, for example, Stockdale 1991). The middle classes of Dublin are turning counties Kildare, Meath, and Wicklow into ribbon-like suburban garden communities. Protestants in search of security stream out of Derry and ghettoise the Waterside. The middle classes of Belfast's Malone Road further consolidate their colonisation of County Down's 'Gold Coast'.[7] And Cork's harbour goes up in flames while American and European tourists consume the image of the bucolic Emerald Isle (the dominance of rural imagery in many forms of tourism and consumer and popular culture are reviewed in O'Connor 1993).

We have suggested that anthropologists have come late to the recognition and analysis of urbanity and urbanisation in Ireland. If we are not careful, we will be late to grasp the significance of social forces at work in Ireland's towns and cities today, in the everyday lives of their people. We repeat, one of the essential values of anthropology, as a social scientific and humanistic enterprise, it that it provides a view of how people actually live (Kenny and Kertzer 1983: 5). To both chronicle and understand their lives, ethnographers of Ireland should shake off the fetters of their anthropological traditions and training, and immerse themselves in the actualities of an Ireland entering the twenty-first century.

Social relevance should not suffice, however, as the goal of an evolving ethnography of Ireland. The anthropology of Ireland has a great deal to contribute to the comparative understanding of urban process in this era of globalization and post-industrialism. Urban cultures in Ireland are representative of much that concerns the people and the nations of the first and third worlds; their ethnographic study should give Irish anthropology a larger presence on the wider scholarly stage. Ireland's towns and cities are small, but are growing. This mirrors much that is happening throughout the European Community (and much that is in need of more anthropological attention, see Smith 1993). Irish cities have diverse ethnic, national and religious populations, but on a smaller scale than most of the world, and thus more manageable in terms of field research. Smaller size and scale do not make the structures and problems of urban life less intense or meaningful for the people who deal with them from day to day. Urban Ireland is as much a test case for the 'New Europe' (of the European Community and beyond) and the 'New World Order' as is urban France or urban Croatia. The most contested border in western Europe divides Ireland, while the cities of Northern Ireland are the battleground in an ethno-nationalist war that, in its current phase, is entering its second quarter century. And although the cities of the Irish Republic are not torn by nationalist and sectarian violence, they are 'still in the process of being shaped' (O'Toole 1991) as they experience the problems of late urbanisation in an era of post-industrial malaise.

Unemployment, emigration, drug trafficking, joy-riding, vandalism, organised crime, homelessness, and random violence are endemic to Irish urban life. Like cities everywhere, Irish cities are arenas wherein the crucial conflicts over secularisation, reproductive rights, gender equality, race, nationalism, and workers' rights are happening now and will continue to take place; they are the sites for the study of ordinary people's responses to forces which often seem beyond human control (Burawoy et al. 1991). These conflicts will be part of, and will determine the course of, the everyday lives of all Irish people as they attempt to "domesticate" or "humanise" those parts "of the city which pertain peculiarly to themselves" (Cohen 1993: 6). If anthropologists want to understand how Irish people actually live, they must shift their attention to Ireland's cities. In doing so, they may begin the process of de-peripheralising Ireland, and allowing it to inform the comparative analysis of modern life, in Europe and beyond.

We conclude this introduction with a reminder that one of the over-riding achievements of anthropology has been in the comparison of cultures. Ireland is not a homogeneous island in which any study of islanders off the west coast, border residents in the north, countrymen in Clare, or inhabitants of inner city Belfast can stand for or represent the whole. The anthropological project of exploring culture - that is, viewing culture as the context for research, as a metaphor for the totality of a group of people's ideas and actions, and as a descriptive device for capturing aspects of people's experiences - is alive and well in Ireland's towns and cities. The contests over space, power, history and image in the urban areas of Ireland are inextricably linked to the ways people adapt to the perturbations of their urban environments. The diversity of these experiences, including the ways they mirror life elsewhere in Ireland and the world, gives substance to the dynamic urban cultures of Ireland today. We suggest that these cultures will also be a critical element in the future anthropology of Ireland.

Notes

1. Throughout this chapter 'Ireland' and 'Irish' refer to the whole island, while the 'Republic/the south' and 'Northern Ireland/the north' refer to its component polities.
2. Urban expansion and industrialisation need not occur together, of course, though they mostly did in Ireland where only limited urbanisation was a result of emerging commercial and administrative centres (for an overview see Royle 1993; see also Clarkson 1985).
3. Royle (1993), for example, charts the uneven pattern of urban growth throughout Ireland since the mid-nineteenth century, identifying a range of factors which ensured that the bulk of urban development took place to the east of the island. Graham and Proudfoot's (1993) collection also includes two chapters which re-evaluate the debate on urban origins, as well as chapters on the complexities of urbanisation in medieval, eighteenth century and nineteenth century Ireland.
4. Clearly other developments, such as the 'culture of poverty' notion (see Lewis 1966) have influenced urban anthropology, but there is not space to elaborate on them here.
5. Agreement on a definition of 'urban', 'town' and 'city' has been similarly elusive (see Hannerz 1980: ch. 3, for a review of the problems; see also Sanjek 1990: 153, who cites the best of such efforts). For examples of how some particular formulations have been deployed, see Southall (1973) and Fox (1977: 29-32). The definition of a town in the Irish census is a community of more than 2,000 people.
6. Since a number of important articles and books have authoritatively reviewed the origins and development of distinctly anthropological approaches to urbanism and urbanisation, compared them with other disciplines, and set research agendas, it would serve little purpose to rehearse the issues again here (see, for example, Eddy 1968; Weaver and White 1972; Cohen 1974; Southall 1973; Foster and Kemper

1974; Eames and Goode 1977; Fox 1977; Basham 1978; Collins 1980; Hannerz 1980; Gmelch and Zenner 1988).
7. Recently described by O'Faolain (1993) as an 'enclave of power, privilege and prosperity'.

References

Ansari, G. and P. Nas (eds.), 1983. *Town-talk: the dynamics of urban anthropology.* Leiden: E. J. Brill.

Arensberg, C. M. and S. Kimball 1968 [1940]. *Family and community in Ireland.* Cambridge: Harvard University Press.

Basham, R. 1978. *Urban anthropology: the cross-cultural study of complex societies.* Palo Alto: Maryfield Publishing Co.

Bax, M. 1976. *Harpstrings and confessions: machine style politics in the Irish Republic.* Amsterdam: Van Gorcum

Beckett, J. C. 1969. Introduction. In W. H. Crawford and B. Trainor (eds.), *Aspects of Irish social history 1750-1800.* Belfast: HMSO.

Beckett, J. C. et al. (eds.) 1983. *Belfast: the making of the city 1800-1914.* Belfast: Appletree Press.

Bell, C. and H. Newby 1971. *Community studies: an introduction to the sociology of the local community.* London: Allen and Unwin.

Bell, D. 1990. *Acts of Union: youth culture and sectarianism in Northern Ireland.* London: Macmillan.

Bennett, D. 1984. Maggie Feathers and Missie Reilly: hawking life in Dublin's City Quay. In C. Curtin, M. Kelly and L. O'Dowd (eds.), *Culture and ideology in Ireland.* Galway: Galway University Press.

Boal, F. 1970. Social space in the Belfast urban area. In N. Stephens and R. E. Glasscock (eds.), *Irish geographical studies.* Belfast: Queen's University.

_____. 1976. Ethnic residential segregation. In D. T. Herbert and R. J. Johnston (eds.), *Social areas in cities: spatial processes and form.* Chichester: John Wiley.

_____. 1981. Residential segregation and mixing in a situation of ethnic and national conflict: Belfast. In P. A. Compton (ed.), *The contemporary population of Northern Ireland and population-related issues.* Belfast: Institute of Irish Studies.

_____. 1982. Segregation and mixing: space and residence in Belfast. In F. Boal and J. N. H. Douglas (eds.), *Integration and division: geographical perspectives on the Northern Ireland problem.* London: Academic Press.

Boal, F., Murray, R. C. and M. A. Poole 1976. Belfast: the urban encapsulation of a national conflict. In S. E. Clarke and J. L. Obler (eds.), *Urban ethnic conflict: a comparative perspective.* Chapel Hill: University of North Carolina, Institute for Research in Social Science.

Brewer, J. D. 1990. *Inside the RUC: routine policing in a divided society.* Oxford: Clarendon Press.

Brody, H., 1973. *Inishkillane: change and decline in the west of Ireland.* Harmondsworth: Penguin Press.

Buckley, A. D. 1982. *A gentle people: a study of a peaceful community in Northern Ireland.* Cultra: Ulster Folk and Transport Museum.

Bufwack, M. S. 1982. *Village without violence: an examination of a Northern Irish community.* Cambridge, Mass: Schenkman.

Burawoy, M., A, Burton, A. A. Ferguson, K. J. Fox, J. Gamson, L. Hurst, N. G. Julius, C. Kurzman, L. Salzinger, J. Schiffman, and Shiori Ui. 1991. *Ethnography unbound: power and resistance in the modern metropolis.* Berkeley: University of California Press.

Burton, F. 1978. *The politics of legitimacy: struggles in a Belfast community.* London: Routledge and Kegan Paul.

Byrne, D. 1984. Dublin: a case study of housing and the residual working class. *International Journal of Urban and Regional Research* 8, 402-20.

Camblin, G. 1951. *The towns in Ulster.* Belfast: Mullan and Son.

Castells, M. 1983. *The city and the grassroots: a cross-cultural theory of urban social movements.* London: Edward Arnold.

Cawley, M. 1991. Town population changes 1971-86: patterns and distributional effects. *Irish Geography* 24, 106-16.

Cecil, R. 1993. The marching season in Northern Ireland: an expression of politico-religious identity. In S. Macdonald (ed.), *Inside European Identities: ethnography in western Europe.* Oxford: Berg.

Clark, S. 1979. *Social origins of the Irish land war.* Princeton: Princeton University Press.

Clarkson, L. A. 1985. Population change and urbanisation 1821-1911. In L. Kennedy and P. Ollerenshaw (eds.), *An economic history of Ulster 1820-1939.* Manchester: Manchester University Press.

Cohen, A. (ed.). 1974. *Urban ethnicity.* London: Tavistock.

Cohen, A. P. 1993. Introduction. In A. P. Cohen and K. Fukui (eds.), *Humanising the city? Social contexts of urban life at the turn of the millennium.* Edinburgh: Edinburgh University Press.

Collins, T. (ed.) 1980. *Urban anthropology: cities in a hierarchical context.* Athens: University of Georgia Press.

Crozier, M. 1985. *Patterns of hospitality in a rural Ulster community.* Unpublished PhD dissertation, Queen's University Belfast.

Curtin, C. and A. Varley 1986. Bringing industry to a small town in the west of Ireland. *Sociologia Ruralis* 26, 170-85.

Curtin, C. and T. M. Wilson (eds.) 1989. *Ireland from below: social change and local communities.* Galway: Galway University Press.

Darby, J. 1986. *Intimidation and the control of conflict in Northern Ireland.* Dublin: Gill and Macmillan.

Donnan, H. and G. McFarlane. 1986. Social anthropology and the sectarian divide in Northern Ireland. In R. Jenkins and H. Donnan & G. McFarlane, *The sectarian divide in Northern Ireland today.* London: Royal Anthropological Institute Occasional paper No. 41.

_____. (eds.). 1989. *Social anthropology and public policy in Northern Ireland.* Aldershot: Avebury Press.

Eames, E. and J. Goode 1973. *Urban poverty in cross-cultural context.* New York: Free Press.

_____. 1977. *Anthropology of the city: an introduction to urban anthropology.* Englewood cliffs, NJ: Prentice Hall.

Eddy, E. M. (ed.), 1968. *Urban anthropology.* Athens: University of Georgia Press.

Eipper, C. 1986. *The ruling trinity: a community study of church, state and business in Ireland.* Aldershot: Gower.

Epstein, D. G. 1972. The genesis and function of squatter settlements in Brasilia. In T. Weaver and D. White (eds.), *The anthropology of urban environments.* Society for Applied Anthropology Monographs No. 11. Washington D.C.: Society for Applied Anthropology.

Fardon, R. 1990. Localizing strategies: the regionalization of ethnographic accounts. In R. Fardon (ed.), *Localizing strategies: regional traditions of ethnographic writing.* Edinburgh: Scottish Academic Press.

Feldman, A. 1991. *Formations of violence: the narrative of the body and political terror in Northern Ireland.* London and Chicago: University of Chicago Press.

Foster, G. and R. Kemper (eds.), 1974. *Anthropologists in cities.* Boston: Little, Brown and Company.

Fox, R. G. 1972. Rational and romance in urban anthropology. *Urban Anthropology* 1, 205-33.

_____. 1977. *Urban anthropology: cities in their cultural settings.* Englewood Cliffs, NJ: Prentice-Hall.

Garvin, T. 1974. Political cleavages, party politics and urbanisation in Ireland: the case of the periphery-dominated centre. *European Journal of Political Research* 2, 307-27.

Geary, F. and W. Johnson 1989. Shipbuilding in Belfast 1861-1986. *Irish Economic and Social History* 16, 42-64.

Gibbon, P. 1973. Arensberg and Kimball revisited. *Economy and Society* 2, 479-98.

Gibbon, P. and C. Curtin 1978. The stem family in Ireland. *Comparative Studies in Society and History* 20, 429-53.

_____. 1983. Irish farm families: facts and fantasies. *Comparative Studies in Society and History* 25, 375-80.

Glassie, H. 1982. *Passing the time: folklore and history of an Ulster community.* Dublin: The O'Brien Press.

Gmelch, G. 1977. *The Irish tinkers: the urbanization of an itinerant people.* Menlo Park, California: Cummings Pub. Co.

_____. 1980. A fieldwork experience: Irish Travellers in Dublin. In G. Gmelch and W. Zenner (eds.), *Urban life.* Boston: St Martins Press.

Gmelch, G. and W. P. Zenner (eds.), 1988. *Urban life: readings in urban anthropology.* Prospect Heights, Illinois: Waveland Press.

Gmelch, S. 1989. From poverty subculture to political lobby: the Traveller rights movement in Ireland. In C. Curtin and T. M. Wilson (eds.), *Ireland from below: social change and local communities.* Galway: Galway University Press.

Graham, B. J. and L. J. Proudfoot (eds.) 1993. *An historical geography of Ireland.* London: Academic Press.

Haddon, A. C. and C. R. Browne 1891. *Ethnography of the Aran Islands, Co. Galway.* Proceedings of the Royal Irish Academy 18, pp. 768-830.

Hannerz, U. 1980. *Exploring the city: inquiries toward an urban anthropology.* New York: Columbia University Press.

Harkness, D. and M. O'Dowd (eds.) 1981. Introduction. In D. Harkness and M. O'Dowd (eds.), *The town in Ireland*. Belfast: Appletree Press.

Harris, L. 1984. Class, community and sexual divisions in north Mayo. In C. Curtin, M. Kelly and L. O'Dowd (eds.), *Culture and ideology in Ireland*. Galway: Galway University Press.

Harris, R. 1972. *Prejudice and tolerance in Ulster: a study of neighbours and 'strangers' in a border community*. Manchester: Manchester University Press.

——. 1988. Theory and evidence: the 'Irish stem family' and field data. *Man* 23 (3), 417-34.

Hepburn, A. C. and B. Collins 1981. Industrial society: the structure of Belfast 1901. In P. Roebuck (ed.), *Plantation to partition*. Belfast: Blackstaff Press.

Horner, A. 1988. Developments in early morning public transport: an indicator of change in the Dublin City region. *Irish Geography* 21, 45-47.

Hourihan, N. 1978. Social areas in Dublin. *Economic and Social Review* 9, 301-18.

——. 1982. In-migration to Irish cities and towns, 1970-71. *Economic and Social Review* 13, 29-42.

——. 1991. Culture, politics and recent urbanisation of the Republic of Ireland. In M. Bannon, L. Bourne and R. Sinclair (eds.), *Urbanisation and urban development: recent trends in global context*. University College Dublin: Social Services Research Centre.

Howe, L. 1990. *Being unemployed in Northern Ireland: an ethnographic study*. Cambridge: Cambridge University Press.

Humphreys, A. J. 1966. *New Dubliners*. London: Routledge.

Jarman, N. 1992. Troubled images: the iconography of Loyalism. *Critique of Anthropology* 12 (2), 133-65.

——. in press. Intersecting Belfast. In B. Bender (ed.), *Landscape: politics and perspectives*. Oxford: Berg.

Jenkins, R. 1982. *Hightown rules: growing up in a Belfast housing estate*. Leicester: National Youth Bureau.

——. 1983. *Lads, citizens, and ordinary kids: working class youth lifestyles in Belfast*. London: Routledge and Kegan Paul.

——. (ed.), 1989. *Northern Ireland: studies in social and economic life*. Aldershot: Avebury in association with the Economic and Social Research Council.

Kane, E., Blacking, J., Donnan, H. and G. McFarlane. 1988. A review of anthropological research in Ireland, north and south. In L. O'Dowd (ed.), *The state of social science research in Ireland*. Dublin: Royal Irish Academy.

Kellegher, P. and M. Whelan 1992. *Dublin communities in action*. Dublin: CAN and Combat Poverty Agency.

Kenny, M. and D. I. Kertzer. 1983. Introduction. In M. Kenny and D. I. Kertzer (eds.), *Urban life in Mediterranean Europe: anthropological perspectives*. University of Illinois Press.

King, A. D. 1990. *Urbanism, colonialism, and the world-economy: cultural and spatial foundations of the world urban system*. London: Routledge.

Komito, L. 1989. Dublin politics: symbolic dimensions of clientelism. In C. Curtin and T. M. Wilson (eds.), *Ireland from below: social change and local communities*. Galway: Galway University Press.

Larsen, S. A. 1982a. The two sides of the house: identity and social organisation in Kilbroney, Northern Ireland. In A. P. Cohen (ed.), *Belonging: identity and social organisation in British rural cultures.* Manchester: Manchester University Press.

———. 1982b. The Glorious Twelfth: a ritual expression of collective identity. In A. P. Cohen (ed.), *Belonging: identity and social organisation in British rural cultures.* Manchester: Manchester University Press.

Leeds, A. 1988. Towns and villages in society: hierarchies of order and cause. In T. W. Collins (ed.), *Cities in a larger context.* Athens: University of Georgia Press.

Lewis, O. 1966. *La Vida.* New York: Random House.

Leyton, E. 1974. Opposition and integration in Ulster. *Man* 9, 185-98.

———. 1975. *The one blood: kinship and class in an Irish village.* St John's, Newfoundland: Institute of Social and Economic Research, Memorial University of Newfoundland.

Lloyd, P., 1979. *Slums of hope: shanty towns of the Third World.* Harmondsworth: Penguin Books.

Lomnitz, L. 1977. *Networks and marginality: life in a Mexican shantytown.* New York: Academic Press.

MacNiocaill, G. 1981. Socio-economic problems of the late medieval Irish town. In D. Harkness and M. O'Dowd (eds.), *The town in Ireland.* Belfast: Appletree Press.

McCann, M. 1987. 'Tribal Northern Ireland': an analysis of a stereotype. Paper presented to conference on Ireland and the Irish: a study of stereotypes. Youngstown, Ohio, 25-26 April 1987.

McKeown, K. 1986. Urbanisation in the Republic of Ireland: a conflict approach. In P. Clancy, S. Drudy, K. Lynch and L. O'Dowd (eds.), *Ireland: a sociological profile.* Dublin: Institute of Public Administration.

Messenger, J. C. 1969. *Inis Beag: isle of Ireland.* New York: Holt, Rinehart and Winston.

National Economic and Social Council 1979. *Urbanisation and regional development in Ireland.* National Economic and Social Council Report No. 45, Dublin: Stationery Office.

Nelson, S. 1984. *Ulster's uncertain defenders: Loyalists and the Northern Ireland conflict.* Belfast: Appletree Press.

O'Connor, B. 1993. Myths and mirrors: tourist images and national identity. In B. O'Connor and M. Cronin (eds.), *Tourism in Ireland: a critical analysis.* Cork: Cork University Press.

O'Dowd, L. 1987. Town and Country in Irish ideology. *The Canadian Journal of Irish Studies* 12 (2): 43-53.

O'Faolain, N. 1993. The discreet charm of the northern bourgeoisie. *The Irish Times,* 10 July 1993.

O'Malley, E. 1985. The problem of late industrialisation and the experience of the Republic of Ireland. *Cambridge Journal of Economics* 9: 141-54.

O'Toole, F. 1991. Institutionalised non-culture in the city. *The Irish Times,* January 1991.

Peace, A. 1989. From arcadia to anomie: critical notes on the constitution of Irish society as an anthropological subject. *Critique of Anthropology* 9 (1), 89-111.

Redfield, R. 1941. The folk culture of Yucatan. Chicago: University of Chicago Press.

Rollwagen, J. R. 1980. Cities and the world system: toward an evolutionary perspective in the study of urban anthropology. In T. Collins (ed.), *Urban anthropology: cities in a hierarchical context.* Southern Anthropological Society Proceedings No. 14. Athens: University of Georgia Press.

Rosaldo, R. 1988. Ideology, place, and people without culture. *Cultural Anthropology* 3 (1), 77-87.

Royle, S. A. 1993. Industrialization, urbanization and urban society in post-famine Ireland, c. 1850-1921. In B. J. Graham and L. J. Proudfoot (eds.), *An historical geography of Ireland.* London: Academic Press.

Ruane, J. 1989. Success and failure in a West of Ireland factory. In C. Curtin and T. M. Wilson (eds.), *Ireland from below: social change and local communities.* Galway: Galway University Press.

Sanjek, R. 1990. Urban anthropology in the 1980s: a world view. *Annual Review of Anthropology* 19, 151-86.

Scheper-Hughes, N. 1979. *Saints, scholars, and schizophrenics: mental illness in rural Ireland.* Berkeley: University of California Press.

Shanks, A. 1987. The stem family reconsidered: the case of the minor gentry of Northern Ireland. *Journal of Comparative Family Studies* 18 (3), 339-61.

Silverman, M. and P. H. Gulliver (eds.) 1992. *Approaching the past: historical anthropology through Irish case studies.* New York: Columbia University Press.

Sluka, J. A. 1989. *Hearts and minds, water and fish: popular support for the IRA and INLA in a Northern Irish ghetto.* Greenwich, CT: JAI Press.

____. 1990. Participant observation in violent social contexts. *Human Organization* 49 (2), 114-26.

Smith, M. E. 1993. The incidental city: urban entities in the EC of the 1990s. In T. M. Wilson and M. E. Smith (eds.), *Cultural change and the New Europe: perspectives on the European Community.* Boulder and Oxford: Westview Press.

Southall, A. 1973. *Urban anthropology: cross-cultural studies of urbanization.* London: Oxford University Press.

Stockdale, A. 1991. Recent trends in urbanisation and rural repopulation in Northern Ireland. *Irish Geography* 24 (2), 70-80.

Varley, A. 1983. 'The stem family in Ireland' reconsidered. *Comparative Studies in Society and History* 25, 381-91.

Vaughan, W. E. and A. J. Fitzpatrick. 1978. *Irish historical statistics: population, 1821-1971.* Dublin: Royal Irish Academy.

Vincent, J. 1989. State and community: a case study of Glencolumbkille. In C. Curtin and T. M. Wilson (eds.), *Ireland from below: social change and local communities.* Galway: Galway University Press.

Weaver, T. and D. White (eds.), 1972. *The anthropology of urban environments.* Washington, DC: Society for Applied Anthropology.

Wilson, T. M. 1984. From Clare to the Common Market: perspectives in Irish ethnography. *Anthropological Quarterly* 57 (1), 1-15.

_____. 1987. Mythic images of the Irish family in the works of Flaherty, deValera, and Arensberg and Kimball. *Working Papers in Irish Studies,* Northeastern University, 87 (2-3), 14-31.

Wirth, L. 1928. *The ghetto.* Chicago: University of Chicago Press.

Wolfe, A. W. 1980. Multinational enterprise and urbanism. In T. Collins (ed.), *Urban anthropology: cities in a hierarchical context.* Southern Anthropological Society Proceedings No. 14. Athens: University of Georgia Press.

2 Belfast: whose city?

Kay Milton

To whom does a city "belong"? Who allocates its resources and determines access to its facilities? Who shapes the quality of urban life, planners or people, affluent or poor, commuters or residents? These questions, addressed by Pahl in the essay from which the title of this chapter is borrowed (Pahl 1969), occupied the citizens of Belfast and the pages of the local press between the spring of 1987 and the end of 1989. The focus of this attention was the Belfast Urban Area Plan (BUAP, referred to below as "the Plan"), the statutory document which would set the guidelines for development in the city until the year 2001. This chapter will address the question of "whose city is Belfast?" by examining the influences that shaped the final content of the Plan.

The analytical perspective used here has been informed by ideas derived from discourse analysis, which, following the work of Foucault (1972; 1982), has been influential in sociology for some years and, through the efforts of some scholars (in particular van Dijk 1985; Fairclough 1992), is emerging as a discipline in its own right. In social theory, discourse has both a processual and a substantive meaning. In the first sense it refers to the constitution of social reality through communication; in the second sense it refers to a field of communication defined by its subject matter or the type of language used. There is no implication that any particular discourse, defined in this second sense, will be internally consistent. A discourse may itself comprise a number of diverse and/or competing discourses. In many social scientific uses of the term, both the processual and the substantive meanings are simultaneously implied. Thus, "political discourse" is not just communication about politics or which uses political language, it is the process through which we come to understand what politics is.[1]

One way of analysing the constitution of social reality through discourse is to consider how knowledge is made to count (Harries-Jones 1986: 234; 1991) through political debate. In this way, discourse analysis has been embraced by political anthropology through an emphasis on language as an instrument of power (Grillo 1989; Fairclough 1989; Bourdieu 1991). Political debates are treated as "sites of struggle" (Seidel 1985: 44; 1989: 223), in which meanings are contested and negotiated. In order to interpret the course and outcome of a political debate, it is important to identify the processes whereby some meanings acquire precedence over others (cf. Peace, in press).

In the debate analysed here, the protagonists are the planning authority, which in Northern Ireland is the Department of the Environment (DoE(NI), referred to below as "the Department"), and a number of individuals and protest groups (referred to below as "the objectors"). The Plan whose contents the objectors strove to influence is regarded as an important document. It will form the framework for all planning decisions taken in Belfast during the period of its operation (1989-2001). It was assumed, by planners, developers and the interested public, that development proposals which contravene the guidelines set in the Plan would be unlikely to proceed, while those which accord with the Plan would be difficult to oppose effectively. In the formulation of the Plan, personal fortunes and livelihoods, as well as social needs, rights and privileges, were seen as being at stake.

The production of a strategic development plan is a complex operation, only the barest outline of which need be presented here. The Department, through its Town and Country Planning Service, is obliged to produce development plans covering the whole of Northern Ireland, and to provide for public participation in this process. In May 1987, the Department published its Preliminary Proposals for the Belfast Urban Area (DoE(NI) 1987a) and invited public comment. The Draft Plan (DoE(NI) 1987b) was published in November of that year, with further invitation to comment. As a result of the high number of responses received,[2] a Public Inquiry, to air the objections, was held in June 1988. The following year, the Planning Appeals Commission (PAC) presented its report on the Inquiry, with recommendations, to the Department (Guckian and Hawthorne 1989). The final decision on a plan's content rests with the Department, which may accept or reject the recommendations of the PAC. At the end of 1989 the Department formally adopted the Plan, with modifications (DoE(NI) 1989). The final Plan was published in 1990 (DoE(NI) 1990).

The analysis presented here focuses on just one of several major issues debated during the production of the Plan, i.e., the allocation of resources between public transport, new road developments and car parking facilities. The main sources of information used in the analysis are documents produced by the planning authorities and objectors; specifically, the Plan itself, in its various stages (DoE(NI) 1987a; 1987b; 1989; 1990), statements prepared by non-governmental organisations and protest groups (Community Technical Aid 1987; 1990; Stop the By-Pass Campaign 1987) and the report of the PAC (Guckian and Hawthorne 1989), which is a particularly important source of information since it presents in detail the views of the Department and the objectors. The Public Inquiry and meetings organised by protest groups, which I attended on behalf of the Belfast Urban Wildlife Group, provided valuable opportunities for participant observation and for informal conversations with planners and objectors.

The issue: public vs. private transport

Belfast's transportation strategy underwent a major reappraisal in the 1970s, which resulted in a new strategy being adopted in 1978. Its aim was to bring about "improvements for all transport users through a broad balance in the allocation of resources between public transport, new and improved roads and car parking" (DoE(NI) 1987b: 64). A further review (Halcrow Fox and Associates 1987), commissioned by the Department in preparation for their drafting of the Plan, was interpreted by them as having broadly endorsed the 1978 strategy. Transportation proposals in the Plan therefore represented a continuation with the past and were intended to maintain what the Department perceived as a balance between public and private transport.

The measures proposed in the Plan included the general maintenance of public transport services "to ensure reasonable access to jobs, shops, schools and recreation", the continued development of bus services, including improved bus station accommodation, the possible consideration of new railway stations and halts and the continuation of concessionary fares. Alternative public transport technologies, such as light rail systems, would be "kept under review" (DoE(NI) 1987b: 66-67). Proposed improvements to the city's road network included extensive road building and road improvement on the eastern and southern approaches to the city. These approaches serve the densely populated suburban commuter belt of North Down and the dormitory villages and rural areas beyond (DoE(NI) 1987b: 67-72). Car parking facilities within the city would be developed at a level "sufficient to meet demand" (DoE(NI) 1987b: 72). In financial terms, the proposed allocation of resources was 57 per cent on private transport (roads and car parking) and 43 per cent on public transport (Guckian and Hawthorne 1989: 347).

From their initial appearance in May 1987 (DoE(NI) 1987a), these proposals attracted considerable and often vociferous criticism.[3] Several new community groups were formed with the specific aim of opposing these and other aspects of the Plan. The general gist of the objections was that, far from achieving a "balance" between public and private transport, the Department's proposals were heavily weighted towards car users. It was argued that Belfast's road network was already more than adequate, whereas the city's public transport system was far from satisfactory and received less

financial support from the Government than any other such system in
Western Europe (*Belfast Telegraph* 2 September 1987). It was claimed that
the Plan made no attempt to address the transportation needs of
disadvantaged sectors of the population, and that alternative methods of
transport such as light rail, small bus schemes, cycle lanes, and so on, had
not been adequately considered (Community Technical Aid 1987: 16). The
proposed new road schemes would, it was claimed, have serious and
undesirable environmental consequences in their immediate vicinities,
including increased noise and air pollution and the loss of valuable recreation
facilities and wildlife habitat (Stop the By-Pass Campaign 1988: 7; *Belfast
Telegraph* 24 July 1987).

One of the central questions underlying the differences of opinion
between the Department and the objectors was, "Who is the Plan for? - Who
benefits from its proposals?" The Department held assumptions which
enabled it to argue that its transportation policies would benefit the majority
of Belfast citizens. The objectors were adamant that the Department's
proposals would benefit a minority, while their own various alternative
proposals would benefit the majority. Also underlying the disagreement was
a difference in perception of the Plan's purpose. The Department stressed
that the Plan was intended as a basis for decisions on land use, and could not
be expected to solve social problems (DoE(NI) 1987b: 3; Guckian and
Hawthorne 1989: 5). Many objectors treated the Plan as a device which
might at least address social needs if not fulfil them (Guckian and Hawthorne
1989: 327ff, 330, 332, 344).

The Department's model

The Department perceived the transport-using population as divided into two
categories: "those who depend on public transport and those who use the
private motor car" (Guckian and Hawthorne 1989: 339). This distinction
formed a basis for the Department's policy guidelines, which defined the
purpose of public transport as being primarily, "to cater efficiently for the
demand for travel from people with no access to a car or who cannot drive"
(Guckian and Hawthorne 1989: 350, 360). The implicit assumption is that
the car was, and would remain, the preferred form of transport. The
possibility of car owners ever turning to public transport was not entertained,
and was therefore ruled out as a basis for policy. When questioned about the
feasibility of one possible public transport scheme, a representative of the
Department at the Public Inquiry stated that he,

> did not consider it realistic to expect the middle class population to rush out
> in the morning and file into a fleet of buses which would take them to bus

shelters where they would leap on larger buses to head for the city centre (Guckian and Hawthorne 1989: 357).

If the users of public transport and car users are distinct categories of people, it follows that policies which favour one at the expense of the other are discriminatory and therefore bad. The Department recognised the "interests, needs and rights" of both categories, and was concerned to avoid discrimination: "For example, the department could not justify the exclusion of private motorists from the Belfast City Centre simply in order to boost the use of public transport" (Guckian and Hawthorne 1989: 339). On the other hand, given that public, as well as private transport "is a significant user of the roads system" (Guckian and Hawthorne 1989: 340), the Department was able to argue that its proposals for road development and improvement would benefit both categories of traveller. In the light of these arguments, it was suggested, the proposed division of expenditure between private (57%) and public (43%) transport was not unreasonable.

The Department also used a broad economic argument to justify its support of private transport. Stimulation of the urban economy was one of the stated objectives of the Plan (DoE(NI) 1987b: 16-17). During the years of political unrest which preceded the Plan, Belfast experienced considerably higher levels of unemployment than other UK cities.[4] Although, as the Department emphasised, the Plan was a basis for land use, and was not intended directly to influence social trends, it was considered important, as far as possible, for the Plan to create the physical conditions under which economic development could flourish, "and to ensure that there are no unnecessary obstacles of a land use nature which would inhibit job creation" (DoE(NI) 1987b: 31). Easy access to the city centre by car users was presented as a factor which would contribute to economic development, by helping to make Belfast an attractive area for investment in commerce and retailing (Guckian and Hawthorne 1989: 347).

Through this argument, the Department identified the interests of the car-using commuter with the interests of the community as a whole. Economic development, it was assumed, is self-evidently good for everyone. Not only does it enable the already affluent to become more so; by creating employment it also increases the wealth, and therefore the options, of those at the bottom of the economic scale. Anything which encourages economic development thus contributes to the well being of the whole population. Easy access for private transport attracts investors; therefore, supporting private transport indirectly helps everyone.

The objectors' model

Unlike the Department which, like all government departments, is obliged to present a united public face (Milton 1990: 29-31), the objectors presented a range of opinions which reflected their varied interests, some economic, some environmental. There were, however, two main arguments which were common to most of the objections. The first was that support for private transport helps a minority rather than a majority, and much less the community as a whole. The second was that it is not only possible, but highly desirable, to persuade car users to give up their cars in favour of public transport.

Fundamental to the first argument was the statistic, accepted by all parties to the debate, that only 47 per cent of households in the Belfast Urban Area owned a car in 1986; this was expected to rise to between 51 and 59 per cent by 2001 (Guckian and Hawthorne 1989: 396, 412). It was argued that this left a very large proportion of the population potentially dependent on public transport (Guckian and Hawthorne 1989: 396). This category would include, not only those households without a car, but also the members of car-owning families whose wage earners took the car to work each day, depriving others of its use (Guckian and Hawthorne 1989: 412). On this basis it was argued that policies aimed at improving conditions for car users would benefit only a minority.

Furthermore, the level of benefit that would accrue to this minority was, it was argued, insignificant when measured against the potential harm and inconvenience of road-building schemes. For instance, one witness at the Public Inquiry, objecting to the proposed road developments through East Belfast, was reported as saying:

> the main reason for spending £21 million of public money was so that the motorist could be in bed later and get to and from work quicker and in doing so, inflict air pollution, noise, vibration, severence, visual pollution, pedestrian delay, intimidation, risk of accidents and dirt on fellow citizens living in East Belfast . . . What right had a minority to abuse a majority in pursuit of minimal advantages to the minority (Guckian and Hawthorne 1989: 353).

The inconvenienced majority would include, not only the residents of East Belfast but also, by implication, the general public, whose £21 million could, presumably, be better spent.

Perceived rights of ownership underlie several of the objections to specific road development proposals. Those living in an area were seen as having more right to its facilities, and to a say in its future development, than those who merely drive through it twice a day on their way to and from work.

Road development schemes, which change the immediate environment of residents for the benefit of commuters, were seen as a direct violation of these rights (Guckian and Hawthorne 1989: 424).

The second main argument which predominated in the objections, that it is both possible and desirable to persuade car users out of their cars and onto public transport, was clearly based on a perception of public transport as the preferred mode of travel. This evaluation did not reflect the objectors' views of Belfast's public transport service as it was in the mid-1980s, but rather of what it could be if given adequate government support. Comparisons were made between public transport in Belfast and in other cities in the UK and Europe (Guckian and Hawthorne 1989: 351, 354, 375), in order to demonstrate that the standard in Belfast, and the level of government subsidy (Guckian and Hawthorne 1989: 370), were much lower than they could be, and that appropriate policies could persuade people to switch from private to public transport.

The perceived benefits of this approach were seen as extending far beyond the sector of the population dependent on public transport. All travellers (including car owners, who would have the option of not using their cars) would benefit from the provision of an efficient, comfortable and fully integrated public transport system. If such a system were attractive enough to persuade a significant number of drivers out of their cars, the overall reduction in road traffic would bring benefits to the whole community in the form of less noise, less pollution, less risk of accidents, less need for expensive new road schemes and all the environmental damage they cause (Guckian and Hawthorne 1989: 352-3, 357, 385).

The outcome

It is widely assumed by those who participate in the planning process that, in any planning issue, considerable weight will be given to the recommendations of the Planning Appeals Commission (PAC),[5] whose role, among other things, is to hold and report on public inquiries. Public faith in the PAC depends on how far it is seen to act independently of the Department. Government planners argue that the PAC guards its independence fiercely, and its record indicates that it is prepared to side with objectors against the Department (Milton 1990: 26, 51-2). In the case of the BUAP Public Inquiry, the PAC was convinced by arguments on both sides of the debate on transportation policy.

The PAC accepted the objectors' view that greater emphasis on public transport was needed and that the persuasion of car users onto public transport was desirable:

In acknowledgement of the vital role which public transport must play throughout the Plan period, Transportation Strategy and Policy TR1 should reflect the need for enhancement of public transport services with a further objective being the achievement of diversion of private car usage to public transport (Guckian and Hawthorne 1989: 413).[6]

In pursuit of this objective, the PAC also recommended the introduction of measures to discourage car parking, particularly long-stay parking, within the city centre (PAC 1989: 1).

They agreed with the Department that the demand for access to the city along its eastern and southern approaches was likely to increase and, therefore, that some new road-building would be justified. Accordingly, they recommended that some of the road development schemes proposed for East Belfast should proceed, despite the inevitable undesirable environmental consequences (Guckian and Hawthorne 1989: 463ff). They were less convinced by the Department's proposals for the city's southern approaches and recommended that,

[a] comprehensive reassessment of the entire Southern Approaches Strategy be undertaken immediately taking account of all optional road systems (including those abandoned in the present Plan) and other transport developments (Guckian and Hawthorne 1989: 432).

They also recommended that, in order to make maximum use of the existing road network in the south of the city,

innovative public transport services should be introduced if only on an experimental basis which could demonstrate the possibility of significant diversion from private car use (Guckian and Hawthorne 1989: 432).

In summary, then, the PAC were in broad agreement with the objectors on the need to improve the public transport service, to divert road users away from private cars onto public transport and, with this aim in mind, to test the feasibility of alternative transport systems and restrict car parking in the city centre. They agreed with the Department that, whatever else was done, some road developments would be necessary in the east and possibly in the south of the city.

The Department's response to these recommendations was to accept some and reject others and to ignore completely one of the PAC's (and the objectors') main arguments. The Department appeared convinced by the argument that there is a high demand for public transport and that services should therefore be "improved to ensure better access" to facilities, rather than merely "maintained to ensure reasonable access" (DoE(NI) 1987b: 66); Policy TR1 in the Plan was amended accordingly (DoE(NI) 1990: 66). The

Department also accepted the PAC's recommendations on proposed road developments; selected developments in East Belfast were accordingly confirmed for implementation "as and when resources permit" (DoE(NI) 1990: 71), while those in South Belfast would be subject to the outcome of a further public inquiry following the reassessment of the Southern Approaches Strategy (DoE(NI) 1989: 26; 1990: 69).

The Department did not accept the PAC's recommendation that car parking in the city, particularly long-stay parking, be restricted, arguing (again) that "a level of provision is necessary to the commercial life of the City Centre" (DoE(NI) 1989: 24). Indeed, they would not rule out the possibility of new long-stay parking facilities in some areas, but conceded to omit the words "long-stay" from some policy statements and to review the issue further in a separate City Centre Plan. The Department also rejected the recommendation that innovative public transport services be tested on the city's southern approaches, but declared that a study of "the potential for new public transport measures" would form part of the reassessment of the Southern Approaches Strategy (DoE(NI) 1989: 26).

The recommendation that attempts be made to divert transport use away from private cars towards public transport (Guckian and Hawthorne 1989: 413, 432) received no acknowledgement, not even a rejection, in the Department's adoption statement (DoE(NI) 1989), nor in the final Plan (DoE(NI) 1990). This omission is all the more conspicuous because all the PAC's other recommendations were explicitly addressed, and because the arguments supporting this recommendation played such a prominent role in the objectors' case.

Interpreting the outcome

Throughout the debate over Belfast's transportation policy, the Department resisted attempts to persuade them to try to influence the demand for public and private transport, rather than merely to cater for it. It might be said that the Department's stance on transportation was non-interventionist. Their aim was to give transport users what they appeared to want, rather than to try to direct their choices away from some forms of transport and towards others. If this non-interventionist policy appeared to favour the car user (as the objectors felt it did), it was because the Department assumed that all transport users would prefer to use cars, and that, as economic recovery progressed and people became more affluent, car ownership would grow.

But why did the Department persist in pursuing a non-interventionist approach in the face of opposition from objectors and, eventually, from the PAC? This persistence might appear more comprehensible if the Department's policies throughout the Plan were consistently non-interventionist, but this was not the case. For example, a declared aim of the Plan was to "halt population loss and maintain a stable level of population" (DoE(NI) 1987b: 16) after a marked decline in the city's population during the years of political unrest (DoE(NI) 1987b: 12). It was thus apparently acceptable for the Department to try to influence people's choice of whether or not to live in Belfast. It was also considered appropriate, and was a major objective of the Plan, to promote economic growth by creating a physical environment in which it could flourish (DoE(NI) 1987b: 17). This strategy would inevitably entail an attempt to direct people's investment choices towards the city. Indeed, the whole concept of land-use planning is interventionist; its very essence is constraint on individual choice for the supposed benefit of the wider community.

The Department's refusal to adopt a more interventionist transportation policy can be understood in the context of "the encapsulating power structure", to use Pahl's phrase (1975: 185). In 1972, in an attempt to exert control over the political unrest in Northern Ireland, the British government imposed direct rule from Westminster and the responsibilities of local and central government were reorganised. Until then, many planning responsibilities had rested with local government, as is the case in Great Britain. Since 1972, responsibility for all planning functions, from the production of area plans to decisions on individual planning applications, has rested with the Department of the Environment (NI) (see Milton 1990: 51). This has had two significant effects on Northern Ireland's planning system, both of which are reflected in the debate discussed here: a) it has made it less accountable to public opinion, and b) it has made it more subject to the constraints of central government policy.

It might be expected that, where the planning authority is an elected local council, its decisions will take some account of public opinion. The extent to which this actually happens is, of course, questionable. The repeated public rows and debates over specific planning issues in Great Britain and the Republic of Ireland, where responsibility for many planning functions rests with local government, demonstrate that the public accountability of elected planning authorities is a matter of considerable debate (Sandbach 1980: 114-20). The converse situation, however, that where a planning authority is not an elected body it need not take account of public opinion, seems less open to question. In Northern Ireland, public opposition to planning decisions does not impinge upon the power of the planning authority as it might in Great Britain or the Republic.

I would not wish to suggest, however, that the Department is generally, in practice, insensitive to public opinion about its policies. I have argued elsewhere that the Department's Planning Service has been sensitive about its lack of public accountability and has been concerned to be seen to consult public opinion (Milton, in press b). In the case of the BUAP, the

Department was able to convince the PAC that it had exceeded its statutory obligations to provide for public consultation (Guckian and Hawthorne 1989: 12). Nevertheless, the lack of accountability remains, and was an important contributory factor in the outcome of the debate over Belfast's transportation strategy.

Equally important in this outcome was the fact that the Department, as part of the UK's central government, is heavily constrained by the policies of that government. During the years in which Margaret Thatcher was Prime Minister, government policies were driven by a commitment to promote conditions in which economic development could flourish. In some policy areas, this meant intervening to remove what were perceived as obstacles to economic progress (for instance, though the privatisation of public services and reductions in the power of trade unions). The Department's concern to foster economic development in Belfast by trying to stabilise the population and create an environment attractive to investors is consistent with this general commitment.

The effects of this commitment on the Thatcher government's transportation policy were revealed in the White Paper on Britain's environmental strategy (HMSO 1990). "Our great car economy", as Mrs Thatcher once called it, was seen as playing a vital role in economic development:

> the Government welcomes the continuing widening of car ownership as an important aspect of personal freedom and choice. The speed and flexibility of motoring make it indispensable for much of business travel, which in turn is vital for the economy (HMSO 1990: 73).

Accordingly, the Thatcher government's extensive programme of road-building in Great Britain was presented as an important economic strategy, and also as one which would bring environmental benefits by reducing congestion (HMSO 1990: 74). The benefits of public transport were acknowledged, but policy was directed at meeting, rather than influencing, demand.[7] The echoes of this approach in the Department's plans for Belfast's transport system are quite clear. The Department could not allow itself to be persuaded that the use of private transport should be discouraged, since this would have contradicted the declared policies of the government of which it is a part.

Objectors at the Public Inquiry claimed that other UK cities have succeeded in implementing interventionist transport policies. If this is indeed the case, it is almost certainly because the elected local authorities in Great Britain have considerable responsibilities for transport and planning in their areas, and are therefore not only less constrained by the wishes of central government, but also more sensitive to the wishes of the electorate. Thus it would seem that, following a significant transfer of power from local

authorities to central government in 1972, the planning system in Northern
Ireland became more Thatcherite in character than elsewhere in the UK.

Conclusion

I suggested above that understanding the course and outcome of a political
debate depends on identifying the mechanisms by which some meanings
acquire precedence over others. In its final form (DoE(NI) 1990), the BUAP
was very similar to the draft version (DoE(NI) 1987b). The two-year process
of public consultation resulted in very few changes, and the objectors
emerged from the debate over transportation policy with the clear impression
that Belfast belongs to the planners, who may dispose of it as they wish. And
yet, at the Public Inquiry, the objectors had won some important arguments.
How can such victories, gained in a public and supposedly independent
arena, be rendered insignificant in the final outcome?

It the final version of the Plan, the Department made some concessions,
but these hold little promise of action. Policy TR1, which declares the
intention to improve, rather than merely maintain, public transport services,
is qualified by the phrase, "subject to the level of resources available"
(DoE(NI) 1990: 66). The actual provision of public transport services is, in
any case, largely in the hands of local bus and rail companies and other
commercial concerns. The promise to study "the potential for new public
transport measures" as part of the reassessment of the Southern Approaches
Strategy (DoE(NI) 1989: 26) is a pale response to the PAC's recommendation
that innovative services should actually be tested.

Perhaps more significant than the nature of these concessions, is the fact
that the objectors' most important victory (in their view) at the Public
Inquiry, the PAC's recommendation that demand be directed away from
private car use towards public transport, was completely ignored by the
Department. While it must be assumed that the Department rejected this
recommendation (CTA 1990: 84), its omission, assuming that this was not
an accidental oversight, would seem to suggest something more: that they did
not know how to counter the argument, other than by admitting that it was
against central government policy. To have done this would have been to
acknowledge the overriding influence of the British government in Northern
Ireland's planning policy, and this in turn, apart from being politically highly
sensitive, would have exposed the public consultation exercise as a sham.

Planning systems throughout Britain and Ireland contain elaborate
procedures for the airing of public opinion. Peace (in press), borrowing a
term from Thompson (1978), has dubbed such procedures "modern theatres
of control", suggesting that, while they appear to create an arena for public
participation in decision making, they are structured in such a way as to

render that participation ineffective. An appropriate task for political anthropology, through its treatment of political discourse as a site of struggle in which meanings are contested, is to demonstrate precisely how this happens. If the debate on Belfast's transportation strategy had taken place outside the formal planning process, in a less tightly structured arena, it is likely that the Department's failure to defend its policy against a major opposition argument, would have been seized upon and exposed. As it was, the structure of the planning process removed any need for the Department to defend itself effectively. The planning system gives the Department the last word; once the Public Inquiry was over, there was no further opportunity for the objectors to make their voices heard.

From the discursive process analysed in this chapter there emerged a tangible product, the final Plan, which stands as the official basis for the future development of Belfast. According to the guiding principles on which the planning system is based, this document should have been the joint creation of the planning authority and the interested public. But the effects of direct rule and the legal constraints of the planning system conspired to deny the people of Belfast an effective voice in its creation. Although their opposition is on public record, the Belfast Urban Area Plan, an immaculate, high profile document to which developers, planners and other interested parties continuously refer, carries no hint of the ownership struggle that preceded its publication.

Notes

1. For a more detailed discussion of the concept of discourse, see Milton (in press a).
2. There were 2,486 objections, including 31 petitions (DoE(NI) 1989: 1).
3. See, for instance, reports and letters in the local press: *Belfast Telegraph*, 24 and 30 July, 11 August, 7 September; *Belfast Newsletter*, 10 August; *Sunday News*, 2 August; *Irish News*, 5 August (all 1987).
4. In 1986, during the preparation of the Plan, unemployment in the Belfast Urban Area was 20 per cent overall (DoE(NI) 1987b: 31) and over 50 per cent in some parts of the city.
5. The Planning Appeals Commission was set up under Part XII of the Planning (Northern Ireland) Order 1972, to arbitrate in cases of disagreement between developers and the Department and to hold public inquiries on planning issues.
6. In the Plan, specific policy statements are labelled in the manner of "TR1" (see DoE(NI) 1987b, 1989).
7. For a more detailed analysis of these policies, see Milton 1991.

References

Bourdieu, P. 1991. *Language and Symbolic Power*. Cambridge: Polity Press.

Community Technical Aid 1987. *Report on the All Belfast Open Conference on the Belfast Urban Area Draft Plan 2001*, held in Central Hall, Rosemary Street, 25 November 1987. Belfast: Community Technical Aid.

_____. 1990. *BUAP 2001: summary of outcome*. Belfast: Community Technical Aid.

van Dijk, T. (ed.) 1985. *Handbook of Discourse Analysis*, 4 vols. London: Academic Press.

DoE(NI) 1987a. *Belfast Urban Area Plan - 2001: Preliminary Proposals*. Belfast: HMSO.

_____. 1987b. *Belfast Urban Area Plan 2001* (Draft). Belfast: HMSO.

_____. 1989. *Belfast Urban Area Plan 2001: Adoption Statement*. Belfast: HMSO.

_____. 1990. *Belfast Urban Area Plan 2001*. Belfast: HMSO.

Fairclough, N. 1989. *Language and Power*. London: Longman.

_____. 1992. *Discourse and Social Change*. Cambridge: Polity Press.

Foucault, M. 1972. *The Archaeology of Knowledge*. London: Tavistock.

_____. 1982. The order of discourse. In *Language and Politics* (ed.) M. Shapiro. Oxford: Blackwell.

Grillo, R. 1989. Anthropology, language, politics. In *Social Anthropology and the Politics of Language*, Sociological Review Monograph 36 (ed.) R. Grillo. London and New York: Routledge.

Guckian, F. G. and Hawthorne, R. S. 1989. *Article 6 Report to the Planning Appeals Commission on a Public Inquiry on Belfast Urban Area Plan 2001*. Belfast: Planning Appeals Commission.

Halcrow Fox and Associates 1987. *A Review of Transportation Strategy for Belfast, 1986-2001*.

Harries-Jones, P. 1986. From cultural translator to advocate: changing circles of interpretation. In *Advocacy and Anthropology: First encounters* (ed.) R. Paine. St Johns, Newfoundland: Institute of Economic and Social Research, Memorial University of Newfoundland.

_____. (ed.) 1991. *Making Knowledge Count: Advocacy and social science*. Montreal and Kingston: McGill-Queen's Press.

HMSO 1990. *This Common Inheritance: Britain's environmental strategy*. London: HMSO.

Milton, K. 1990. *Our Countryside, Our Concern: The policy and practice of conservation in Northern Ireland*. Belfast: Northern Ireland Environment Link.

_____. 1991. Interpreting Environmental Policy: a social-scientific approach. In *Law, Policy and the Environment* (ed.) R. Churchill, L. Warren and J. Gibson. Oxford: Blackwell.

_____. in press a. Environmentalism and Anthropology. In *Environmentalism: The view from anthropology*, ASA Monograph 32 (ed.) K. Milton. London: Routledge.

_____. in press b. Land or Landscape: Rural Planning Policy and the Symbolic Construction of the Countryside. In *Rural Development in Ireland* (ed.) M. Murray and J. Greer. Aldershot: Avebury.

PAC 1989. *Report on a reference to the Commission under Article 6(2) of the Planning (Northern Ireland) Order 1972 (as amended) in respect of objections to the Belfast Urban Area Plan 2001*, 29 September 1989. Belfast: Planning Appeals Commission.

Pahl, R. E. 1969. Whose City? In *New Society* 23 January 1969: 120-22.

_____. 1975. *"Whose City?" and Further Essays on Urban Society*. Harmondsworth, Middlesex: Penguin.

Peace, A. in press. Environmental Protest, Bureaucratic Closure: The politics of discourse in rural Ireland. In *Environmentalism: the view from anthropology*, ASA Monograph 32 (ed.) K. Milton. London: Routledge.

Sandbach, F. 1980. *Environment, Ideology and Policy*. Oxford: Blackwell.

Seidel, G. 1985. Political Discourse Analysis. In *Handbook of Discourse Analysis, Volume 4: Discourse analysis in society* (ed.) T.A. van Dijk. London: Academic Press.

_____. 1989. We condemn apartheid, BUT...: a discursive analysis of the European Parliamentary debate on sanctions (July 1986). In *Social Anthropology and the Politics of Language* Sociological Review Monograph 36 (ed.) R. Grillo. London and New York: Routledge.

Stop the By-Pass Campaign 1987. *The Road To Nowhere: Comber Route (1), a case of tunnel vision.* A report prepared by an *ad hoc* committee drawn from "Stop the By-Pass" Campaign, Belfast Civic Trust and professional, commercial and political interests.

Thompson, E. P. 1978. Folklore, anthropology and social history. *The Indian Historical Review* 3 (2): 247-66.

3   Craigavon: locality, economy and the state in a failed 'new city'

Liam O'Dowd

The research project[1] on which this chapter is based seeks to challenge a pervasive compartmentalisation in the study of socio-economic change in Northern Ireland. This compartmentalisation has taken a number of forms. First, the analyses of the dramatic transformation of Northern Ireland's economic structure since the 1960s have remained unconnected with the study of its impact on specific localities. More particularly, apart from some crude estimations, there has been little in-depth examination of the links between ethnic-national conflict and economic change at either local or regional level.[2] Second, the ethnic-national conflict has been linked to space and locality, especially in the work of Jones (1960) and Boal (e.g., Boal and Douglas 1982). While carefully underlining the centrality of sectarian geography, this approach sees the latter as merely the outcome of inter-communal conflict. It pays relatively little attention to how the state and wider processes of economic restructuring interact with locality and ethnic conflict. Third, a variety of local community studies do exist but they too are largely compartmentalised from the study of structural changes at the political and economic level. Moreover, they have tended to concentrate less on urban industrial than on rural settings. They have shared the perspective of much of the anthropology of modern Ireland which has focused on the degeneration and decline of traditional rural society (important exceptions to this pattern are Eipper 1986; Jenkins 1983; Dilley 1989; and Howe 1990). The research reported here, however, concerns an urban environment with a long history of industrialization - now marked by a combination of industrial change and decline as well as by an intensification of ethnic-national conflict.

Cast in broader terms, our research problem addressed an age-old issue in the social sciences - the links between structural change and the experiences and responses of local actors in specific communities. The initial problem was whether to begin the study with an account of structural

Irish Urban Cultures

change or alternatively with an examination of a de-limited territorial area. The former posed serious data problems. While much socio-economic information exists for Northern Ireland as a whole, information was extremely patchy at lower levels of disaggregation. Two decades of changing local and administrative boundaries made historical comparisons difficult and, moreover, ensured that many of these local entities failed to correspond with popular territorial identifications.[3]

Starting from de-limited territorial areas also posed problems. Existing studies of such areas often failed to address wider structural and political change adequately. There was little systematic comparative study of local communities (see Donnan and McFarlane 1986: 396), in part because of the practical difficulties of studying more than one community at a time. Existing ethnographies also seemed to concentrate on areas of limited size, i.e., small rural communities or urban housing estates. In the face of these kinds of problems it seemed to many observers that the 'community studies' tradition generally had run out of steam (Day and Murdoch 1993).

On the other hand, in the 1980s, a tradition of 'locality studies' had emerged which seemed to link wider processes of economic change to particular localities (see, for example, Hausner 1987; Cooke 1989; Bagguley et al. 1990). Many social scientists argued that, far from homogenising social space, modern capitalist development was a differentiating force - heightening the economic, social and political significance of localities (Urry 1981: 464). This perspective appeared promising in a Northern Ireland context, where the ethnic-national conflict also seemed to be enhancing the significance of localities. Regional analyses in Northern Ireland had underlined the central role of the state in mediating economic change (O'Dowd 1986; Rowthorn and Wayne 1988). It was also clear that the state was a key element in the relationship between the Catholic and Protestant communities. Thus, it appeared that the state provided a bridge between general processes of economic restructuring and local community consciousness heightened by the continuing conflict.

The Craigavon new city project neatly brought together all these issues. Craigavon was both a product of the radical economic change of the 1960s and a key means employed by the state to direct and influence that change. It underlined the territorial dimensions of state policy and brought the latter face to face with the problem of restructuring sectarian geography. By the early 1970s, sectarian geography was being exacerbated by the eruption of the Northern Ireland conflict which in turn was to have a decisive impact on the prospects of the new city. The overall result was the exposure of the territorial and ethnic strategies of the Northern Ireland state to critical scrutiny, an exposure which was to lead to the reshaping of the state itself.

The 'new city' plan was an attempt to merge two long established towns, Lurgan and Portadown, into an enlarged urban area, Craigavon. In terms of local perceptions, at least, the plan failed. Not only have the two towns preserved their distinctiveness, a third entity has emerged - Brownlow - a legacy of new city housing policy. Although Craigavon is the official name for all three areas, significantly, locals identify only Brownlow as Craigavon, seeing its severe socio-economic problems as conclusive testimony of the ill-advised nature of the new city plan. Whatever the final outcome, however, the experience of the 'new city' to date allows us to examine the interface between economic change, state management and established local identities.

The first part of this chapter outlines the historical and 'structural' context of the new city project, drawing on official documents, newspapers and interviews. This project, which generated political controversy from the outset, was severely hampered by the international economic downturn after 1973, by political upheaval in Northern Ireland, by the vagaries of government economic and planning policy, and, not least, by popular resistance to the new city idea. The second part of the chapter probes the basis for this resistance among local residents who are coping with, and reflecting on, the 'failure' of the new city twenty-five years after its inception. The concluding section suggests that the 'failure' of Craigavon has arisen from the interaction of state policy, economic change, and local identity and local action. In particular, it highlights the importance of the interaction of state and local territorial strategies in a society marked by deep ethnic-national divisions.

Background, origins and development

The Craigavon project was conceived and partially implemented against a background of radical socio-economic and political change. Not only was the project perhaps the most ambitious example of urban planning in twentieth century Ireland, it was initiated at a time when there was a major shift in how Northern Ireland was being incorporated into the international economy. Indeed, the new city was intended as a means of influencing and shaping this incorporation. The global economy was undergoing radical alteration itself as multinationals were beginning to develop effective global strategies, including the decentralization and dispersal of production processes, which were undermining more locally-based industry in the towns and cities of the province.

The British government in the post-1945 period and, more belatedly, the Northern Ireland government (Stormont), had become committed to an interventionist role in influencing the geography of global economic change. This meant *inter alia* developing growth-centres, new cities, and industrial estates to act as poles of attraction for industry. In peripheral regions of the United Kingdom (UK) and the Irish Republic, this policy meant state sponsorship of branches of multinational corporations. The subsequent move away from interventionist policies in the 1970s and 1980s to more "market-led" strategies of development was to have far-reaching effects for Craigavon.

However, by the early 1960s, pressure was building on Stormont to take a more active role in promoting regional economic development. Persistent high unemployment in the province contrasted with near full employment in Britain. Large scale redundancies among Protestant workers in the Belfast engineering and shipbuilding industries had led to defections from the Unionist Party to the Northern Ireland Labour Party. The British Conservative government had begun to revitalise regional policy by attempting to re-direct employment to peripheral regions of the UK - a policy taken further by the new Labour government between 1964 and 1970. Moreover, multinational corporations were generating more mobile international investment and the Irish Republic had already embarked on its programme of state-sponsored multinational investment. Within the Northern Ireland civil service, there was mounting concern over the rapid and unplanned growth of the Belfast urban area (see e.g., Oliver 1978). A small group of civil servants, in conjunction with some younger modernising government ministers (including the new Prime Minister Terence O'Neill, Brian Faulkner and William Craig), embarked on a regional development strategy which was to have far-reaching ramifications. By the 1960s, Stormont was ready to embrace a policy of new towns, growth centre planning, and the provision of industrial estates, roads and other infrastructural developments.

Two key reports were commissioned: one on physical planning (Matthew Report 1963) and one on economic development (Wilson Report 1965). These reports introduced the fashionable British planning rhetoric of the time without acknowledging the highly charged nature of Northern Ireland's sectarian geography. Matthew proposed a stop-line to Belfast's development. He urged that labour and industry be redirected to two major growth centres, Antrim/Ballymena and Lurgan/Portadown, and to a number of secondary centres in the east of the province. Among Matthew's more dramatic recommendations was a proposal for a new "regional city", incorporating the market and linen towns of Lurgan and Portadown, with a population of 20,000 each. This new city was to cater for a large overspill of population from Belfast and for unemployed migrants from the west of the province. The target population set for it was 120,000 by 1980 and 180,000 by the year 2,000.[4] Matthew (1963) declared the new city to be the "first priority" of the Plan and claimed that it would be "a major symbol of regeneration within Northern Ireland".

Matthew justified his choice of location on the grounds of proximity to Belfast, existing transportation routes with potential for expansion, land availability, and the existence of two established urban centres, Lurgan and

Portadown. Significantly, unemployment rates were not a criterion. Both Lurgan and Portadown rates were generally at or below the Northern Ireland average and much lower than in other potential locations such as Armagh, Derry and Newry. Nonetheless, the subsequent Wilson report on the economy, published two years later, endorsed Matthew's plans claiming that the new city could "weld the area together and provide a growth point capable of adding significantly to Northern Ireland's capacity to attract industry" (Wilson 1965: 29-30). Even prior to the Wilson document, the O'Neill administration had moved with great alacrity to implement Matthew's new city recommendations despite considerable hostility from opposition members at Stormont. The latter accused the government of favouring a predominantly Protestant area over Catholic areas with higher levels of unemployment.[5]

Hostility provoked by the choice of location was further intensified by the Cabinet's decision to name the new city after the first Prime Minister of Northern Ireland (James Craig) and by the failure to appoint any nationalists to the new Development Commission. The debate over Craigavon continued in the midst of controversy over a series of other locational decisions, the alleged neglect of the west of the province, the closure of railway lines to the predominantly nationalist towns of Derry and Newry, and, subsequently, the preference of "unionist" Coleraine to Derry as the site of the province's new university.

Despite these objections, and many others by both nationalists and unionists (see Blackman 1988), the plan for Craigavon was prepared and a New Towns Act (NI) was passed in June 1965. In July 1965, the Ministry of Development designated a development area of approximately 100 square miles (67,553 acres), incorporating the boroughs of Lurgan and Portadown and the rural districts of Lurgan and Moira in County Armagh. The designated area had a population of 61,700. In June 1966, a Vesting Order was made and 68,000 acres of land were acquired for the project; a considerably larger area than acquired for similar new town developments in Britain (Carolan 1987).

The first major conflict was between the government and local farmers concerning the value of vested land. The farmers' campaign, which temporarily brought together Protestants and Catholics, was unsuccessful. In October 1965, the Craigavon Development Commission was appointed to manage the development of Craigavon in accordance with the Plan. There was little representation of local interests, possibly to minimise competition between Lurgan and Portadown, while anti-unionists were excluded altogether. Neither was there any mechanism for public participation or consultation. The whole project had been the brainchild of a small elite of politicians, planners and civil servants. In conception and design, it paid little attention to the attachment of Northern Irish people to their localities, nor did it contemplate how difficult it would be to construct a new over-arching urban entity to which both locals and migrants could give their allegiance. The Craigavon Master Plan provided for a sharp segregation of residential, industrial and retail zones reflecting the planning wisdom of the time and the belief that the new city dwellers would be car-owners.[6]

Although the Brownlow sector was the first to be initiated, it was already behind target by 1969. Its population in June of that year was only 1,600 against a target of 5,000. By 1969, the managing director of Goodyear was claiming major labour recruitment problems. Labour turnover was also becoming a problem. The company lost 254 employees in the first four months of 1969 and 'screened' the unemployed in Belfast, Strabane, Newry and Enniskillen with little success. The manager also claimed that new city housing was "too rich for the pocketbook" of potential workers (*Belfast Telegraph* 17-19 June 1969). It seems likely that labour shortages and turnover were partly due to work-related factors and partly to a reluctance to move to, or remain in, an unfamiliar new city environment.

Problems in attracting migrants persisted. In 1971, a mobility office was established in Belfast to provide advice, publicity and financial assistance in the form of cash grants to encourage movement out of Belfast. The resettlement grant scheme met with little success and was often abused by 'moonlighters' who moved to Craigavon until they received the cash grant and then returned, mainly to Belfast (*Lurgan Mail* 11 March 1982). The Craigavon Development Commission went on to build a total of 3739 houses in 22 estates. The Commission succeeded in making major investments - amounting to £500 million - in roads, advance factory units, housing, a government training centre and a 492-bed hospital with a projected employment of 750. Five new industrial estates were established at Annesborough, Silverwood, Seagoe, Carn and Mahon.

By the late 1960s, however, the development of Craigavon was becoming caught up in the general escalation of the 'troubles'. The reluctance of families of both communities to move away from their home territories or to live in mixed communities was now exacerbated. Belfast Catholics began to retreat back into West Belfast, while Protestants tended to move to the new estates on the fringes of the Belfast urban area. Neither were attracted to Craigavon in large numbers, although some 'problem families' were assigned housing there. Conversely, sectarian conflict in Lurgan and Portadown encouraged locals to move to Brownlow, to escape the violence. From the outset, Brownlow gained a reputation as being relatively free from sectarian conflict. However, it did not escape a considerable degree of physical segregation of Protestants and Catholics.

The planners intended to create an integrated community in Brownlow. They sought to avoid the physical separation of denominational facilities by grouping schools, churches, and shops near the centre of neighbourhoods.

The sector was to be a model of integration located between two towns which had a long history of sectarian segregation. As early as 1973, however, there was considerable Protestant-Catholic segregation in Brownlow (Reid 1973). The eastern area contiguous to the Catholic estates in Lurgan was predominantly Catholic, while those in the west nearest Portadown were largely Protestant. This tendency was confirmed by the later building of the Parkmore estate. Closer to Portadown, it became almost exclusively Protestant. While a mixed buffer area exists in the middle of Brownlow (Reid 1973), Brownlow has remained a predominantly Catholic area. Demands for jobs and housing were greater among Catholics and from the outset the Goodyear factory near Lurgan employed large numbers of unskilled Catholic workers. Brownlow's subsequent image problem, however, derived less from sectarian considerations than from problems of marginalization, deprivation and unemployment.

By the early 1970s, other obstacles were mounting for the new city. As part of the reorganisation of local government in 1973, the Craigavon Commission was abolished. It had proved to be one of the shortest lived of any of the UK new town commissions, and its abolition removed the major agency with overall responsibility for coordinating development in Craigavon. The new Borough Council remit did cover the new city, but it had very limited powers. Moreover, it was dominated by rival Portadown and Lurgan interests with minimal representation from Brownlow. The dominant political interests were highly sceptical of the new city in any case, and argued that Brownlow had been developed at the expense of Portadown and Lurgan.

In fact, quite apart from local government re-organisation, regional and growth-centre policy was going out of fashion nationally. In 1975, a new Regional Development Strategy reversed the Matthew/Wilson plans and favoured the dispersing of development among 26 District towns. This further down-graded Craigavon, as did a subsequent shift in priorities to regenerating housing and infrastructure in Belfast and in the older towns. These changes in conjunction with the 'troubles' and international recession made industrial promotion more difficult. Unemployment began to rise rapidly in Craigavon in line with the overall Northern Ireland level. As happened in Britain, the juxtaposition of areas of low and high unemployment became apparent. While industrial employment in Portadown proved resilient, it declined considerably in Lurgan and disastrously in Brownlow with the demise of Goodyear. Brownlow was developing, not as a housing sector of an integrated new city, but, in the words of one state official, as a "collection of problem housing estates, located somewhere between Portadown and Lurgan". In fact, the fragmented nature of Brownlow was expressed physically in the layout of its housing estates. Built for a skilled, fully employed, car owning population, it has proved unsuitable to a population characterised by low skill levels, low incomes, mass unemployment and limited mobility.

Overall, the story of Brownlow in the 1980s was one of continuous crisis involving housing surpluses, high tenancy turnover rates, declining job opportunities, and high debt levels. Over 800 houses were demolished (circa 20% of the total housing stock) and others privatised. While this reduced the housing surplus, it did not prevent the high tenancy turnover or the drift of people back to refurbished or new dwellings in Lurgan, Portadown and Belfast.

The politics of Brownlow in the 1970s and 1980s were not those of unionism and nationalism but of community groups, housing and social welfare issues. The Brownlow Community Council (1979) strongly criticised the ward boundaries which led to under-representation of Brownlow compared to Lurgan and Portadown. It suggested that the only hope for the area was a strong voice to offset the rivalries of the towns. This demand was to recur regularly from umbrella groups of community activists.

In spite of its internal divisions, a separate identity began to develop in Brownlow, rooted in part in its neglect and stigmatisation by Lurgan and Portadown interests and in part due to its dependency on state agencies. By the time our research got underway the Brownlow Initiative (and subsequently Brownlow Ltd.) had been set up as a "partnership" between state agencies, community groups and business to develop an economic strategy for Brownlow *per se*. Soon after, the government designated the area as the sole Northern Ireland recipient of funds under the EC's third anti-poverty programme. The Brownlow Community Trust was established as a partnership between statutory, voluntary and community organisations to administer the programme and tackle the social problems of the area. It seemed that the government was acquiescing to demands to have Brownlow treated as a separate local entity - yet another sign that the vision of an integrated new city had been laid to rest.

A deteriorating economic environment, lack of consistency in state policy, and a loss of political enthusiasm all combined to undermine the new city. Yet, such a general and 'top-down' assessment misses an important dimension to the story, i.e., the interaction of local identity and local action with state policy. At the outset, the Craigavon project seemed to meet two key requirements: for planners and administrators, it represented the opportunity to translate 'best' British economic and 'new town' strategy to Northern Ireland; for Stormont ministers, it was consistent with maintaining unionist economic and political dominance. Neither group reckoned with the strength of local resistance, however, and the difficulty of transcending deeply rooted communal and territorial identifications in Lurgan and Portadown. Our research in Craigavon, almost three decades after its designation as a new city, highlights not just local residents' reaction to failed state policies, but how local responses and perceptions helped ensure such failure in the first place. Perhaps the most striking failure of all, was the failure of the new city advocates to grasp the problematical nature of state-locality interaction in a society torn by territorially based ethnic national divisions.

Local responses and perceptions in a 'failed' new city context

By 1989, when this research began, residents of Craigavon were agreed that Lurgan and Portadown had retained their separate identities. Typically, Brownlow was also seen as distinct - a failed remnant of a failed new city. One life-long resident of Portadown remembered the rivalry between Lurgan and Portadown from her schooldays, adding:

> There's always rivalry between Lurgan and Portadown. . . . But the two towns are very similar, even in the shape of the towns. You would never get a Lurgan person saying that Portadown's a better town or vice versa. I've often thought that was the reason why the city didn't join up. Although we're supposed to be from Craigavon, if anybody asked me where I came from, I'd never think of saying I came from Craigavon. I come from Portadown. There are two main towns in themselves and a piece in between that's an outsider.

The long-standing rivalry between both towns was a recurrent theme among our informants. It was clear also that overarching local identities transcended the Protestant-Catholic divide. However, this did not mean that the internal communal divide was unimportant. Indeed, there were considerable differences in the population balance in each locality. The percentage of Catholics ranged from approximately 30 per cent in Portadown, to about 50 per cent in Lurgan and 70 per cent in Brownlow.[7] Moreover, religious affiliation fused in different ways with social class and local identity in each area. A senior manager in the Southern Health and Social Services Board made the issue of intra-locality division explicit:

> Portadown people are Portadown . . . you could say there's two separate communities in Portadown and two separate communities in Lurgan; they wouldn't even talk to themselves, let alone acknowledge this big lump in the middle. I think they are reasonably insular and it's a disaster in social planning for everyone to come together into one big brave new town with new industry and big jobs.

A male community worker in Brownlow noted the perception of the place as a dumping ground for 'problem-families':

> Every Tom, Dick and Harry has been shoved in here, and the place has a
> name for all sorts of perverts and weirdoes. This has been said to me by
> people I knew from Portadown . . . morale is low, self-esteem is low.

Brownlow's identity was portrayed generally in negative terms. An official
in the Craigavon Training Centre located in Portadown observed that there
was very little difference in trainees from Lurgan and Portadown but that
those from Brownlow:

> would tend to have a very erratic attitude, and would tend to drop out -
> they'd have discipline problems, time-keeping and attendance problems. . . .
> I feel that people who were encouraged to come into it [Brownlow] were
> possibly troublesome cases from elsewhere.

Brownlow Ltd. and Brownlow Community Trust aimed to reverse this
negative image by generating improved job opportunities, welfare provision,
and identification with Brownlow as an entity distinct from either Portadown
or Lurgan.   The development of separate strategies for Brownlow even
included a proposal by the Brownlow Initiative to build a traditional town
centre to give the area a focus. Such attempts to establish a separate identity
for Brownlow were met with a mixture of scepticism and enthusiasm by state
officials and voluntary sector workers dealing with the area.[8] Community
activists, on the other hand, saw little alternative, given the stigmatisation
and isolation of the area by Portadown and Lurgan, though they felt
ambivalent about the possibility of success.

A leading voluntary sector worker involved in the regeneration plans
acknowledged that "historically Brownlow was a white elephant" and "an
administrative embarrassment" and that "a lot of senior civil servants would
hope that it would go away". The consultants appointed to develop the
Brownlow Initiative noted that there were only a few scattered shops in the
area and one manufacturing business employing six people (four of them on
training schemes) in an area of 10,000 people (Mackey 1989). This was a
sharp reminder of the difficulties of creating a settled urban identity
comparable to that in Lurgan and Portadown.

Lurgan and Portadown: contrasting business cultures

In terms of origins, size, location, and common industrial base in the linen
industry, Lurgan and Portadown seem to have much more in common with
each other than they do with Brownlow. Yet, our respondents' images of
Lurgan and Portadown not only stressed their differences from Brownlow,
but the contrasts between one another. Portadown was uniformly represented
as the most successful local economy, while Lurgan was portrayed as less

well off - a point supported by our survey research. Both towns were perceived as very different in terms of business and trade union culture, and highly competitive historically vis-á-vis employment, trade and other resources. These responses illuminate the difficulties of merging the two towns into a wider urban entity. For example, one Catholic industrialist claimed that there was more "entrepreneurial flair in Portadown than in Lurgan", adding:

> I think there are more people owning their houses[9] and there's more of a
> sense of commitment in the community and to the community. It may have
> something to do with the Catholic/Protestant links . . . you have a higher
> percentage of Catholics in Lurgan than in Portadown. And for some reason
> there has never been as much capital available in the Catholic community.

A retired businessman active in bringing new industry to Portadown in the post-war period saw the ascendancy of Portadown in terms of a more proactive civic culture:

> You can get Portadown people to respond more quickly to a public need
> (for example, set up a committee). The Portadown Chamber of Commerce
> is an example - it has been going for 50 years, whereas Lurgan Chamber of
> Commerce, you never hear about them.

Our historical research into local economic initiatives in Portadown and Lurgan confirmed the pro-activity of a small business elite in the former and the relative inactivity in the latter. As early as 1946, an elite group of businessmen formed the Portadown New Industries Council (PNIC) to attract industrial investment to the town as the local linen industry began to decline. The PNIC was largely informal in nature with five permanent members: a store-owner, a solicitor, a builder and two linen industrialists. It linked the local Chamber of Commerce with the Junior Chamber, the Rotary Club and the Borough Council. Its first chairman was a highly influential linen industrialist at both local and regional level. For example, he used his position on the Electricity Board for Northern Ireland to persuade Unidare to locate in the town, and he was able to persuade existing local employers to adapt to a more diversified industrial base. In the late 1950s, the PNIC was the first local body to produce an industrial promotion brochure to "sell the town" to potential investors.[10]

Not only was the Portadown business elite more active than its Lurgan counterpart, it pre-figured the systematic sponsorship of multinational investment by the Stormont government in the 1960s. Craigavon Development Commission took over the functions of the PNIC on its creation in 1966. Nevertheless, when the Commission disbanded in 1973 the newly formed Craigavon Borough Council expressed an interest in the old PNIC and in 1980 the Craigavon New Industries Council (CNIC) was established and re-named the Craigavon Industrial Development Organisation (CIDO) in 1985.

The old gulf between Lurgan and Portadown re-appeared, however. Although the CNIC was to act for Craigavon as a whole, representatives from Lurgan withdrew their participation within 18 months, claiming that the new body was primarily Portadown-oriented. CIDO took advantage of the Thatcher's government commitment to 'enterprise culture' to establish small business units in Portadown, while, belatedly, an Enterprise Trust was established in Lurgan in 1989. The slowness of Lurgan to respond to the new enterprise policies was explained by the manager of the Lurgan Job Market in terms of the absence of locals at management level in industry:

> If we had industrialists who were local, maybe they would band together and get things going. There are some, but not as many as other towns would have. They say that the Rotary here is more commercially-orientated than manufacturing-orientated.

Certainly, evidence of employment change suggested that Portadown had succeeded better than Lurgan in diversifying its economy and combating global economic changes. Between 1950 and 1970 both towns had similar unemployment rates - at or below the Northern Ireland average. Initially, both were heavily dependent on linen manufacture, but as this industry declined Portadown's economic diversification helped it to combat recession. Between 1971 and 1978 Portadown lost only 10 per cent of its manufacturing jobs, as compared to Lurgan's 21 per cent. In the same period, unemployment increased by 85 per cent in Portadown and by 139 per cent in Lurgan.[11] Thus, the Craigavon project coincided with a widening gulf between the economies of Portadown and Lurgan - a gulf that may be partly rooted in the history of their business communities. Both towns have seen the replacement of indigenous industry by national and multinational interests. Portadown, however, has retained a larger core of locally owned manufacturing which seems to provide the impetus for a more positive response to economic change and shifts in government economic policy.

Trades union culture

Business, of course, constitutes only one element in a complex local identity. Different trades union histories also distinguished the two towns. For example, unlike Portadown, Lurgan had a long history of trade union activity associated with the linen trade - a difference which lived on in the perceptions of local activists. One retired trade union official in Lurgan claimed that Portadown would not join the trade union in the 1950s while

"Lurgan was 100 per cent trade union". Whereas Portadown had its leading business activists, Lurgan had a prominent and influential union organiser called Mick Casey. While there was a trade union in Portadown, "there were never trade union principles . . . they accepted everything that was offered to them, whether they liked it or not". He felt that Portadown employees were always very respectful to their bosses.

Another trade union activist supported the point about worker deference in Portadown claiming that, in one factory, fully organised by the ATGWU, workers called their bosses 'Master' and were called by their surname in turn. He also noted the historical resistance in Portadown to trade union organisation claiming that it was 'a religious thing'.

As in the case of business culture, religion is seen as interwoven with the history of trade unionism in both towns. According to the retired trade union official: "it was always considered a Catholic thing to be a member of a trade union . . . all the shop-stewards in the linen trade were Catholic . . . people were looked down on because they were associated with a 'Communist/Catholic' organisation" (i.e., the trade union).

Trade unionists acknowledged, however, that Portadown's better employment record and improved trade union organisation had led to a strengthening of trade union membership, whereas economic decline had undermined Lurgan's trade union tradition. Nevertheless, as another ATGWU official pointed out, Lurgan remained the traditional centre for trade union protests and parades.[12] These were unlikely to occur in Portadown. Although trades union membership was seen to have increased in the latter due to active local officials, membership was not to be confused with militancy. This view was supported by several female trade unionists concerned with opposing the privatisation of services in Craigavon Hospital (located near Portadown). They complained about the difficulty of mobilising opposition to privatisation of services in Craigavon Area Hospital (near Portadown) blaming it on conservatism, status snobbery and "culture". Although religion was not explicitly mentioned as a factor, unfavourable comparisons were made between the lack of militancy in Protestant Craigavon and the more militant response in Catholic Newry to the same privatisation plans.

The different business and trade union cultures in Lurgan and Portadown were compounded by local political rivalry between the two towns. While this rivalry found expression on Craigavon Council in terms of intra-unionist politics, it was also evident in wider lobbying for facilities and resources.

Ethno-sectarian geography and local identity

The origins of both Lurgan and Portadown can be traced directly to the plantation of Ulster in the early seventeenth century. In Lurgan, for example, a planter family, the Brownlows, built the town and maintained an unbroken connection with it until recently. Memories of plantation and revolt are preserved in local culture. Perhaps one of the more striking examples of this was the ceremony on the bridge in Portadown in 1991, presided over by the head of the Orange Order to commemorate the Protestants massacred there 350 years earlier in the Catholic rising of 1641. Both towns were strong centres of Orangeism from the inception of the Orange Order in the late eighteenth century.

Against this background, geographers and historians have noted how communal segregation became an integral part of the rapid development of both towns in the second half of the nineteenth century. The pattern of segregation established in Lurgan by 1911, after forty years of industrial growth, has changed little in the twentieth century - in 1971, it was the most segregated middle-sized town in Northern Ireland (Poole 1982: 298-305).

Our interviews revealed a sharp awareness of religious segregation. Respondents spoke of an "invisible line" which divided Catholic from Protestant Lurgan. There was a sharp sectarian polarisation in working class estates in both Lurgan and Portadown and signs that these divisions were being replicated in Brownlow. Some of our respondents referred to cases of intimidation and assassination which led to the enforced movement of population in the early 1970s and a reversal of the degree of mixing that was beginning to occur in some of the newer estates.

Early signs of the failure of the planners' attempt to create religiously integrated areas in Brownlow were confirmed in the 1980s. The estates nearest Lurgan were overwhelmingly Catholic and became, in a sense, an extension of the Catholic part of Lurgan. Protestants in Brownlow, on the other hand, gravitated towards Portadown. Central Brownlow was more mixed but the demolition of some of the central estates was reducing its size. In the words of a Brownlow community worker, this demolition is:

> creating a lot of problems for the central area. The nationalist side is gravitating towards Lurgan, the loyalist side to the Portadown end, and the middle being totally devastated. I think that's going to create difficulties in the future - it could exacerbate sectarian difficulties of which there has not been much so far.

The housing schemes and industrial estates of the new city, far from providing new "integrated environments", soon began to demonstrate the power of popular as opposed to planners' definitions of locality. In our interviews with householders,[13] there was a tendency to distinguish between workplace and where it was located. Generally, there was a feeling that both religions can and do work together but that the location of the workplace and/or the areas through which one had to travel to get to it, could be problematic. A female Protestant factory worker in Lurgan commented:

> There isn't anything, you know, between Protestants and Catholics in work really. You know, everybody seems to be sort of friends like. It's a funny thing, that like. You can have a mixture of people and the troubles would never be mentioned at work.

This woman said her factory was in a Catholic area of Lurgan and that she had no fears at all about going to work. Her husband, however, remembered difficulties in persuading Catholics to travel through Protestant areas to work at his previous place of employment.

An unemployed Protestant in Portadown mentioned a food processing plant located in a Catholic area pointing out that: "there's no Protestants that would apply for that because of where it is". His wife added: "it's not in a really bad area but to get to it you have to go through a really bad area". The husband then referred to a Protestant factory where Catholics had similar problems.

A part-time Catholic shop assistant in central Craigavon was in no doubt that shops in Lurgan and Portadown employed workers on the basis of religion and that people would refuse to work in certain factories because of their religion. She then added: "I wouldn't go to Portadown - I'd go to Lurgan. There's girls I work with who've never been to Lurgan - they stay in Portadown." This comment is revealing in that it illustrates the self-contained nature of Portadown and Lurgan and the orientation of the Catholic part of Brownlow to Lurgan.

The manager of Lurgan job market stressed the separateness of Lurgan and Portadown and noted the difficulty of working with "three separate communities" within the Craigavon area. He mentioned the reluctance of Lurgan people to travel to work in Portadown, four or five miles away, although they would travel to industrial estates on the outskirts of Portadown or to work in Lisburn and Belfast. The reluctance to travel was particularly marked among Catholics who saw Portadown as a Protestant town. The Lurgan job market manager mentioned, in particular, the efforts being made to get people to attend the Job Club in Portadown, observing: "you can't tell whether it's a genuine fear or just an excuse or a perceived notion. There was always confrontation between Lurgan and Portadown anyway".

The difficulties posed by sectarian geography were underlined by an unemployed 35 year old Catholic man in Portadown:

> You don't go to certain factories because they are in bad areas. . . . I've seen Manpower or the job market as it's called now, asking me to go to a job and

I wouldn't go to it because of the area it was in. Because I can't drive and I've no form of transport and I'd have to walk or go on a bike, or whatever. But I thought it was highly dangerous going through the areas y'know.

The impact of sectarian geography on young people's opportunities was stressed by some of our key informants. A Portadown community workshop (training) manager noted:

Ninety per cent of the trainees would come from the Tunnel (Catholic working class area of Portadown). Those trainees have a ghetto mentality - they won't go outside of this area. . . . We had some trainees going for a job here this morning [mentions another Catholic area of Portadown], which is a quarter of a mile from here, and they wanted to know how they would get there. They have this ghetto mentality reinforced at home.

His opposite number in Lurgan also noted the reluctance of young Catholic trainees: "(they) will go to Protestant employers, but they won't go to a predominantly Protestant area to work". Employment that serviced the whole Craigavon area posed particular problems in negotiating sectarian geography. A Brownlow woman whose husband was a taxi-driver worried about him being "an easy target":

If you are going around you're just stopped and asked who you are and what you are. . . . There would be certain areas they would be afraid to go into. People would ring a certain company because they know what they are.

The difficulties of constructing an integrated local labour market in Craigavon are clear from our interviews, which show that there is more mixing at work than in housing, education and leisure pursuits. Nevertheless, workplaces are lodged within a sharply defined sectarian geography which they also help to shape. Mobility and willingness to travel to work are constrained not just by religious affiliation but also by age, gender and class. While none of our middle class, and few of our female, respondents indicated that their own access to work was limited by sectarian considerations, clearly they were a major consideration for our working class interviewees, especially for males in the younger age groups.

Territorial and ethnic-sectarian divisions, far from being undermined by economic change and state planning, were in many respects consolidated by them. One key indicator is unemployment rates. Our survey research reveals major territorial and religious variations in unemployment rates, ranging from 26.4 per cent in Brownlow to 17.3 per cent in Lurgan to 11.5 per cent in Portadown (the unemployment rates for the Craigavon Travel to Work Area and Northern Ireland as a whole were 13.7 per cent and 15.4 per cent respectively). These figures obscured very large variation within localities. In Brownlow, for example, a survey undertaken in 1989 (prior to our survey) reveals rates of zero and 9 per cent in two owner-occupied estates and a range from 30 to 38 per cent in the publicly owned estates (Mackey 1989).

Differential unemployment rates by religion in each of the three areas further confirm the durable economic underpinnings of sectarian geography in Craigavon (see Table 1).

Table 1
Unemployment rates by religion, gender and locality (percentages)

	Lurgan	Brownlow	Portadown
Catholic males	29.4 (51)	29.6 (27)	27.6 (29)
Other denominations males	12.8 (47)	36.4 (11)	10.0 (70)
Catholic females	13.3 (30)	17.4 (23)	15.4 (26)
Other denominations females	5.9 (34)	14.3 (7)	3.7 (54)
Total Catholics	23.5 (81)	24.0 (50)	21.9 (55)
Total other denominations	9.9 (81)	27.8 (18)	7.3(124)
Total	17.3(162)	26.4 (68)	11.5(179)

Table 1 lends support to information from our other sources that Portadown is the most successful local economy followed by Lurgan and Brownlow. However, "equality of misery" between Catholic and Protestant, as measured by unemployment rates, holds only in Brownlow. Although care must be taken in interpretation because of small numbers, the figures indicate that all denominations share the common economic marginalization of Brownlow. The position is very different in the two established towns where it is much closer to the Northern Ireland picture as a whole. Catholics are three times more likely to be unemployed than others in Portadown and 2.4 times more likely in Lurgan. Interestingly, the gap is widest in the most successful economy, suggesting that success in creating new jobs does not necessarily mean greater inter-communal equality. It is clear also that inter-communal inequality is generally greater for males than for females with the striking exception of Portadown, where Catholic women are over four times as likely to be unemployed as women from other denominations.

Territorial and communal identity, therefore, is not merely a matter of perception but is rooted also in material inequality. Differential experiences of work and unemployment, for example, combines with residential segregation to help define Catholic and Protestant communities. Inter-communal inequality seems to have been consolidated rather than undermined by the experience of the new city. Portadown has maintained a strong economy, benefiting from new industrial investments and government policy. Lurgan, and especially Brownlow, have suffered in comparison.

Conclusion

It now seems that the vision of an integrated new city at Craigavon has been finally abandoned, yet the project has had a major effect on the area, notably in the creation of Brownlow and in the investment of substantial government expenditure in a skeletal framework which links industrial estates, roads, housing estates, and an incomplete city centre. The elaborate, and now inappropriate, urban layout still visible in Craigavon is a reminder of the optimistic assumptions which informed the project in the early 1960s. These included beliefs in the efficacy of 'top-down' planning as an instrument of socio-economic change, in the continuation of economic expansion, and in a future of political stability in Northern Ireland, where communal divisions could be managed, if not avoided altogether. In the event, international economic downturn coincided with political upheaval, ensuring that multinational investment would no longer serve as the engine of new city development in the 1970s and 1980s.

Such broad explanations of failure, while necessary, are insufficient in themselves, however, and ignore the salience of local identities and local action. Craigavon is testimony to the durability and adaptability of territorial and communal identities despite the challenge which the new city project seemed to pose to the local *status quo*. In Northern Ireland, any attempt to implement a new spatial or territorial strategy inevitably means modifying the ethno-sectarian geography which comprises the province as a territorial unit. Territorial decision-making has always been a matter of contention since the creation of Northern Ireland, notably with respect to the location of housing and jobs, as well as the delineation of local electoral boundaries. Territorial strategies, however, are not just a matter for policy makers, they are of central significance in everyday life in the construction of local and communal identity. Our research suggests some of the ways in which communal affiliation, business, trade unions, the experience of work and unemployment are interwoven to forge local identities. The formation and negotiation of sectarian geography in Craigavon is not just a matter for policy makers, it is a matter for local residents also. They are influenced by historical and cultural memory, by fear and intimidation, and by the class, gender, religion and age group to which they belong.

The fate of the new city reveals the capacity of local groups to fit the altered urban environment to the contours of established sectarian geography. The polarised sectarian geography of Lurgan and Portadown has survived and has extended into the new Brownlow district. Superficially, both towns seemed to have common origins and a shared history of industrial development making them appropriate candidates for merger into the new city. Closer study, however, reveals significant differences in local culture which are expressed in intense rivalry - a rivalry which has survived a shared suspicion of the new city. Different local histories of inter-communal relations, of access to work and political power, and antagonisms over the state and over territory all contributed to resistance to the new city project. Far from the latter ameliorating such differences, it seems to have exposed and underlined them.

In societies where ethnic or national divisions are central, territorial strategies are routinely employed to link the economic, political and cultural dimensions of everyday life. Of course, such links are made in all societies, but in stable states they appear consensual, opaque or only partially contested. Where ethnic-national divisions persist, however, and where the state is largely identified with one ethnic group, state and local boundaries are routinely problematical and even violently contested because they delineate different ways of linking economy, polity and culture. Moreover, the various specialised functions of the state are regularly co-ordinated to protect ethnic dominance, which in turn is identified with the state itself.

The Craigavon project linked economic and spatial strategies while initially obscuring their political and cultural dimensions. It seems likely that, for some of the planners and economists involved, building a new city as a means of economic modernisation constituted an end in itself or held out prospects for greater political and cultural integration of both ethno-religious communities in Northern Ireland. From the outset, the nature of local response to the project, the emergent and enveloping Northern Ireland conflict, and changing international economic conditions, demonstrated the limitations of the Craigavon strategy. It failed, but it is an instructive failure for students of locality formation and locality-state relationships.

Locality formation is a complex dynamic process shaped by the interplay between local action, the state and the international economy. Confronted with the complexity of this process, a social science of compartmentalised disciplines is tempted by spatial, economic, political and cultural reductionism. Here the social scientist falls back on abstraction, either by choosing to privilege economic, political or cultural variables, or else by arbitrarily defining a locality as a fixed territorial and physical entity. While abstraction is necessary, the form it should take is debatable. This research suggests that abstraction should not obscure process.

Economists and sociologists who study local economies and labour markets must realise that these are not synonymous with 'locality'. This research supports Howe's (1990:72) observation in his Belfast study that local economies and labour markets are simultaneously cultural constructions which sustain the sectarian divide. As he points out, each ethnic group feels a 'proprietary right to jobs in its own area'. However, as Craigavon shows, what is 'its own area' is contestable. Many jobs in Craigavon service the whole area and demand territorial strategies to deal with a mosaic of segregated communities. Of course, joblessness also has territorial dimensions, which are particularly constraining on young males in the Craigavon area. Students of global economic development have underlined how modern business and technological innovation have allowed capitalist firms a growing freedom from territorial constraints. The history of Goodyear in Craigavon is a good example. Yet, ironically, such a capacity to transcend spatial boundaries has made territoriality and locality more, not less, important. Firms can choose where to locate; and localities and state agencies must compete for the jobs they provide. As a result, localities are often reshaped by processes to which they can only react, rather than control.

Recognising the impact of international economic change in ethnically divided societies should limit the temptation to reduce locality formation to accounts of ethnic struggle. Ethnic groups are typically heterogeneous with respect to their business and workplace cultures and their class composition. Such groups, and their internal divisions, relate to the economy and the state in different ways. Indeed, the state and the economy play a key role in constituting inter- (as well as intra-) ethnic relations and in building up the patterns of conflict and accommodation which mark these relations in particular localities. Access to power (state or otherwise) or degrees of powerlessness can in themselves constitute crucial elements of local and communal identity.

There is, therefore, no simple correspondence of ethnicity and territory. Lurgan, Brownlow and Portadown, are internally divided on ethnic lines (and in different ways). Each area is characterised by different patterns of inter-ethnic conflict and accommodation, and by different relationships to the state and the economy. Yet, in Lurgan and Portadown, and to a growing extent in Brownlow, there are types of overarching popular identifications strong enough to prevent the three areas from being merged into an integrated new city. Day and Murdoch's (1993) critique of locality studies includes a plea to restore 'community' to its place in the study of social space. They argue that the tendency to replace 'community studies' with 'locality studies' discounts the capacity of local actors to shape their environment. They criticise the way in which locality studies have accorded primacy to economic factors, thereby conceptualising localities as simply the contingent outcomes of wider processes. When greater weight is accorded to local action by these studies, Day and Murdoch (1993:85) argue, the term 'locality' takes on many of the connotations of 'community'.

While they are correct in warning against ascribing to localities the capacity to act, Day and Murdoch (1993) seem to leave open the possibility of using both terms, 'community' and 'locality'. Certainly, Craigavon suggests the utility of this approach. Each ethnic group may be seen as an 'imagined community' pursuing territorial strategies which help shape localities. As argued above, local identification can be different from communal identification. The construction, defence and management of local boundaries allows us to grasp the processes of interaction between economic actors, the state, and local groups.

Territorial strategies remain critical in all societies where states and communities seek to domesticate the dynamics of socio-economic change. However, they are particularly transparent in societies characterised by ethnic-national conflict. More stable, homogeneous societies are characterised by a popular amnesia about the degrees of historic conflict, coercion, and even duplicity involved in constructing national boundaries and in incorporating localities within states. Some of the thinking behind the Craigavon project seems to have assumed that the prospect of the new city would induce such amnesia, locally at least. In this, it failed to recognise the importance of local actors and of the historical and cultural memories they brought to the 'new city'. The significance of these memories, however, resides not in some pathological fixation with the past, but in the way in which they are provoked and re-activated by the territorial strategies of states and capitalist firms, by the politics of locational decisions, and by the continued material inequalities within and between communities. By giving a voice to local actors, social scientists and policy makers can begin to grasp the importance of historical and cultural memory and the local and communal identities to which it contributes.

Notes

1. This research project, "Local Responses to Industrial Change in Northern Ireland: A Comparison of Newry and Craigavon", was funded by ESRC Research Grant: R000 23 1161. I would like to acknowledge the contribution of two research officers on the project: Michael Maguire, 1988-89, and Colm Ryan, 1989-91. The research, carried out between 1989 and 1991, employed a variety of methods including semi-structured (taped) interviews with local businessmen, officials, community activists, politicians and householders, as well as a questionnaire survey of 250 households randomly selected from the Craigavon area.

2. Economists have tended to incorporate 'the troubles' as a rather crude and undifferentiated variable into their analyses, estimating their effect on employment, unemployment, job promotion, external investment and public expenditure. Rowthorn and Wayne (1988) have provided the most detailed study of the links between economic change and the conflict but have focused on the regional, rather than the locality level. Studies of employment inequality and discrimination (e.g., Smith and Chambers 1991; Cormack and Osborne 1991) also concentrate on the regional rather than on the local levels. Eversley (1989) makes strenuous attempts at sub-regional analysis of labour market inequality between Catholics and Protestants but his analysis is greatly hindered by imperfect census data, by shifting administrative boundaries and by the lack of correspondence between popular and administrative definitions of locality.

3. While Northern Ireland is relatively well provided with statistical information at regional level, this is not the case at local level. Major data sets such as the

Continuous Household Survey, the Labour Force Survey, and the Family Expenditure Survey cannot be disaggregated to local level because of sample size. Analysis of the census is also hampered by problems of non-response and non-completion in specific areas and by the shifting ward boundaries between censuses.

4. In fact, by 1991, the population of Craigavon Borough Council area had only reached 74,986, an increase of only 1,726 since 1981. Far from attracting new migrants, Craigavon showed a net out-migration of 7.8 per cent between 1981 and 1991 (Northern Ireland 1992).

5. Portadown and Lurgan were significant centres of local Unionist power, even if they had relatively large nationalist populations. Early Catholic civil rights activists had criticised Lurgan's 15 person local council for operating "large religious ghettos". Although the 1961 census indicated that Catholics accounted for over 45 per cent of Lurgan's population, a system of block voting (i.e., every elector voting for every councillor with no ward divisions) ensured that there was no anti-unionist representation on the local council. In central and local government in the town, it was claimed that there was only one Catholic in a salaried position. Lurgan council's 156 employees included only 25 Catholics, 23 of whom were labourers (McCluskey 1989). An early account of the Northern Ireland 'problem' indicated similar difficulties with the block voting system in Portadown. In 1962, there was no direct Catholic representation on Portadown Council, although Catholics comprised over a quarter of the population (Barritt and Carter 1962: 125).

6. In 1966, the whole project got a major boost when the Minister of Commerce, Brian Faulkner, announced that Goodyear was to locate a £6.5 million factory between Lurgan and Brownlow, with a promise of 2,000 jobs. Goodyear, it appeared, would be at once the industrial anchor and launching pad for Craigavon as a whole. In fact, after a chequered local history, it reached a peak of nearly 1,800 workers in 1977. Thereafter, its workforce was run down to its eventual closure in 1983 with a loss of 770 jobs.

7. In our random survey of 250 households, 33 per cent were Catholic in Portadown, 52 per cent in Lurgan, and 70 per cent in Brownlow.

8. Some officials pointed out the need to plan for Craigavon as a whole. Others, such as the outgoing Director of Social Services in the region, placed more emphasis on the need to develop a separate strategy for Brownlow. The Department of the Environment, as owners of the land in the area, was a major force behind the economic regeneration plan. However, community activists and some voluntary sector workers believed that the plan was aimed more at reducing state expenditure in Brownlow than a genuine attempt to develop it as an urban locality in its own right.

9. Interestingly, this point was not confirmed by our survey of households.

10. This information is from an interview with a former secretary of PNIC.

11. Employment and unemployment data are derived from Northern Ireland (n.d.), Ministry of Health and Social Services, Abstract 8, page 8 for 1953-67 figures. Subsequent figures come from unpublished Department of Economic Development sources.

12. David Calvert, a former Democratic Unionist Party councillor in Craigavon, remembered Lurgan in the 1960s not as a trade union centre, but as a great location for (Protestant) religious meetings (BBC, "Places Apart, Lurgan" 2 July 1990).

13. In-depth interviews were undertaken with fourteen households in the Craigavon area. Interviewees were selected from respondents to our random survey of households, to reflect the balance of religion, household location and employment profile in the random sample.

References

Bagguley, P., Mark-Lawson, J., Shapiro, D., Urry, J., Walby, S. and Warde, A. 1990. *Restructuring: place, class and gender.* London: Sage.

Barritt, D.P. and Carter, C.F. 1962. *The Northern Ireland problem: a study in community relations.* London: Oxford University Press.

Blackman, T. 1988. *Housing policy and community action in County Durham and County Armagh.* Unpublished PhD thesis, University of Durham.

Boal, F.W. and Douglas, J.N.H. (ed). 1982. *Integration and division.* London: Academic Press.

Brownlow Community Council. 1979. *The future of Brownlow.* Craigavon: Brownlow Community Council.

Carolan, B. 1987. *The management of the Craigavon housing crisis: an assessment of the Northern Ireland Housing Executive's strategy, 1983-86.* Unpublished MSc thesis, University of Ulster.

Cooke, P. 1989. *Localities: the changing face of urban Britain.* London: Unwin Hyman.

Cormack, R. J. and Osborne, R.D. (eds). 1991. *Discrimination and public policy in Northern Ireland.* Oxford: Clarendon Press.

Day, G. and Murdoch, J. 1993. Locality and community: coming to terms with places. *Sociological Review* 41, 82-111.

Dilley, R. 1989. Boat owners, patrons and state policy in Northern Ireland. In H. Donnan and G. McFarlane (eds) *Social anthropology and public policy in Northern Ireland* Aldershot: Avebury.

Donnan, H. and McFarlane, G. 1986. "You get on better with your own": social continuity and change in rural Northern Ireland. In P. Clancy, S. Drudy, K. Lynch and L. O'Dowd (eds) *Ireland: a sociological profile* Dublin: Institute of Public Administration.

Eipper, C. 1986. *The ruling trinity: A community study of church, state and business in Ireland.* Aldershot: Gower.

Eversley, D. 1989. *Religion and employment in Northern Ireland.* London: Sage.

Hausner, V. (ed). 1987. *Economic change in British cities.* Oxford: Clarendon Press.

Howe, L. 1990. *Being unemployed in Belfast: An ethnographic study* . Cambridge: Cambridge University Press.

Jenkins, R. 1983. *Lads, citizens and ordinary kids.* London: Routledge and Kegan Paul.

Jones, E. 1960. *The social geography of Belfast.* London: Oxford University Press.

McCluskey, C. 1989. *Off their knees: a commentary on the civil rights movement in Northern Ireland.* Galway: Conn McCluskey & Associates.

Mackey, D. 1989. *Brownlow skills survey.* Brownlow: Mackey Consultants.

Matthew Report. 1963. *The Belfast regional survey and plan.* Cmd. 451. Belfast: HMSO.

Northern Ireland. 1992. *Census of population 1991: Preliminary Report.* Belfast: HMSO.

____. n.d. Ministry of Health and Social Services, Abstract 8.

O'Dowd, L. 1986. Beyond industrial society. In P. Clancy, S. Drudy, K. Lynch and L. O'Dowd (eds) *Ireland: a sociological profile.* Dublin: Institute of Public Administration.

Oliver, J. 1978. *Working at Stormont.* Dublin: Institute of Public Administration.

Poole, M. 1982. Religious residential segregation in urban Northern Ireland. In F.W. Boal and J.N.H. Douglas (eds) *Integration and division* London: Academic Press.

Reid, J. 1973. Craigavon: what went wrong? *Lurgan and Portadown Examiner* 27 December.

Rowthorn, B. and Wayne, N. 1988. *Northern Ireland: the political economy of conflict.* Cambridge: Polity Press.

Smith, D. J. and Chambers, G. 1991. *Inequality in Northern Ireland* Oxford: Clarendon Press.

Urry, J. 1981. Localities, regions and social class, *International Journal of Urban and Regional Research* 4, 455-74.

Wilson Report. 1965. *Economic development in Northern Ireland.* Cmd. 479. Belfast: HMSO.

4   Negotiating community: the case of a Limerick community development group

Eoin Devereux

The idea that socio-economic development can be achieved through organising people on a community basis has gathered momentum in both rural and urban Ireland in recent times. For its proponents, development based on the notion of community presents few if any conceptual difficulties, yet for social scientists 'community' remains a long-standing intellectual question.[1]   The development strategy usually referred to as 'community development' raises an interesting set of issues for social anthropology in that 'community' and 'communities' need to be defined by those interested in promoting this development strategy whether from above or from below. Following Cohen (1985), this chapter suggests that communities are defined by local people and outsiders not only in physical or spatial terms, but also symbolically.   Despite the usually positive images implicit in the use of the word by policy makers and development groups, 'community' is often a contested concept which is argued over by competing groups of people and individuals.   It is also used strategically by 'community groups' to give credence to the assertion that their views are representative of *everybody* in a given area.   Thus the ways that people use, construct and understand the term 'community' constitute an important issue not only for anthropologists, but also for those in both the public and private sectors who are interested in development issues.

This chapter explores how some inhabitants of an urban area have responded to social change using a community development model.   I examine the issue of urban collective action involving a Limerick city community development group.   In particular, I am concerned with how community development raises the issues of *what* is the community, *who* is in the community, *how* is community defined and with what effects.   The chapter begins with a discussion of the importance of understanding community in terms of symbolic boundaries (Cohen 1985). It then reviews the way in which interpretations of 'the past' play an important role in the symbolic construction and definition of community.

My focus throughout this chapter is on the origins, structure, and activities of the Parish Group in Limerick city. The Parish Group's roots lie in a dispute over competing versions of community and in response to the changes which were taking place in the locality as a result of an inner city urban renewal project being implemented by outside agencies. The Parish Group is currently involved in a 'partnership' relationship with external statutory groups through its membership of the Social Action Against Unemployment in Limerick project (SAUL), a relationship that has implications for the Parish Group's strategic and symbolic uses of community. This case is of interest in that it points to the importance of understanding community development not only in terms of the symbolic dimensions of community, but also in terms of the significance of social class in the dynamics of local community issues.

Defining and using community

The writings of A. P. Cohen (see, for example, 1985; 1986; 1987) have transformed how many social scientists define and use the word 'community'. Rejecting traditional structuralist interpretations of community, Cohen argues for an understanding of community which takes account of both boundary and symbol. He notes also the important role which the past plays in how people define and understand community. Cohen suggests that the word community implies both similarity and difference; the word's use implies:

> that the members of a group of people (a) have something in common with each other, which (b) distinguishes them in a significant way from the members of other putative groups (1985: 12).

Cohen stresses the importance of boundary in defining community. Boundaries may be physical or symbolic. Whilst the inhabitants of a small island might be a community, defined in physical or spatial terms, the community(ies) on that island might also be defined in terms of a shared history or common belief system. For Cohen, community is:

> Just a boundary-expressing symbol. As a symbol, it is held in common by its members; but its meaning varies with its members' unique orientations to it (1985: 15).

He argues that community is by and large a mental construct:

> whose 'objective' manifestations in locality or ethnicity give it credibility. It is highly symbolised with the consequence that members can invest it with their selves. Its character is sufficiently malleable that it can accommodate all of its members selves without them feeling their individuality to be overly compromised. Indeed, the gloss of commonality which it paints over its diverse components gives to each of them an additional referent for their identities (1985: 108-109).

Many observers of community development have stressed both the ambiguity of the notion of community and the subsequent attractiveness of basing a development strategy on such a vague concept (see, for example, Edwards and Jones 1976).

Cohen makes two further important observations of relevance in the present context. First, he stresses the importance of 'the past' in constructing a notion of community. This view can also be fruitfully applied to the world of community development. On the one hand, a community group may be engaging in development work, such as employment creation, which may contribute to social change in a locality, whilst on the other hand its ideological framework may be rooted in a traditionalist construction of what the community is or should be. Thus community groups can find themselves to be both preservers and developers of community at the same time.

Secondly, Cohen argues that communities are not only symbolically defined but that communities and community groups themselves engage in activity which is in itself symbolic. In his study of Whalsay, for example, Cohen tells us that locals participate in a 'spree', which is a party held on a number of occasions throughout the year. Cohen sees the spree as a symbolic expression by community members of both commitment to the community and an acknowledgement that change has taken place. Similarly, London's Notting Hill carnival, which in itself has changed over time, has been found to have an important symbolic function for young immigrants. Cohen notes that the carnival is important in this regard in that "Each is able to define the community for himself using the shared symbolic forms offered by the carnival" (1985: 55).

In the following two sections, I apply Cohen's understanding of community to a community development project in an inner city area in Limerick. I explore the strategic uses to which community is put by examining the concept of partnership between state and community, a relationship in which the Parish Group is currently involved.

The Parish

Situated on an island between two rivers in the inner city, the Parish Group's activities are based in the oldest part of Limerick. The area's inhabitants live in the streets surrounding a range of medieval buildings, as well as in a number of local authority housing estates. The boundaries of the community which the Parish Group seeks to represent may be defined in both spatial terms, given its island location, and in symbolic terms, which reflect a shared culture and class identity. The word 'parish' in the group's title does not refer to a sub-unit of a diocese, which in this case is Saint Imelda's Parish, but to 'the Parish' as a community famous throughout Limerick. Local understanding of the term 'the Parish' is grounded in a shared sense of history and working class culture. Membership of the Parish therefore depends on a shared stock of knowledge about the past, and not only on inhabiting a specific spatial area.

The area was the site of a Viking settlement in the tenth century and the many ancient buildings in this locality, such as King John's Castle and the Bishop's Palace, bear testimony to the important historical events which have taken place there. Set on an island between the Abbey and Shannon rivers, the Parish is renowned in the city of Limerick as being a place where the city's first settlers resided. Today, locals within and without the Parish still refer to inhabitants of the area as being members of the 'old stock'. Similarly, many of the names associated with the area tell of its Viking connection. The local salmon weir, for example, is known by its Danish name, 'Lax Weir', whilst one local shop is known as 'The Tholsel', which is the Danish for City Hall. The area itself is known locally by a number of names. It is called 'the Island', 'the King's Island', or more commonly as 'the Parish'.

In the folk culture of Limerick city, the Parish is celebrated in poetry and song for its strong sporting traditions, particularly in terms of its rugby prowess. It is also famous for being the home of a traditional Limerick food known as 'packet and tripe'.[2] Predominantly a working class area, the men from the Parish traditionally worked in the city's older industries, such as bacon curing and flour milling, or as labourers in the city's docks. With the decline of these industries and the effects of recent economic recessions, long term unemployment has grown in the area amongst both the older and younger residents. Many of its streets incorporate some of the city's oldest buildings and walls. Much of the area's housing was built by Limerick Corporation earlier this century. In the 1930s, the Parish, which was mainly situated around Mary Street, Bishops Street, Nicholas Street and an area known as The Abbey, was enlarged with the building of the first big local authority housing estate in the Island Field, and more recently attempts have been made to encourage urban renewal by building more local authority housing.

Much of this development has been welcomed by local people, but plans such as those first suggested in the late 1970s to build a section of a proposed ring road through the Parish met with much opposition from the inhabitants. Controversy raged again with the renovation of King John's Castle. Many members of the Parish were not happy with the new design of the castle, which involved the adding of a large glass and steel structure to house an interpretative centre. There was much opposition in the form of street protests to what locals call either 'the Glasstle' or 'the Thing'.

The Parish Group's activities follow in a long line of collective action in the locality. In the 1940s there was a guild of the national community development movement *Muintir na Tire* (People of The Land or Country) at work in the area. Taking the Catholic parish as its focus, the guild carried out some very important relief work during the Second World War. There have been other examples of collective action in the Parish with a 'Stop The Ring Road Committee' opposing the local corporation's road development plans in the 1970s. The committee's membership was made up of people from both inside and outside the Parish. Thus, notions of community can be symbolically extended to include people who reside in different spatial areas but who happen to share common beliefs and values.

In the mid 1980s the Saint Imelda's Parish Council, whose break up eventually gave rise to the Parish Group, attempted with limited success to bring about socio-economic development in the Parish. The area has also been the site of much activity in the city-wide Anti-Water Rates Campaign which was fought against the corporation's plans to impose charges for the supply of water to householders. On the election of the new city council in 1991, The Anti-Water Rates Campaign resulted in the abolition of water charges. One prominent member of the Parish Group was elected as an independent councillor on this issue. He topped the poll in the electoral area which includes the Parish.

The Parish Group, however, is not the only community-based group which is currently at work in the area. There are twenty voluntary organisations active in the Parish, many of which see themselves as community developers. These include the Parish Group, a separate but similarly titled Parish Development Group[3,] and a number of residents' associations. An artists' co-operative has also been formed. Many of these groups use the local community centre as their meeting place, but the Parish Group operates from its Local Action Centre in the main street of the Parish.

Central to the Parish Group's model of community development is the notion of partnership. The attempts at fostering partnership may be seen to operate on two interrelated levels. Firstly, it attempts to bring about partnership at local level by bringing together under its banner the many other voluntary groups at work in the area. Secondly, in dealing with the statutory agencies whose decisions affect the lives of many of the local inhabitants, the group has been involved as part of the SAUL project in a process of partnership building through that organisation's committee system. It is clear that there is a diversity of opinion amongst the Parish Group's members as to how community-state partnership works out in practice.

Although many of the community activists to whom I spoke were unclear as to what model of community development the Parish Group was using in its work, the group may be placed amongst those community development groups who follow a consensus approach. This model of development seeks local consensus on issues and is not unlike that which has been followed in the past in other Irish towns (see, for example, Curtin and Varley 1986; Scott 1985). Thus, at local level, the Parish Group sees itself as an umbrella body which seeks to include many community groups under its canvas.

Despite the conflict amongst community leaders in its early days, the Parish Group has had some success in bringing together many of the interest groups in the locality when critical issues have arisen. It has also been successful in encouraging other local groups, such as residents' associations and women's groups, to become active in the Parish Group's activities, such as the organisation of the annual community festivals. It is interesting to note that amongst the Parish Group's key activists are some who subscribe to very different political viewpoints, but who have come together by having an interest in the welfare of their community.

The Parish Group's commitment to the ideal of partnership, however, also has to be seen in another context. As a community partner in SAUL, the group has attempted to create bonds of partnership between local statutory and voluntary bodies. In the context of the group's watchdog role over environmental issues, partnership has been problematic. However, even those who tend to be critical of the activities of statutory bodies believe that it is better for the group to work through the system rather than being viewed as just another pressure group. Within the Parish Group itself there appears to be differing opinions as to how partnership works out in practice. Most view the development of partnership between the statutory bodies and their group in a positive light. There are, however, others who feel disenchanted and disappointed with the workings of the larger project to which the Parish Group is affiliated. As one activist told me "sitting around the table saying that we are all equal is fine, but what happens when one of the statutory bodies takes a decision which will affect the lives of most of the members of the community without consulting us?" Another of the group's members expressed this relationship as being one where both the statutory and voluntary groups were working together for the common good. The issue of partnership must also be viewed in terms of how community groups use this arrangement for their benefit. In the words of one community activist, partnership means "allowing us to help ourselves". In practice this means that the relationship permits the community group to identify key people within the statutory bodies who are responsible for the provision of resources in the area. The reverse is also true in that the relationship allows the statutory bodies to work with those deemed representative of the locality or community.

Since its formation in 1987, the Parish Group holds an Annual General Meeting which all members of the locality can attend. The meeting is usually well advertised by posters in local shops and through circulars delivered to each household. Typically, about fifty people attend such meetings and twelve officers are selected to serve annually. Regular monthly meetings are also held and, given the group's watchdog role on local issues, extraordinary emergency meetings are often called. The Parish Group's organisational structure allows for the participation of representatives of other local groups in its decision making. It actively canvasses the sports, women's, and residents' groups in the area to work under its banner. The Parish Group is in turn represented by two of its officers in the SAUL project. The Parish Group's membership is predominantly made up of people who live in the Parish. Its key activists, however, reside both in the Parish and in the nearby middle class Quinntown area, which was until recently part of the Catholic parish of Saint Imelda's. Many of those who live outside the Parish have strong connections with it, having been born there or being related to Parish residents through marriage.

As well as drawing on the residential and kinship bases of community for its credibility, the Parish Group has often celebrated the culture of the Parish, usually by reference to the past. It utilises a variety of symbols in this regard. The group's logo is that of 'the Nail', a low limestone pillar capped by a circular plate of copper and kept in a Parish building known as 'the Exchange'. In the past, those engaged in commercial activities paid cash for their transactions on the Nail - giving rise to the well known phrase 'paying on the nail', meaning to pay cash down to purchase commodities. The Parish Group has adopted this symbol as being a sign of its credentials, as well as signifying its concern for the past. It also uses the local buildings of historical interest in a symbolic way. The group not only projects itself as a guardian of these buildings, but celebrates their importance for locals by organising events in which 'the past' is re-enacted. Thus, the castle and the palace are the settings for a yearly pageant in which local residents play the leading roles, thereby renewing their sense of shared history. Other symbols, such as the Danish ancestry of the people as well as local culinary tastes (in the form of packet and tripe), are also used by Parish people to stress their separateness from the rest of the city and to reinforce their own sense of community.

The Parish Group therefore has to be viewed in a number of ways. Firstly, there is a strong tradition of community collective action both in the city and in the locality in which the Parish Group is based. Secondly, the community in which the Parish Group is operating may be defined in both physical and symbolic terms. Thirdly, the Parish Group is not alone in laying claims to 'the community', given the existence of other community-based groups and the fact that the locality is currently host to an external community development initiative, which is attempting to foster better relationships between state and community. Fourthly, the activities of the Parish Group have also to be seen in the context of the social changes which are taking place in the locality.

Contesting and using community

I turn now to discuss how the notion of community is both used and contested. 'Community' can be a focus of contention between outsiders and locals, and between those who wish to develop or preserve the community, including between locals themselves.

The Parish Group's beginnings are rooted in a conflict which took place among community leaders in the late 1980s and in response to the changes which were coming about because of inner city urban renewal. Adopting the slogan 'Developing our Future, Preserving our Past'[4] the Parish Group was formed in late 1987, after a dispute which took place on the Saint Imelda's Parish Council and as a reaction to the inner city redevelopment.

Formed in the early 1980s, Saint Imelda's Parish Council had two main functions. Its first aim, in the words of one former member, was to 'bring about the overall betterment of the Parish' and secondly, it was to be responsible for the voluntary activities associated with Saint Imelda's, the local Catholic church. The council enjoyed some success in both these roles. However, a power struggle took place on the Parish Council in 1987. In what was seen as an attempt to oust certain members, a motion was passed stating that all members of the Parish Council should be practising Catholics and that they must attend mass at the local church. Six members of the Parish Council refused to accept this ruling and left the council accusing it of being sectarian. The underlying reasons for the conflict within the Parish Council seem to have been political. A number of those who left had been active in local left wing politics, but there were also community development issues at stake. As members of the Parish Council those who left had been on the side of those who favoured a strong community development orientation for the council. Those who remained on the Parish Council wanted to reorientate the council towards a predominantly church related role. They failed, and the Parish Council disintegrated in the following year.

The split in the Parish Council may be seen as a dispute over competing versions of community. Those who supported the motion passed by the Parish Council seemed to define community in terms of Catholicism and membership of the Catholic Parish, while those who resigned defined community in terms of 'the Parish', a notion which, as we have seen, incorporates working class culture and a shared stock of knowledge about the area's history. The split might also be understood in terms of a debate over the kinds of strategies which a group attempting to preserve the Parish might take. Those who left the council favoured (initially at any rate) an approach that can be viewed as a conflict model of community development, involving protest about the changes which were coming about in their locality. This row between Parish Council members shows that arguments take place amongst locals over the definition and activities of their 'community'.

Having resigned from the council, the six former Parish Council members were keen to form a new community development group. The impetus for forming the Parish Group must also be seen in the context of the changes being brought about in the Parish as a result of urban renewal and in the plans to renovate some of the key buildings of historic interest in the area. As one of the founder members said "We were concerned at the time about living conditions in this inner city parish. We did not want certain types of 'development' being forced upon us". As well as this environmental issue, the community activists were also concerned that locals might not benefit from the rise in tourism which was an anticipated result of such redevelopment. My interviews with members of the Parish Group indicate that, as their slogan ('Developing Our Future, Preserving Our Past') suggests, members have a strong sense of history and a belief that the area's heritage must be preserved. As one activist commented, "between the four bridges which lead to this island lies the very beginnings of the city's history. We must not lose that". Fostering a pride in the Parish as a place of working class traditions and customs is also one of the Parish Group's aspirations. This view was expressed many times by the group's activists. This stance was strongest among those in the group who felt threatened by the recent tourist developments in the locality. In the first instance, they argued that locals should be the ones to benefit economically from such developments. However, fears were also expressed by some that the 'real' culture of the locality would in some way be masked by those responsible for bringing coach loads of tourists to the Parish. As one informant stated in reference to the Parish Group, "We'll show them real working class Limerick. We won't give them a plastic version of ourselves".

The group's formation can therefore be seen to be centred on competing versions of community emanating from both inside and outside the Parish. Internally, the debate hinged on communities defined by religious affiliation and a consensus development strategy, as opposed to a community based on class identity, the past, and a development strategy which would include conflict with outside development agencies. In terms of external factors, the Parish Group's genesis must also be viewed in terms of the response of some local people to the activities of outside development agencies that wished to modernise and develop the area as part of a city-wide urban renewal programme. The defence of the Parish from such activities illustrates that debate often takes place among outsiders, traditionalists, locals and modernisers, all of whom bring different constructions of the term 'community' to the table. For outsiders, the Parish is an area with resources, such as historic buildings which can be developed and exploited for tourism. It is also a zone which falls within the orbit of plans to modernise the inner city, for it presents possibilities to those in both the statutory and private development sectors. For locals, the Parish represents more than a spatial development zone, it is also the community in which they live.

The Parish Group in action

The Parish Group's activities in its five year history can be divided into four main categories: responding to environmental issues, organising recreational activities, providing locals with information about welfare entitlements and adult education opportunities, and promoting tourism development in the area. Its primary activity has been to highlight environmental issues in the inner city district where it is based. In this regard it plays what one of its activists refers to as a 'reactive or watchdog' role. One of the group's main tasks to date has been to respond to the urban renewal and development plans of the local authorities. It tries to do this by working through the system, and to this end has regularly invited the city's planners and architects to come and speak to the group about their plans. Through such means the group hopes to influence the planning process.

The Parish Group's second activity involves the organisation of local cultural and sporting events. Given its dedication to fostering a positive image of the Parish, the main activity in this regard has been the organisation of a community festival, which in the past has stressed parish pride as its main theme. However, these events are also used by the Parish Group as a means of fund-raising to cover the costs of its other activities. At other points in the year the group has been responsible for organising street theatre, and art and photographic competitions which take the Parish as their theme. All of these actions see this community group engage in activities which are largely symbolic. They are occasions when membership of the Parish is reaffirmed and an identity separate from other identities in the locality or in the city is underlined. An example of how members of this community group see themselves in a distinct light is to be found in the only half in jest suggestion that the Parish Group might issue their own passports to locals and visas to all other visitors to the area.

The Parish Group's third main area of activity is in the provision of information to local people about employment and educational opportunities and in the dissemination of details about social welfare rights and entitlements. A more recent concern of the Parish Group has been to foster employment creation through tourism development. In late 1992, it hoped to attract funding to develop the local river banks as a tourist attraction. In addition, it also planned to expand its tourist information facilities and the marketing of locally produced arts and crafts from its local action centre. The Parish Group's activities defend both the physical and symbolic community which is the Parish. In fact, to the people of the Parish, there is little difference. Yet such definitions entail contradiction. For example, a fundamental tension for the group is their proposed involvement in tourism development, which involves balancing their roles as preservers and developers of their community.

Both community groups and the state use the notion of community to serve their particular interests. This is particularly obvious if one examines the idea of developing partnership links between community and state. For statutory bodies the idea of partnership with community groups is important in a number of regards. Ideally, it facilitates the identification of community needs and interests; it attempts to create consensus between decision makers and 'community people'. Partnership may also be viewed however, as a mechanism of social control whereby 'community people', who might otherwise be a thorn in the side of the decision makers, can be incorporated into the system. For community groups, the prospect of partnership also brings with it a number of important advantages. In forming a relationship with statutory bodies by declaring itself to be representative of the community, a group can attempt to access resources which might otherwise be located elsewhere. The fruits of a community-state partnership can therefore sometimes contribute to the maintenance of the dominant position of a particular community group within a locality.

Conclusion

As was suggested at the outset of this chapter, the notion of community, which is often seen as unproblematic both by policy makers and those involved in community development, is, on closer examination, an area bedevilled by many questions. A clear understanding of the many uses and meanings of the term community is a good starting point if we wish to fully understand development and change.

This case study of an inner city community development group in Limerick is instructive on a number of levels. Community development activities are not only responsible for bringing about social change, but may also arise in response to perceived threats to communities, as a result of social forces such as urban renewal and redevelopment. The Parish Group's use of 'community' has to be understood as being both symbolic and strategic, and as a way of protecting a community by reference to a shared stock of knowledge about the past. In a comparative context, the Parish Group is similar to other community groups operating in urban and rural areas in Ireland and elsewhere. Groups lay symbolic claim to communities from which they derive credence for their endeavours. This claim can perhaps be interpreted in two ways. Firstly, there are those involved in local action who genuinely believe that they represent community feeling and interests. Secondly, however, it is also possible that at this most local political level, there are those who are well aware of the benefits that can accrue from associating the terms community or community development with their activities. Thus, the use of 'community' may in fact be a strategic one. Many of these community groups are made up of a very small proportion of the population of a locality. In some respects, therefore, the term 'community' is appropriated by such groups, irrespective of whether they have the support or interest of the wider population. As one community activist in another part of Limerick city told me:

We are trying hard to do something for the community. It's very hard, however. Most of them [community residents] are not bothered to get involved. Still, we must keep at it, for it is our duty to represent the community.

The Parish Group's identity depends upon a shared sense of history and working class culture. This is used by the Parish Group as a way of identifying the group with the interests of the locality. At the same time, it projects itself as representative of the community by attempting to forge partnerships with other local groups, and with the statutory bodies who work in the area. The Parish Group's story indicates the utility of groups having their constructions of community accepted locally and externally. In terms of the hoped-for partnership with statutory bodies which the Parish Group's membership of the SAUL project has promised, it is interesting to note that the group has met with those agencies whose redevelopment and renewal activities are the very ones which are the perceived threats to the Parish Group's community.

The Parish Group is not unique in its claims to be representative of the whole community. Curtin and Varley, for example, in their study of the Laketown Development Association, note that this group, despite its narrow class composition, continually claimed "to be representing the entire community" (1986: 180). Similarly, Harris, in her study of community in North Mayo, notes that "while 'communities' may not exist in Ireland, ideologies of communities do" (1984: 171). These ideologies are regularly put to use by those deeming themselves to be representative of 'the community'.

In terms of its use of the word 'community', and more particularly in its attempts to develop partnership between the state and the locality, the Parish Group is also well aware of the possible gains for the area in a partnership between the state and the voluntary sector. Thus, to a certain extent, the group has begun to develop its strategic skills in dealing with the state. There are clearly gains to be had for local government and state authorities as well. Partnership relationships (if real partnership can be said to exist) allow the statutory bodies to identify 'community needs and interests', and to work with 'community people'. This serves as an important mechanism of social control whereby otherwise radical voices can be co-opted into or marginalized by the system.[5] The state therefore may be shown to have its own agenda in its use of community. Citing Harris (1984) and O'Carroll (1985), Tovey notes that community is "nothing more than an ideology used by the state or by local capitalist interests to secure compliance from less powerful groups or to maintain consensus around a state-imposed development process" (1992: 110).

The Parish Group's story is also of interest in that it points to the possibility of conflicts within a locality over the direction and concerns of community development groups. In the case of the Parish Group, the divisions on Saint Imelda's Parish Council gave rise to both a split in, and the reorientation of, community development activity, thus underlining the notion that 'community' is in fact a symbolic construction, which is continually negotiated. Moreover, several layers of opinion exist among local activists about how issues such as partnership and community development work out in practice. This case study of how one local group has responded to the changes in its midst may also have significance beyond Limerick. For example, it illustrates how the workings of a major European Community programme (Poverty 3) is dependent on local community support, which is defined in a number of symbolic ways. Communities do not just exist *per se;* they are ideas and arenas which are negotiated, constructed, and contested.

Studies of collective action in Ireland involving groups claiming to represent 'the community' have been predominantly rural in their orientation (Devereux 1992; Varley et al. 1990; Varley 1991). Accounts of activities by development groups in urban areas are rare, despite the existence of large numbers of groups attempting to tackle a wide range of problems in Irish cities and towns. In the field of social anthropology, a start towards helping our understanding of the workings of Irish urban-based community groups has been made by Bennett (1988).[6] Bennett's study, set in Dublin city, is concerned with a community group's response to the problem of drug pushing. The activities of community groups in smaller towns outside Dublin have been examined by both Eipper (1986) and Harris (1984). In Northern Ireland, the ethnographic approach has perhaps been put to greater effect in studies of community politics. Ogle (1989), for example, examined the strategies for tenant participation in improvements to housing estates. As this chapter has demonstrated, social anthropology has the potential to play an important role in understanding the many forms of cultural constructions of 'community' that are used by the state and the voluntary sectors, and in examining the diversity of interpretations and constructions of the term by groups of people who perceive themselves to be communities.

Notes

1. The research was carried out in 1992 and 1993 through participant observation and semi-structured interviews. The author has also been involved in a number of projects in the area, including training some members of the group under study in research skills.
2. This dish consists of the boiled lining of a sheep's stomach, and a pudding made by filling a cow's intestines with blood and cereal. Packet and tripe is believed by locals to be the best cure for a hangover.
3. This group, which has a similar title to the group under study here, was set up as a separate entity by one of the Parish Group activists. Its key function is to organise courses in personal development.
4. The Parish Group was not the first local group to adopt this theme. In 1977, the King's Island Community Week used the slogan 'A Future for our Past'.
5. For a discussion of this topic, see Varley 1991.
6. For an equally interesting descriptive account of the activities of inner city community groups see Sheehan 1985 .

References

Bennett, D. 1988. Are They Always Right? Investigation and Proof in a Citizen Anti-Heroin Movement. In *Whose Law and Order* Tomlinson. M. (ed.) Studies in Irish Society Series, Sociological Association of Ireland, Belfast.
Cohen, A. P. 1985. *The Symbolic Construction of Community*. London: Tavistock.
_____. (ed.) 1986. Of Symbols and Boundaries, or Does Ertie's Greatcoat Hold the Key? In *Symbolising Boundaries: Identity and Diversity in British Cultures*. Manchester: Manchester University Press.
_____. 1987. *Whalsay*. Manchester: Manchester University Press.
Curtin, C. and Varley, A. 1986. Bringing Industry to a Small Town in the West of Ireland. *Sociologia Ruralis* 26 (2).
Devereux, E. 1992. Community Development Problems in Practice: The Muintir na Tire Experience 1931-1958 *Administration* 39 (4): 351-69.

Edwards, A. D. and Jones, D. G. 1976. *Community and Community Development.* The Hague: Mouton and Co.

Eipper, C. 1986. *The Ruling Trinity.* Aldershot: Gower.

Harris L. 1984. Class, Community and Sexual Divisions in North Mayo. In Curtin, C. et al. (eds.) *Culture and Ideology in Ireland.* Galway: Galway University Press.

Ogle, S. 1989. Housing Estate Improvements: An Assessment of Strategies for Tenant Participation. In Donnan, H. and McFarlane, G. (eds.) *Social Anthropology and Public Policy in Northern Ireland.* Aldershot: Gower.

O'Carroll, J. P. 1985. Community Programmes and the Traditional View of Community. *Social Studies* 8 (3/4): 137-48.

Scott, I. 1985. *The Periphery Is The Centre: A Study of Community Development Practice in the West of Ireland, 1983-1984.* Edinburgh: Arkleton Trust.

Sheehan, R. 1985. *The Heart of the City.* Dingle: The Brandon Press.

Tovey, H. 1992. Rural Sociology in Ireland - a review. *Irish Journal of Sociology* 2: 96-121.

Varley, T., Curtin, C. and O'Donohue, K. 1990. Theory and practice of Community Development in two West of Ireland Community Councils. In Buller, H. and Wright, S. (eds.) *Rural Development: Problems and Practices.* Aldershot: Avebury.

Varley, T. 1991. Power to the People? Community Groups and Rural Revival in Ireland. In S. Healy (ed.) *Rural Development Policy: What Future For Rural Ireland.* Dublin: Conference of Major Religious Superiors.

5   Personalism and brokerage in Dublin politics

Lee Komito

The Republic of Ireland is often portrayed, by residents and outsiders alike, as a society where everybody knows everyone else, and, especially, knows everybody else's business. In the political arena, this has been referred to as 'personalism'. In academic discourse, this has often been translated in terms of clientelism and brokerage: voters going to politicians in order to obtain benefits from the government. There has been a wealth of discussion about clientelism and brokerage in Irish politics; indeed, it is one of the major topics for ethnographic research in the Republic of Ireland (see, for instance, Gibbon and Higgins 1974; Bax 1976; Sacks 1976; Higgins 1982; Komito 1984; 1989a; 1989b; and Wilson 1989). Although 'personalism' is often used as a coded allusion to political clientelism, it can be used simply to emphasize the personal and informal dimension of Irish politics (e.g., Schmitt 1973).   This is especially true in the relationships between politicians, between politicians and partisan supporters, and also between politicians and voters. It is this personal dimension, as evidenced in Dublin politics, which this chapter addresses.[1]

Most anthropological descriptions of Irish politics have been based on rural research, and the extent to which similar behaviours exist in urban settings has not been established. My research in Dublin shows the ways in which urban politics is both similar to and different from rural politics. The nature of party politics appears to be the same; a rural party activist would feel quite at home at a Dublin constituency meeting.   However, Dublin politicians and activists notice that they have less contact with constituents than their rural counterparts, and this perception is supported by at least one recent survey (*Irish Marketing Surveys* 1991).   The converse is also true: Dublin constituents have less contact with politicians and activists than their rural counterparts. This raises an interesting question: if urban constituents are less likely to have personal contact with politicians, what are the consequences for the clientelist behaviour that has been characteristic of rural politics? Do constituents realize that they can go directly to state bureaucrats, or do they continue to use politicians as brokers? The answer is that they do neither. The search for trusted intermediaries remains important, but the strategies of that search are different. Urbanites extend their search wider than their rural counterparts, and contact a wide variety of figures who have no political connections. Personalism and trust remain features of politics in Dublin, for both middle-class and working-class locales, just as they are features of rural politics. Why should this be the case, and what does this say about politics in Ireland?

In order to develop these points, this chapter compares different aspects of rural and urban politics. It examines the daily activities of Dublin politicians to illustrate the amount of constituency work in which politicians engage. A short description of Dublin party politics provides evidence of the similarity between urban and rural party activities. The decrease in the amount of contact between politicians and voters in Dublin, as compared with rural Ireland, is then explored. The class dimension of urban brokerage is discussed, before raising some general issues about urban politics.

A Dublin politician's diary

Government in the Republic of Ireland operates at both a local and a national level, with independent elections for each tier. Unlike many such parliamentary democracies, most Irish national politicians also hold local office. The only exceptions are Ministers and Ministers of State, who are expected to resign from local office once appointed to their Ministerial position. Local office is usually a stepping stone to national office but, because of the nature of competition in Irish politics, most national politicians prefer to retain their local office even after election. Thus, many politicians are first elected as councillors to Dublin Corporation or County Council, and also are members of one of the houses of the Oireachtas (parliament): either Dáil Éireann or Seanad Éireann. The 'lower' house, Dáil Éireann, is the more powerful, and successful politicians are likely to be Teachtai Dála (commonly abbreviated as TD, and the equivalent of a British Member of Parliament) as well as local councillors (for a fuller description, see Coakley and Gallagher 1992 or Chubb 1992).

Partly as a result of wearing both a local and a national hat, the daily diary of a national politician from Dublin makes impressive reading. He or she will attend the national parliament three days a week, and also have at least one day of local government meetings. Until the 1980s, national politicians were dependent on other income; salaries were too low for anyone to live on a politician's salary alone. Many politicians also held full-time jobs outside politics (this is less likely to be the case now, as salary increases have enabled national politicians to give up, or take leave from, non-political employment). Earning a living, combined with attending local and national government meetings, accounts for their weekday activities, and parliamentary sittings may last until early or even late evening.

Other meetings are held in the evenings or at weekends. These fall into three categories: party, community, and individual meetings. Political parties have a three-tier structure of national, constituency, and branch organisation. Both local and national politicians are dependent on the support of the fifteen to twenty-five branches in their constituency, and these branches meet, individually, about once a month. Politicians try to attend the meetings of branches, which means that politicians could have fifteen to twenty-five evening meetings a month.[2]

Secondly, there are community meetings. One finds politicians at all community events, such as the opening of a new church or new community hall. If a local benefit is taking place, politicians will make an appearance. Community groups and residents' groups expect politicians to attend their meetings and respond to their problems. Thus, during any week, politicians could easily have up to seven or eight such local events or meetings to attend.

Thirdly, politicians also hold advice 'clinics' one to four times a week. These are well publicised through local papers, information sheets put into houses, and notices in community centres. Anyone in the area can consult about their problems or difficulties, and politicians see twenty or thirty people at each clinic session. Even at home, politicians receive phone calls, letters, and personal visits regarding constituents' cases.

Taken together, these obligations mean a very hectic political life. Many a politician leaves a local government council meeting in order to briefly attend a community or residents' meeting after which he might have a party branch meeting where he wants to have a drink and chat with branch activists. Politicians clearly cannot be full participants at any of the meetings, but they are seen to be there, and are able to keep in touch with all the various happenings in their constituency.

Rural politicians or politicians from other urban centres have equally hectic lives; ethnographic reports (e.g., Higgins 1982) and interviews with rural politicians indicate that all politicians devote an enormous amount of time to constituency activities. A review of government salaries asked TDs to estimate how much time they spent on political business other than attending the Dáil (Review Body on Higher Remuneration in the Public Sector 1972: 211) . Forty-four percent said 31-50 hours a week, and thirty-seven percent said over 50 hours. In addition, the TDs were asked to list the kinds of expenses they incurred. This partial list illustrates the cost of maintaining a social presence: subscriptions to organisations (mentioned by 52% of TDs), travel in constituency (52%), entertainment (46%), telephone

(18%), attending clinics (17%), funeral offerings (7%), maintaining
constituency office (7%), telegrams (5%), and wedding presents (4%).

Politicians maintain that keeping in touch with government bureaucracy,
political party, and community, even if hectic, has one major advantage: they
keep their hand on the public pulse, and know what concerns people. This
image corresponds with the one derived from numerous ethnographic studies
of rural politics in the Republic of Ireland (Bax 1976; Sacks 1976; Carty
1981). These rural studies describe politicians who are well connected with
all the happenings in their constituencies. In these ethnographies, it is clear
that close attention is paid to the constituency in order to monitor political
support. Politicians are constantly 'nursing' their constituencies to maintain
their electoral support, and are keenly aware, at any given time, where their
support comes from. A quintessential symbol of Irish politics was an
interview broadcast over Irish television in the early 1970s. It pictured two
political activists, one from Fianna Fáil and one from Fine Gael, standing on
a hill, looking out over a valley in Donegal. The two of them discussed each
of the houses visible from the hill, and were able to identify how members of
each household voted. This is personalism exemplified.

Party politics

Rural ethnographies are also replete with stories of politicians trying to
denigrate party rivals, trying to control the local party structure, trying to
make bigger public claims than rivals, getting jobs for 'special' friends, and
so on. Political life in rural areas of the Irish Republic seems to be continual
party in-fighting, as well as maintaining personal links with the voters (see
Bax 1976 for the most vivid description). The picture of urban party politics
that emerged from a study of politics in Dublin in the late 1970s and early
1980s is little different (Komito 1985). Political competition is largely intra-
party, rather than inter-party. This is the result of structural factors. The
Irish electoral system combines proportional representation with multi-seat
constituencies. Thus, in a five seat constituency, voters can rank order their
preferences, choosing amongst all candidates. Since there has been, until
recently (Laver and Marsh 1992), a tradition that voters support only 'their
own' party, politicians have been in competition with other politicians from
the same party for the votes of loyal party supporters. Between elections,
politicians are always aware that, when the next election is called, it is their
party colleagues that will pose a threat and so it is those colleagues who must
be feared and watched. The local party structure is one arena for these
conflicts, as politicians try to prevent their rivals from gaining control of the
local party machinery.

While this conflict is latent much of the time, tensions manifest themselves during nominating conventions. Politicians cannot control which of the party candidates the voters choose, but they can at least control who is nominated in the first place. Candidates are nominated by representatives of the constituency branches; if politicians can control the branches and the nominating convention, they can ensure that potential rivals do not receive a nomination. Preparations for nominating conventions are made years in advance. Politicians do their best to make sure that supporters hold important positions (such as secretary or president) in the branches; these are the individuals who can persuade other branch members to support particular candidates and are usually the branch representatives at selection conventions. In the course of research, I found that one politician had planted three of his close relatives in three different branches, rather than waste them all in one branch. Politicians are often suspected by rivals, and party headquarters, of maintaining 'paper branches'; which exist as far as the party organisation is concerned but whose only active members are the branch officials who vote as the politician wishes.[3]

While 'paper branches' and loyal kin in control of other branches are preferred means of safeguarding one's position in the constituency party, most branches in a constituency are either controlled by no single politician or are themselves factionalised into different camps. The monthly branch meetings are very complex; beneath the surface of conviviality and commitment to party ideals, there exist plots and counter-plots. Politicians and their supporters spend much of their time trying to deduce the significance of every minor event: does it imply that someone's support is shifting? Will that action somehow enhance councillor 'L's' position? For example, at one constituency-wide meeting, the constituency secretary placed a local councillor in the front row of the meeting, while a local TD and also a visiting party dignitary (a TD from another constituency) were at the table facing the audience. This was an exception to the normal practice of seating all elected politicians at the head table. The TD thus received more public attention than the councillor. The councillor felt he could not make a fuss, as this would appear mean-minded, but he was annoyed and also worried: had the secretary done this deliberately (thus aligning himself with the TD whose position was increasingly threatened by the councillor)? Since no direct question could be asked to settle the matter, the councillor could only watch the secretary more closely in the future. At selection conventions, the conflicts manifested themselves more transparently. In one convention, attempts to control votes involved late night phone calls, sometimes using outright lies about rivals, to change the votes of delegates. The convention ended with almost overt accusations of betrayals, as the deceptive phone calls made the previous night were revealed in an angry post-mortem.

During the selection convention, various procedural and rhetorical strategies are used in the competition for position. Such conflict takes place beneath the surface; many of those attending these meetings accept the apparent harmony and shared goals at face value. Indeed, such shared goals are often used as a weapon in party rivalries, in a manner which recalls Bailey's (1969) observation that the moral rules shared by members of a political community can be used in a pragmatic manner by leaders. In one case, an aspiring activist tried to obtain a nomination, and threatened to supplant the established councillor. The aspirant had more votes, and would have won an election. However, the established councillor warned of the dangers of factionalism and divided loyalties. To avoid a divisive vote, he said, they should ask the national executive to permit both to run as candidates. If the aspirant had fought this, he would have seemed concerned only with personal ambition (in contrast to the other's concern for the party). He had no choice but to agree. The established politician was easily able to use his national contacts to influence the national executive; as he had expected, they decided to permit only one candidate, which was the established politician himself.

Competition between members of the same party sometimes becomes so intense that politicians can favour the election of members of opposition parties, rather than rivals from their own party. In one case, this preference led to a sitting TD keeping the opposition informed regarding the campaign schedule of an up and coming party rival. In this way, any publicity tactics could be countered by the politician in the other party; as far as the TD was concerned, far better that a politician from another party get elected than a rival within his own party have a chance to build his electoral base. Needless to say, the party leadership would have taken quite a dim view of this, had they known, but the sitting TD was more concerned with his career than with the overall success of his party.

These descriptions of complex party machinations would be familiar to anyone studying politics in the Republic of Ireland. Party politics appears to be much the same anywhere in the Republic, whether one examines a rural or an urban constituency. Party activists are clients of patrons, or rivals of other clients, but never simply neutral participants. Party politics in Ireland is pyramid shaped, and the opposing groups at each level have links with higher level opposing groups. Thus, one faction in a branch would have links with a constituency politician, while the other faction would have links with another constituency politician. At the next level, those two politicians would constitute opposing blocs, and would also have links to opposing national level politicians. This is a picture that would find echoes in factional politics elsewhere, as first evidenced by Barth's model of bloc alliances composed of opposing groups at each level of the political hierarchy (Barth 1959). Factional politics in the Republic of Ireland exists in the context of party solidarity and collective identification. Fianna Fáil activists talk of "a Fianna Fáil person" or "family"; and the label carries with it specific obligations of behaviour towards other members of the same moral community. They contrast themselves with Fine Gael, who are less than fully Irish, too closely linked with British interests, and not really close to "the people". Fine Gael activists, on the other hand, see themselves as morally upright and honest, while characterising Fianna Fáil as immoral and capable of doing or saying anything for the sake of a single vote. It is only within the context of these strongly held loyalties, uniting politicians, activists, and voters, that internal party factions exist.

Politicians and the community

As noted, party politics and the constituency activities of politicians in Dublin are similar to politics in rural Ireland. However, the picture changes considerably when one looks at the relationship between politicians and voters. In rural ethnographies, politicians are described as having close personal contacts with voters. These contacts are developed through business and community activities, and also arise out of extensive networks of blood, marriage, and friendship relations. Politicians relate to voters not simply as constituents but also as friends, relations, customers and so forth. These are multiplex, overlapping relationships (Southall 1973; Hannerz 1980). In Dublin, it would appear that politicians are unable to cultivate, and exploit, such an extensive network of political support. Politicians and activists tend to exist in their own private world, somewhat apart and isolated from the broader society of their constituents.

One indication of this is the process, already discussed, by which party candidates are selected. There is often some effort to choose candidates who will bring in votes from particular geographical areas of the constituency (similar to the process observed by Sacks 1970). The presumption is that people will vote for their local candidate and, having then voted, will vote for other candidates of the same party. However, this public rhetoric does not match the reasons given by politicians in private. They are happy to select candidates representing a geographical spread because they do not want their own local power base threatened by giving publicity to an aspiring candidate in the same locality. The number of electoral votes which potential candidates might obtain is rarely the basis for selection; in a number of cases, individuals selected performed very poorly in the election. This became such a problem in the 1980s that the party headquarters, for all parties, began to impose candidates on the local organization, if the local selection procedures did not appear to maximize the party vote. This problem does not appear to have diminished over time. As recently as April 1993, a prominent member of Fianna Fáil, who had been given the task of improving party performance in urban areas, noted that: "Too many candidates spend two or three years trying to win a nomination rather than out canvassing and dealing with the public" (*Irish Times* 20 April 1993). In the largest political party, activists and politicians in Dublin are still out of touch with voters.

Another indication of the distance between voters and politicians in urban areas is a change in election rules. Until 1965, only the names, and not the party affiliation of candidates, appeared on ballot papers. After 1965, however, the election rules were changed so that party affiliation would also be displayed alongside each candidate's name. The implication is clear: up to that point, political parties had been confident that voters knew to which parties the candidates belonged. In the 1960s, however, the parties recognized that such a link would now have to be explicit. No longer could parties assume that voters knew, personally, the politicians who were looking for electoral support. It is hardly a coincidence that the 1966 Census reported, for the first time, over fifty percent of the population living in town as opposed to rural areas. Ten years earlier, only forty-four percent had been classified as living in towns (Central Statistics Office 1972).

Local party organisation differs between urban and rural constituencies, with implications for the relationship between politicians and voters.[4] Branch numbers tend to be higher in rural areas; in 1979, Fianna Fail had about 50-150 branches per rural constituency, and 20-30 branches per city constituency (Chubb 1982: 112). One informant suggested that, in Fianna Fáil, fifteen would be about the smallest number of branches for an urban constituency, with an average of twenty-five, whereas a rural constituency could have as many as seventy, subdivided into four sub-groups. Although some rural branches might have a small membership, another Fianna Fáil activist estimated that a rural branch could have 100 members to an urban branch's 15, with the same catchment area (in terms of voting population). Furthermore, as another activist noted, 100 members would probably include members of the same families, whereas only heads of households seem to belong in urban families. Party activists from all parties in Dublin (particularly those from middle-class constituencies) repeatedly emphasized how isolated they were from the community, as contrasted with their rural counterparts. Urban activists might not see one another in the normal course of daily life, and formal branch meetings are necessary to sort out problems and discuss tactics. For rural branches, however, the formal meeting is more of a ritual; members would already have seen each other, naturally, in the course of their non-political lives, and would have had ample opportunity to make decisions in advance.

The greater separation of politicians from voters is also confirmed by a survey carried out in 1991 at the time of local elections (Irish Marketing Surveys 1991). One of the survey questions was "Since the last Local

Elections in 1985, have you had contact with any member of your Local Authority, in person, by phone, or in writing, to seek their help?" The results show both a class and an urban/rural division. Only twenty percent of middle class respondents had contacted a local politician, while between twenty-five and twenty-seven percent of working class respondents had contacted politicians. Similarly, only twenty-one percent of urban respondents had contacted politicians, while twenty-eight percent of rural respondents had contacted politicians. While this question measures brokerage frequency, it tends to confirm the view of political activists that rural voters tend to be more closely involved with politics and politicians than their urban counterparts.

This apparent gulf between the political parties and the urban social environment in which they are situated arises for a number of reasons. One factor is the structure of political representation, in which the number of politicians per head of population varies widely. At national level, the constitution requires that representation, numerically, "shall so far as it is practicable, be the same throughout the country" (Article 16.2.3, 1937 Constitution). However, there is no rule as to the number of councillors for a particular area, and wide variation is possible. Urban areas tend to have fewer councillors than rural ones; the ratio in County Dublin was, in 1980, 1:7,151 voters and in Dublin City 1:8,088 voters. At the same time, there was a ratio of 1:942 in Leitrim and 1:1,875 in Clare (Roche, D. 1982: 312-20). This means there is closer contact between councillors and voters in rural areas, simply by force of numbers. This also alters the relationship between councillors and TDs, since rural counties have a large number of councillors relative to TDs while urban ones have a small number. In 1980, there were 806 city and county councillors and 166 TDs, or a ratio of 4.86:1; yet, in the Greater Dublin area the ratio was less than 1.7:1. In rural politics, the TD must tolerate councillors who are simultaneously his helpers and also potential rivals. In the urban constituencies, since most TDs remain councillors, rivals of TDs can be denied the stepping stone of local elected office, which helps explain the degree of factionalism evidenced at selection conventions.

A feature of rural politics is the ability of politicians to develop personal links with voters, so that politicians have their own blocs of votes as well as the support of intermediate brokers who can deliver blocs of votes. Bonds of consanguinity and affinity alone can, in a stable community, deliver hundreds of votes and constitute a strong core of electoral support. Other personal links, once developed, can also be relied upon. In the Irish context, Sacks (1976: 111-136) offers the most detailed description of the importance of kinship in rural politics. One Donegal councillor estimated that twenty percent of his votes came from kinship connections (1976: 97). In Dublin, the resources, if not the rules of the game, change. As individuals move from one house to another, or one job to another, any existing links to politicians become irrelevant, as the voter moves to a new constituency, or a different part of the same constituency. Politicians consider urban communities to be more amorphous and anonymous than rural communities, due to geographical mobility and a perceived weakening of the extended family.[5] Even in working class urban areas, politicians complain that, when they assist someone by getting them a house, the house is usually in a different electoral area, with the consequent loss of grateful voters.

The lack of a personal link with voters is evidenced by Dublin politicians at election time. They know the areas where they are strongest and most likely to obtain votes, but this bears no necessary relation to the areas in which voters visited clinics. People clearly do not vote on the basis of favours owed as a result of personal efforts on behalf of individuals. As has been noted elsewhere (Komito 1989a), much of a politician's time is spent trying to transform an instrumental exchange relationship (from the voter's perspective) into a personal and moral relationship. While this may be the politician's goal, the starting point is the voter who feels no particular moral obligation or personal connection with any particular politician.

Interestingly, one Dublin politician who successfully built up a network of personal contacts, did so on the basis of pre-existing links in the west of Ireland. The politician, as a new candidate in the constituency, organised his campaign through a pyramid of personal contacts. Contacting people who had moved to Dublin from his home county in the west, and whom he knew through friends, secondary school, and university, he asked some to organize small meetings and he asked others to name ten friends who might help him. He held numerous `coffee mornings' where he met small groups of housewives. Thus, he literally organised `friends of friends' to quickly penetrate the constituency. The result in the election was that he was the first person to reach the election quota.

In this context, the previous description of a politician's daily diary takes on a new meaning. Rather than evidence of being in touch with individuals throughout their constituency, it demonstrates how out of touch politicians know themselves to be. They are trying, with the busy schedule of activities, to make up for those bonds of personalism that their rural compatriots can largely take for granted. Politicians are also clear that many of their activities are a waste of time. Clinics, for instance, appear to epitomise personalistic politics -- individuals are asking politicians for personal assistance, and, as they receive it, they become clients of the politician and vote accordingly. The evidence is otherwise. Voters make the rounds of all the politicians, trying to play one off against the other. Even if they are helped, there is no certainty that they will vote for the politician at the next election. Politicians are obviously aware of this; the major reason given for holding clinics is their publicity value. It is important that voters in an area feel they are getting some attention from the politician; without it, they might decide to transfer their votes to a politician who demonstrates greater concern for the area. Thus, the clinics are part of the general strategy of maximising a reputation in the local community, rather than a means of obtaining the support of specific individuals.

The weekly round of meetings can also be given a different interpretation. Politicians do not believe that all contacts made at such meetings create personal bonds of electoral obligation; instead, past participation at these meetings and membership in local community groups become, at election time, a basis for attracting support from anonymous voters. The constituency of Dublin North provides an example of local connections which a politician creates, and depends on, for recognition. Thomas Wright was an aspiring Fianna Fáil candidate in the 1982 election. In addition to owning a fish and poultry business in the centre of Malahide, he was Malahide 'Community Personality' for 1981. He was chairman of Malahide Festival for the previous six years, a current member of Bord Iascaigh Mhara (the National Fisheries Board), Portmarnock Community Centre, Malahide Chamber of Commerce, and the Malahide Tennis and Cricket Club. He further noted that he was the coach of the Irish schoolgirls' international basketball team, as well as a member and former player in the local Gaelic Athletic Association (GAA) club. His Fine Gael rival for the marginal seat was Nora Owens. She advertised that she had previously been editor of the local newsletter, as well as having been involved with residents' associations, community councils, school boards, the Old Malahide Society, and the Tidy Towns Committee. Both candidates hoped to create an identification with the locale, in hopes of gaining extra votes. Neither presumed that previous activities in these groups were sufficient to ensure votes at election time, as subsequent events demonstrated: Wright lost the 1982 election, but then gained a seat in 1987.

Voters, trust and personalism

Descriptions of rural politics emphasize the personal link with politicians, and, even though politicians may cultivate such a link to ensure electoral support, it seems clear that the voters themselves want that personal link. In ethnographic accounts, this personal link is demanded because people do not trust anonymous civil servants in Dublin or anonymous local officers in the county council. They can only extend trust to individuals who are known to them personally (Sacks 1976: 47-48; Bax 1976: 184). Part of the mythology of modernization was that people would eventually realize that a personal relationship is not a prerequisite for fair treatment; thus, as modernization proceeds, one should see a move from politicians as personal mediators to direct approaches to bureaucrats. While such views about social change have become less supportable in the last twenty years, it is still not clear why the personal brokerage link has been the preferred means of access to the state. Does the situation in Dublin provide any additional evidence in this regard? Ethnographic evidence certainly shows the lack of personal links between voters and politicians in Dublin. If voters are faced with a choice between going to anonymous bureaucrats or somewhat less anonymous politicians, do they turn their attention to bureaucrats?

The evidence suggests that urban voters do not approach agents of the state directly; they, like rural voters, want relations of trust with people they know personally. However, since the structure of social and political relations is different in Dublin, the strategies by which those personal relations are exploited are also different. Part of the evidence for this comes from a survey designed to compare Irish 'civic culture' with that of other countries (see Almond and Verba 1965; Raven and Whelan 1976). The survey asked: "If you should have any problems with the authorities, which of the people here in the street (area) would you think of consulting? (We do not assume that you are personally acquainted with the person)." Only one person could be named; those who indicated they did have someone in mind were then asked to name the person's occupation. It is a particularly interesting survey because respondents were free to choose anyone; most comparable surveys only permit respondents to choose between politicians and civil servants. While the question does not directly measure brokerage activity, it is a useful index of frequencies of voter-politician contacts. The survey did not specify Dublin versus other respondents, and the categories used to classify respondents were somewhat problematic, so it is only possible to distinguish, in a general way, between urban and rural respondents.[6]

In accordance with the expectations of modernization theory, the survey indicated that individuals in urban areas are less likely to choose politicians as the preferred broker. However, in contradiction to modernization theory, there is only a marginal increase in preferences for bureaucrats. Respondents who do not prefer to go to politicians choose, instead, someone else in the local community, who, by definition, is neither a politician nor an employee of the state. These individuals have been referred to, in Table 1, simply as members of the 'community'.

Table 1
Percentage distribution of respondents,
by brokerage preferences and residence
Source: Komito 1992

	politician %	community %	official %	N	
Rural	61.9	35.6	2.4	491	(57.9%)
Urban	42.0	51.5	6.4	357	(42.1%)

Out of a sample size of 848, just under sixty per cent of respondents were classified as rural, and just over forty percent were classified as urban. This is roughly similar to the 1971 Census figures.[7] While sixty-two percent of rural respondents would go to a politician, only forty-two percent of urban respondents would make the same choice. However, in the urban context, those going to officials (local authority officials, civil servants, social welfare workers, community health nurses, and so on) only increased to just over six percent. It is the residual category of `community figure' that shows a marked increase; in other words, urban dwellers may no longer go to politicians, but they still go to some mediator rather than deal with the state directly.

The actual occupations which constitute this residual category of 'community figure' is as interesting as the size of the category. Firstly, if urban and rural respondents are taken together, the occupations grouped together as 'community figure' include solicitor (chosen by 8.3% of respondents), priest (7.1%), farmer (4.7%), businessman (2.9%), and shopkeeper (2.1%). These high-status occupations are the ones most likely to be consulted when individuals need assistance. Looking only at the urban respondents, the same high-status individuals remain important: solicitor (10.9%), priest (7.3%), businessmen (4.2%), farmer (2.0%)[8], shopkeeper (2.8%). But, in addition, new figures emerge as significant choices: guard (2.5%), printer (2.0%), housewife (3.4%), chairman of residents' association (2.0%), teacher (1.4%), and publican (1.4%). There is a further 10 per cent comprising occupations too diverse to summarize. Overall, the figures indicate a greater diversity of brokerage choices in urban areas than in rural areas.

There is a relatively clear consensus about appropriate brokers in rural contexts: politician, solicitor, priest, and farmer account for 82 per cent of respondent choices. However, no such consensus exists in the urban context, where a similar selection of occupations accounts for only 62 percent of choices. Urban dwellers utilize a wider range of brokers than rural respondents. It is also notable that, in many cases, there are no obvious links of economic or political dependency between the individual and the broker, which would explain why that person was approached. Why, for instance, should an individual choose a printer or a housewife, except that they are choosing 'friends'? Thus, the decrease in personal contacts with politicians has not led voters to turn to officials; in their search for trusted mediators, they simply cast their brokerage net more widely.

There is some indication from the survey that middle class respondents were more likely than working class respondents to choose 'friends' rather than politicians as brokers, although the number of respondents is too small to be statistically significant. This would be in line with another survey (Komito 1989b), and interview data also suggest that middle-class urbanites are likely to have friends who can act as brokers or mediators. Individuals who have obtained a third-level education have a pool of potential brokers to draw on. In many cases, they know someone in the civil service or, failing that, someone in one of the professions (such as law or medicine) who can act as intermediary. This also happens in working class areas (one political activist worked for the telephone company and could provide contacts), but there are fewer instances of this, and the contacts provided are less likely to have any significant resources at their disposal. Thus, in working-class areas, voters are less likely to have any effective alternative to politicians.

One common feature of brokerage, whether middle-class or working-class, is the conspicuous absence of class rhetoric. In one sense, this is unremarkable, since its absence is a feature of politics in the Republic, whether rural or urban, working-class or middle-class. It is remarkable, however, if one compares Irish urban politics with urban politics elsewhere in Europe, where class, ethnicity or religion are often the basis of collective political action (Mair 1992a; 1992b). Most of the brokerage that occurs in Dublin is either individual or community oriented. That is, people usually want something for themselves as individuals (social welfare assistance, medical assistance, or public housing), or as a member of a residents' group (community parks, improved street lighting, or provision of public buses). The only context in which class differences manifest themselves is that working-class voters are more likely to want individual benefits for themselves, while middle-class voters are more likely to be concerned with community amenities.

Although urbanites approach politicians less often than do rural people, 'politicians' remains the major occupational category (42%) of urban broker. Nevertheless, Dublin voters tend to approach politicians with suspicion rather than trust, especially since they are less likely than rural voters to have kinship or friendship claims upon them. In politicians' clinics, the rhetoric of exchange between politician and voter is imbued with the sense of a bargain being struck. People do not overtly say "I voted for you, so you should now come through", but this is the implication. Certainly constituents say, when explaining why they expect politicians to fill out forms that they could fill out themselves: "Sure, isn't that what he is elected for?" The voters are uncertain how much they can trust politicians, and hope that they have some hold over politicians by virtue of the vote. This helps explain the relative lack of interest in Community Information Centres. These Centres are staffed by volunteers, who have received training from the National Social Services Board. There are 77 such Centres around the country, and they provide information about administrative services on a confidential basis. Both local and national officials recognize that inquiries from such Centres are legitimate -- that is, they will respond as they would to a politician's inquiry (although not always as quickly). These Centres are used to some extent (according to the National Social Services Board (1991), they dealt with 130,987 queries in 1990), but not to the same extent as politicians' clinics. People do not believe the Centres are as effective as politicians, and, more significantly, they also do not believe they will work as hard as politicians. At least with a politician, one has the threat of the vote as a bargaining stick; one has no moral or personal hold over a stranger in a Community Information Centre. Thus, the preferred basis for assistance in Dublin continues to be some bond of trust, rather than any alternative institutionalised assistance; when that is not available, the next best alternative is an implicit transactional bargain between voter and politician.

Conclusion

To summarize, party politics in the Republic of Ireland remains the same whether one speaks of urban or rural areas. Party politics is built on a pyramid of patron-client links. At each level (branch, constituency, national), individual activists and politicians compete with others, use the support of their clients in that competition, and are, in turn, clients of higher level patrons. These factional conflicts exist within each political party, membership of which is similar to the moral community of ethnicity.

The major difference between Dublin and many rural communities is the relationship between political activists and the voters. In rural communities, politicians provide a relationship of trust, linking voters with a distrusted state. Although politicians provide such links in order to advance their own political careers, that does not alter the perception of individuals that such a trusted link is both needed and provided. In Dublin, such relations of trust are still sought by voters. However, due to a widening gulf between politicians and voters, politicians are unable to provide that relationship. In the absence of such a link, voters continue to look for individuals who can act as personal links to the state. These individuals do not necessarily hold positions of power or prestige in the local community (in the 'civic culture' survey, individuals also chose low prestige occupations such as housewife and printer); the main prerequisite is that they are trusted.

To some extent, this differs from the expectations implicit in earlier rural ethnographies. In these ethnographies, brokerage was a consequence of beliefs and behaviours that were stereotypically 'traditional', such as a distrust of impersonal bureaucracy and a distance from central authority. In such a context, one would have expected Dubliners to be less likely to be dependent on personal contacts with politicians, and more likely to deal directly with state functionaries. Surprisingly, although Dubliners are indeed less likely to depend on personal contacts with politicians, they did not directly approach state functionaries. Instead, they continue to prefer personal links, but with other potential mediators.

Personalism and trust are features of Dublin politics, just as they are features of rural politics. This illustrates the importance of the personal dimension in the way individuals relate to the state (see Eisenstadt and Roniger 1984). Is there any reason, specific to Ireland, that would explain this preference for personal contacts? The Irish civil service is criticised as secretive, authoritarian, and unresponsive; not only is little attempt made to release information, it seems there are positive attempts to conceal even trivial items of information. As one expert on Irish public administration said:

> the operations within government departments and within state-sponsored bodies are almost entirely closed to public scrutiny. We know about what goes on within them only in so far as a conscious decision is taken to publish a decision or report, often presented as a remarkable act of magnanimity on the part of the body concerned (Barrington 1980: 191-2).

One politician observed that there was an "almost paranoid refusal by public agencies to divulge even the minimum information about projects or concerns of public interest" (Chubb 1982: 379; see also Roche, R. 1982; Komito 1985). Perhaps this lack of access, which excludes middle-class as much as working-class Dubliners, explains the dependence on trusted personal contacts. Irish bureaucracy has become more accountable and accessible in recent decades; will this encourage direct access to the state and reduce people's dependence on trusted intermediaries?

The preference by Irish people for personal contacts has been noted before (Pyne 1974). Even though few people actually need brokerage assistance, they still want politicians to be available as brokers (Komito 1989b). That is, despite people's experience of a system that works reasonably well, they still distrust it and believe instead in the need for personal contacts. Furthermore, such personal contacts are perfectly possible in Ireland. As one famous Irish politician (quoted in Chubb 1982: 316), remarked in the 1960s:

> there is hardly anyone without a direct personal link with someone, be he Minister, TD, clergyman, county or borough councillor or trade union official, who will interest himself in helping a citizen to have a grievance examined and, if possible, remedied.

In the 1980s, people could still, if they so desired, find a personal advocate to act on their behalf. The significance of personal networks in organisations is well known; such networks are crucial to an organisation's adaptability and efficiency. The significance of such networks in urban politics is less clear. The idea that urban communities are impersonal and anonymous lost currency many decades ago; cities as large as New York or London are often described as collections of urban communities. However, when applied to the entire urban political system, the description usually implies some degree of immoral activities. In Dublin politics, personal contacts are the normal style of political interaction for all individuals. Nevertheless, the evidence suggests that these personal contacts exist without any wide-spread corruption or illegality.[9]

What, then, of personalism in Dublin politics? When comparing Dublin with rural Ireland, it is clear that personalism is a common feature of politics throughout the Republic. The difference is that, in Dublin, politicians are often not part of those networks of trust. So the question should be, what of personalism in the Republic generally? Is this personalism a universal preference, but one which manifests itself in such an extreme manner only in a small-scale society like Ireland? Or is Irish society, as a whole, a personalistic one, and do people extend, to the political arena, the same assumptions about personal contacts that they use in their other social and economic activities? Alternatively, is this dependence on personal contacts part of the legacy often attributed to Ireland's "post-colonial" heritage? Perhaps this personalism is largely a consequence of the information constraints imposed by the state bureaucracy? These are questions which deserve further examination, but about which there is insufficient ethnographic evidence for many conclusions. Further social network research will help tease out the relationship between personalism, brokerage, and politics in the Republic of Ireland.

Notes

1. The data for this chapter derive from ethnographic research carried out continuously from 1978-81 in Dublin, and from intermittent research in Dublin since 1981. The research focused on two areas: a working class constituency in Dublin city, and a largely middle class constituency in County Dublin. It also involved interviews with politicians and local officials in the Dublin region.
2. Politicians make sure to attend any meetings in their local 'bailiwick' (see Sacks 1970 for a discussion of the bailiwick system), and might miss meetings in other parts of the constituency where their support is weaker.
3. Evidence of this came from interviews with party activists and politicians from three political parties: Fianna Fail, Fine Gael, and the Labour Party.
4. For further detail on party organisation, see Gallagher (1985), Laver and Marsh (1992), or Mair (1987).
5. It is, of course, well known that urban communities are not always either amorphous or anonymous. The classic studies of working class communities in Dublin (Humphreys 1966) and London (Young and Willmott 1957) found dense networks commonly associated with rural communities. For a discussion of the urban

versus rural distinction from a network perspective, see Southall (1973), Hannerz (1980), and Wellman and Berkowitz (1988).

6. Although this question was not extensively analysed in the original publication, the data were made available to the author for further analysis. The survey divided respondents into seven categories: 1) residential area in city centre, 2) main industrial area in town, 3) mixed residential and industrial/business area in town, 4) suburban area/council estate in large town, 5) large village (500+) in rural area, 6) small village, 7) sparsely populated area. The categories are neither clear cut nor unambiguous, and the safest strategy was simply to dichotomise the variable, 'area of residence,' into rural (areas five through seven) and urban (all remaining areas).

7. The Census figures are 40 percent of residents in towns with a population of ten thousand or more, and 44 percent if residents of towns with a population between five thousand and ten thousand are included (Central Statistics Office 1972).

8. The choice of farmers by urban respondents appears puzzling. Within the general category of 'urban', it was those classified as living in a "residential area in city centre" who chose farmers or agricultural labourers. There are a few possible reasons for this choice: these 'farmers' are urban dwellers who own land elsewhere, the respondents chose someone whom they knew but who did not actually live nearby, or some of the respondents actually lived in rural areas and were classified incorrectly. It was not possible to determine which of these was the correct explanation.

9. This is not to suggest that no corruption exists in Dublin; the process by which zoning decisions are made (to determine the use of land for agricultural, commercial, or residential purposes) is particularly open to abuse.

References

Almond, G. A. and S. Verba. 1965. *The civic culture*. Boston: Little, Brown and Co.

Bailey, F. G. 1969. *Stratagems and spoils: A social anthropology of politics*. New York: Schocken Books.

Barrington, T. J. 1980. *The Irish administrative system*. Dublin: Institute of Public Administration.

Barth, F. 1959. Segmentary opposition and the theory of games: A study of Pathan organization. *Journal of the Royal Anthropological Institute of Great Britain and Ireland* 89: 5-21.

Bax, M. 1976. *Harpstrings and confessions: Machine-style politics in the Irish republic*. Amsterdam: Van Gorcum.

Carty, R. K. 1981. *Party and parish pump*. Ontario, Canada: Wilfrid Laurier University Press.

Central Statistics Office. 1972. *Census of population, 1971. volume I, population of district electoral divisions, towns and larger units of area*. Dublin: Government Stationery Office.

Chubb, B. 1982. *The government and politics of Ireland*. 2nd Edition, Revised. London: Longman.

_____. 1992. *The government and politics of Ireland*. 3d ed. London: Longman.

Coakley, J. & M. Gallagher (eds.). 1992. *Politics in the Republic of Ireland*. Galway: PSAI Press.

Eisenstadt, S. N. and L. Roniger. 1984. *Patrons, clients and friends: Interpersonal relations and the structure of trust in society.* Themes in Social Sciences Series. Cambridge: Cambridge University Press.

Gallagher, M. 1985. *Political parties in the Republic of Ireland.* Manchester: Manchester University Press.

Gibbon, P. and M. D. Higgins. 1974. Patronage, tradition and modernisation: The case of the Irish 'gombeenman' *Economic and Social Review* 6: 27-44.

Hannerz, U. 1980. *Exploring the city: Inquiries toward an urban anthropology.* Columbia University Press.

Higgins, M. D. 1982. The limits of clientelism: Towards an assessment of Irish politics. In *Private patronage and public power: Political clientelism in the modern state.* C. Clapham (ed.) London: Frances Pinter.

Humphreys, A. J. 1966. *New Dubliners: Urbanization and the Irish family.* London: Routledge and Kegan Paul.

Ireland, Republic of. 1937. *Bunreacht na Eireann* [Constitution of Ireland]. Dublin: Government Publications Office.

Irish Marketing Surveys. 1991. *Irish Independent/IMS Poll - Local Elections - 1991.* Dublin: Irish Marketing Surveys Ltd.

Komito, L. 1984. Irish clientelism: A reappraisal. *Economic and Social Review* 15: 173-94.

____. 1985. *Politics and clientelism in urban Ireland: Information, reputation, and brokerage.* Ann Arbor: University Microfilms.

____. 1989a. Dublin politics: Symbolic dimensions of clientelism. In *Ireland from below: Social change and local communities.* C. Curtin & T. M. Wilson (eds.) Galway: Galway University Press.

____. 1989b. Politicians, voters and officials: A survey. *Administration* 37: 171-96.

____. 1992. Brokerage or friendship? politics and networks in Ireland. *Economic and Social Review* 23: 129-45.

Laver, M. and Marsh, M. 1992. Parties and voters. In *Politics in the Republic of Ireland.* J. Coakley and M. Gallagher (eds.) Galway: PSAI Press.

Mair, P. 1987. *The changing Irish party system.* London: Frances Pinter.

____. 1992a. Explaining the absence of class politics in Ireland. In *The development of industrial society in Ireland.* J. Goldthorpe and C. Whelan (eds.) Oxford: Oxford University Press.

____. 1992b. The party system. In *Politics in the Republic of Ireland* J. Coakley & M. Gallagher (eds.) Galway: PSAI Press.

National Social Services Board. 1991. *Annual Report 1990.* Dublin: National Social Services Board.

Pyne, P. 1974. The bureaucracy in the Irish republic: Its political role and the factors influencing it. *Political Studies* 22: 15-30.

Raven, J. and C. T. Whelan. 1976. Irish adults' perceptions of their civic institutions and their own role in relation to them. In *Political culture in Ireland: The views of two generations.* J. Raven, C. T. Whelan, P. A. Pfretzschner, and D. M. Borock (eds.) Dublin: Institute of Public Administration.

Review Body on Higher Remuneration in the Public Sector. 1972. *Report on higher remuneration in the public sector.* Dublin: Stationery Office.

Roche, D. 1982. *Local government in Ireland.* Dublin: Institute of Public Administration.

Roche, R. 1982. The high cost of complaining Irish style. *Journal of Irish Business and Administrative Research* 4: 98-108.

Sacks, P. 1970. Bailiwicks, locality, and religion: Three elements in an Irish Dáil constituency election. *Economic and Social Review* 1: 531-54.

_____. 1976. *Donegal mafia: An Irish political machine.* New Haven: Yale University Press.

Schmitt, D. E. 1973. *The irony of Irish democracy: The impact of political culture on administrative and democratic political development in Ireland.* Lexington, Mass.: D.C. Heath and Company.

Southall, A. 1973. The density of role-relationships as a universal index of Urbanization. In *Urban anthropology.* A. Southall (ed.) London: Oxford University Press.

_____. (ed.) 1973. *Urban anthropology.* London: Oxford University Press.

Wellman, B. and S. D. Berkowitz. (eds.) 1988. *Social structures: A network approach.* Structural Analysis in the Social Sciences, vol. 2. New York: Cambridge University Press.

Wilson, T. M. 1989. Brokers' broker: The chairman of the Meath County Council. In *Ireland from below: Social change and local communities.* C. Curtin and T. M. Wilson (eds.) Galway: Galway University Press.

Young, M. and P. Willmott. 1957. *Family and kinship in East London.* Middlesex: Routledge & Kegan Paul.

6   Dublin 16: accounts of suburban lives

Hervé Varenne

As far I am concerned, the only justification for anthropology, the only reason why it should be supported by non-anthropologists, lies in its struggle to construct "holistic" accounts of the life of human beings in their local circumstances.[1] This imperative evolved in the social sciences out of the recognition of the need not to reduce human action to any of its components, levels, or postulated infrastructures. What is interesting about human activity is what might be talked about as its "passionate surplus." Human beings always do more than what we might expect them to do, and the anthropological task is to emphasize this surplus, what we usually talk about as "culture."

It is now clear, however, that the customary means at our disposal -- particularly the scholarly paper -- conspire to prevent us from achieving accounts that emphasize both the facticity of the world people inhabit, and their own activity within this world. There is much about living in suburban Dublin that the listing of such things as census figures or the price of houses, the summarising of religious or ideological beliefs, or quotes from interviews about any of these things, cannot bring out. Pictures, ethnographic film, etc., would help but cannot be used here. Despite the dangers, I engage here in rather mild stylistic plays which may help us to preserve and enhance our peculiar responsibilities for bringing something of the people we have lived with to our readers through our texts.[2] In turn, I use accounts of personal experiences, statistical summaries, symbolic maps, and quoted voices from my neighbours, to make a dual point about the externality of cultural constructions, and the continual concrete work of the people.[3] This chapter is an acknowledgement of this work, and of its conditions. Interpretation may be the means anthropologists must use, but the goal of anthropology is "presentation" -- the making present in some way of both the conditions that frame activity, and the products of this activity.

The view from my window

Black and silver clouds chase each other swiftly under a blue and grey
canopy. Sea gulls play aerial games in the wind. The bushes across the
street shiver and bend. The young trees on the footpath snap back as they
resist the forces that struggle to uproot them. The grass ripples in the little
garden. The house creaks and whistles. The muffled roar of the oil burner
in the background underlines the freedom of the gale as, suddenly, it dies out
and, just as suddenly, gusts up again. A spray of rain splatters on the large
picture windows. The sun breaks through the clouds casting brilliant light
over the glittering lawn. Emerald island...

Four rows of ten identical houses. Fifty cars in forty driveways. Forty
families, two hundred people. The neat street is deserted. No through
traffic. A quiet "cul de sac of mature properties" as a real estate
advertisement might put it. The eye roams over the thirty-eight neat lawns
each with their variety of bushes, small trees, and flower beds through which
a family presents itself to its neighbours. All different, and yet all the same
until one is caught by the two gardens where overgrown grass and unkempt
bushes betray a private tragedy that can no longer hide behind well trimmed
welcomes and kind offers of a "nice cup of tea."

The street is deserted. A flock of crows descends. They busily hold a
conclave and suddenly take off, in a clatter of powerful wings and chilling
cries. A car is carefully backed out into the street, speeds off in the roar of a
stressed first gear, is abruptly slowed at the first corner, then launched again
before coming to a halt at the STOP sign that marks the boundary of, as we
are told by the symmetrical sign that greets those who drive off the main
road, Greenhill, Ballinteer, Dublin 16, Ireland.[4]

The street is empty again. A magpie lands in the grass, cocks its head
once, twice, picks at the ground, and comes up with a fat worm which it
greedily swallows. A marmalade cat purposefully walks along the wall and
smells the air. Another car goes by. The bright windy silence returns. A
child, loaded with a heavy school bag, walks by. Two others glide away on
their bikes. Off to school. The wind and a splash of sun again. Half an hour
goes by. Another car, another bike. A man washes his car in the driveway of
"8." It is now ten o'clock and one, and then a second, and a third woman
walk their three year olds to "14" where another mother will mind the child
for two and a half hours. A brief moment of freedom in exchange for some
pin money to spend on clothes, or a vacation in Spain. A brief conversation
at the door, and then everyone is off by themselves.

Silence. Through the wall, there is the faint buzz of hoovering as the
housewives go about their business. A car stops in front of "23." A woman

gets out of her battered Mini, pulls back the front seat and two toddlers emerge. Two more emerge from the house, and then their mother. For a few minutes, as the two women exchange lively greetings and recent incidents ("Niamh slept through the night but Kate threw up again"), there is a free for all on the lawn before they all disappear through the front door. Half an hour later the scene is repeated in the reverse order and the Mini zips away. In the mean time two women have gone into "12" for morning tea. For two hours, in a cloud of smoke, they talk about children, husbands, the cost of living, the high taxes, the Church, and the altogether desperate state of things in Ireland.

At noon four or five of the older teenagers ride over from their private high school, expecting lunch and a motherly presence. In half an hour the soft whistle of the bikes briefly underlines the silence again. The mother protests, but she is pleased.

Outside, the windy quiet persists. There is nobody home in "4," "5", "9" and "11." Both husband and wife have sped away much earlier to pay the mortgage for their house in Greenhill, one of the better estates in Ballinteer, everyone agrees. They used to live down the road in Queens Gardens. That was better than their first house in Tallaght, but "the houses here are so much nicer, and the people are so friendly."

Around 3, the children come back. Some let themselves in, snatch a snack, start homework perhaps. The door bell rings. Two little girls, munching sweets, ask: "Is Kathy home? Can she come out and play?" The three are off intently, discussing in great earnest their latest discovery. For two or three hours, there will be some animation in the estate as improvised games of tennis, football or curb ball form and dissolve. Some -- against their parents' express instructions -- cross the street to raid the fields where cows still graze. Bikes are ridden up and down. Toddlers are chased off the pavement. Within two hours siblings gather brothers and sisters back in for tea or dinner. The doors close. The street is again the domain of crows, magpies, the odd speeding car bringing a father or mother home from work, the wind.

Questions and evaluations

A quiet day in the life, or is it death, of Greenhill. This is the perennial question that, over a year of fieldwork, an anthropologist like myself who moved into one of the houses in Greenhill, keeps hearing. In scholarly discussion about Ireland, in the newspapers of Dublin, in pubs and at parties, the same kind of questions are asked: Is one to think of the people who have bought houses there as ambiguously successful middle class or struggling working class? Have they escaped poverty, blight, and the infamous provincialism of small towns? Or have they traded the rich community life of small rural villages or dense urban neighbourhoods, for isolation, loneliness, a kind of metaphoric death in an inauthentic world of rootless consumerism?[5]

The debate grinds on among the people of Greenhill themselves as the lawns get mowed, flowers planted, new carpeting put down, and last but not least, mortgages get paid and new housing estates sprout in the fields up the hill and down the road.

"Oh, of course, that's suburban," says the consultant in gynaecology, as we talk about some oddity of local behaviour. He, of course, does not belong in Greenhill, though he has to reside there. But he is planning to buy a house in Blackrock.

"The people here think they are so special, but I have never been in a worse parish," says the curate as he defends himself against the well known charge that "the priests of these parishes don't really care. Look, nothing is happening. Do you know that, last year, they ..." "When I first came here," continues the curate, "I tried to organize masses in people's homes, in each of the neighbourhoods of my area in the parish. And, you know, the people were very proud of it. They invited all their families and friends from all over the city, but none of their neighbours! Once I went to visit a family in Greenhill whose infant child had died. Would you believe that their neighbours didn't know anything had happened?"[6]

"Greenhill is such a nice place, people are so friendly here. I had a real breakdown when we moved away from our first house in Queens Garden to some place in Rathfarnham. I had to tell John that we had to move back, and we did, even though we lost some money on the deals."[7]

In public at least, the debate never goes much further than conversations about the weather: "It's terrible today, but wasn't it lovely yesterday. They say we should get a few more days of this." The state of the economy, the wisdom of buying a first house, or attempting to trade up to a better estate, and the quality of the life that one can make in Greenhill are things that cannot be settled. They are all matters for a stylised form of talk behind which the anxiety that follows a major act in the history of these families is poorly hidden.

In some ways, the very fact that they all have such an act in their past settles the matter: all the people of Greenhill, and the overwhelming majority of the people of Ballinteer, have not (yet?) migrated to London or Long Island. They have migrated to a place in Ireland that has grown by 95 per cent (from 6,404 to 12,307) over the 1970s,[8] a place where they are making a life in uncertainty. Some of them may still migrate further. Migration certainly remains a possibility, and it is a probability for their children. In the meantime, they are all together at work, and an anthropologist has the responsibility of revealing their struggles to those sceptics who may be misled by the contrast between the appearance of the estate, and either the cottages of Connemara, or the streets of North Dublin.

The issue here is not authenticity or identity. As full participants in the more discursive variations of Euro-American ideologies, many of my neighbours could talk about authentic and spurious cultures, about their identity, and that of their country. Performatively, this talk was always somewhat abstracted from the concreteness of their everyday life. Too specific a focus on this talk would have blinded me to their own struggles.[9] My neighbours were not identical to what they had accomplished in their past. They were not -- in any simple way -- "suburbanites" because they were living in a suburb. Living in a suburb was what they were doing at this point in their life. My task, as an anthropologist, is to focus on my neighbours' practical, active survival. It consists of highlighting what is constructed by the acts that the people make within that which they inherit, by the stories they tell, the identifications they make, the responses they perform as the consequences of older acts become inevitable. The semi-detached house, like the thatched cottage and the Georgian Terrace, are symbols that can all too easily hide the travails of the people who move among them. Behind the curtains framing the huge picture windows that face the streets of Greenhill, there are people whom we must continue to follow. That many in Ireland should be wondering whether "Dublin 16"[10] is the "Real Ireland"[11] for whom the heroes of 1916 died, should not make us turn away from it. Quite the contrary, I would say.

Ballinteer[12]

When I first experienced Dublin, in Autumn 1985, I was struck by the wide bay, by the altogether wild hills that frame the basin, by the sky. Being still quite new to Irish studies, I had to be taught to see the town as a cultural space. I had to be taught to talk about it as a series of concentric circles bisected by a river that separates -- not a left bank from a right bank -- but a popular, working class North from an Anglo-Irish, pretentious South. To the North was Irish nature to be found; to the South the inauthentic culture of the doubtfully successful. To the North was the world whose struggles Sean O'Casey celebrated. To the South was the world James Joyce repudiated. To the North was the populist conservatism of Fianna Fail, and more rarely the socialism of the Labour or Workers parties; to the South was the technocratic conservatism of both Fine Gael, and, by the middle 1980s, the Progressive Democrats.[13]

Little by little, in casual conversations, in tourist guides, and also in scholarly accounts that sometimes point out the artificiality of these symbolic distinctions and thus authenticate them as reference points on the cultural map of Dublin, I learned to distinguish the "Centre" from what I now conceive as three tiers of suburban expansion, in the South side of the city at least. As one moves across the canal that marks the boundary of the central city, one first encounters such areas as Rathmines, Ranelagh, Ballsbridge, Blackrock, which are associated with the late nineteenth century Anglo-Irish and the rising Catholic middle classes. One then moves to the region around Rathfarnham, Churchtown, Dundrum, Stillorgan. These were settled in the 1930s, 1940s, and 1950s with older versions of the semi-detached one-family homes that continue to predominate. Altogether, these regions lost up to 4 per cent of their population in the 1970s. Finally, one enters a region now at the edge of Dublin, areas around and beyond Ballybrack, Clondalkin, Tallaght, Terenure. This is a region for which the population increased by 20 to 600 per cent during the 1970s.

This region is now covered by a mass of housing "estates" (what in the United States might be called "developments"), with the attendant shopping centres and schools, and a minimal complement of such services as churches or pubs. Within the region, one can distinguish various ecological areas, often separated by undeveloped farms, parks, industrial estates, etc. Ballinteer is one such area. Each area is itself somewhat homogeneous in terms of income but not absolutely. All areas contain pockets of "official" poverty (state supported "council housing," sometimes in apartment buildings visible from long distances as they rise four or five stories over the rest of the housing stock), some pockets of unofficial poverty (such as "travellers" temporary settlements). They also contain a not insignificant number of invisible poverty (individual households in various stages of bankruptcy). The areas are in fact somewhat heterogeneous amongst themselves, and any attempt at characterising them as a whole would be misleading. Nothing extremely expensive -- say above £80,000 -- was built in this circle of suburbs, and it is home to many a skilled blue collar worker or petty bureaucrat. Still, many estates have houses that are beyond the reach of most in Dublin, except young professionals, middle managers, and other civil servants. At the other extreme is Tallaght where the Irish government deliberately concentrated housing for the often unemployed working class people who lived in the areas of Dublin which were demolished in the 1960s in the name of urban renewal.[14] Though neighbouring estates can be somewhat heterogeneous, each estate within an area is extremely homogeneous, as far as housing style and cost is concerned. This does not mean that estates are not somewhat heterogeneous as far as the social background of the buyers is concerned.

Through the middle 1960s, Ballinteer itself remained a rural area south of Dundrum with no particular centre. It included a small housing estate built in the 1930s with British money for Irish veterans of World War I, a dozen or so "council" houses dating from even earlier, some middling Anglo-

Irish "estates" (in the old sense of the word that referred to a house and a few acres of park land around it), and a few scattered small shops and farms. Only one of these landed gentry estates, Marley Park, was of any size or other significance, and it had been turned into a city park with a playground for children, playing fields, and trails through woods. By the time we lived there only one of these estates was still operated in a traditional manner as a stud farm. It was hidden behind high walls and a screen of trees that made it all but invisible. The rest of the area had been settled, estate by estate with names like Broadford, Ludford, Woodpark, Clonlea, Pine Valley, Marley, etc. The last area of open fields was built up during our stay. As the first estates were developed, the old Anglo-Irish houses were demolished in the process of putting up the hundreds of semi-detached houses that subdivided the park land and fields. One developer told me that only in the late 1970s was it realized that these houses might have value as status symbols around which to create an advertisement image for the emerging development. They are now often preserved, after having been subdivided into small apartments. There is only one, though quite noticeable, city council estate, Hill View Court at Ballinteer's northern edge. There was also a proposal to transform an open field at the southeastern edge into a halting site for travellers. At what may become the centre of the area, one could find one major shopping centre and two smaller ones, two petrol stations, one school, two pubs, one church.[15]

Identifications[16]

On my first drive through Ballinteer and the other suburbs of this belt, I was struck by the grey to pale beige uniformity of the architecture. All the houses are essentially the same -- differing only in floor sizes, detailing, and after a few years, a weathering mitigated or not by the level of upkeep. They are of the semi-detached style favoured in the British Isles, with small gardens in front and back, a low wall facing the street but not blocking views of, or from, the front of the house. The buildings are typically constructed of cement building blocks with a stucco finish, with huge picture windows in the main rooms. On the ground floor one finds an eat-in kitchen and a more or less extensive living room-dining room combination in a corner of which is located the ubiquitous television and VCR. In some estates no provision is made for parking a car other than a paved area in the front garden. Most have car ports, some have enclosed garages.[17] The heating systems vary from nothing but coal-burning fire places in two bottom rooms, to more or less elaborate ones with oil-burning central heating.

The appearance of uniformity is quite misleading, however. Eventually, I learned that all these details (heating system, double glazed windows, car ports transformed into enclosed garages or extra bedroom, floor size, garden size, density, landscaping, etc.) allow for an elaborate system of identifications that differentiate estate from estate, and neighbour from neighbour. Only a mean-spirited critic will say of the houses and of the people that "they are all alike." In fact, people are very sensitive to not so minor variations in floor size, finish, landscaping, etc. They also work to distinguish their house from the one next door. Given the rather short history of these estates, there may not have been time for glaring differences. Still, people will notice who has enclosed the main entrance within a small porch, who plants an elaborate flower garden, and who is content with the original bare square of grass. The construction of a "granny flat" in the back of the house will be discussed at length, and so will the decision to install new carpeting, and perhaps a second bathroom. Each of these things display, for those who know how to read the signs, households, as particular economic, kin, and status entities.

The affirmation of a peculiar kind of diversity may also arise out of the symbols the people use to identify themselves. Of the several thousand adults who lived in Ballinteer in the middle 1980s, not more than a few dozen had been born there. None of the people of Greenhill had been. "I am from Cork," "my parents were both from Co. Meath," "I think my grandfather was born in Arklow," "oh, no my mother was a real Dubliner, we grew up on Eccles Street." The three dozen families who inhabit the houses their parents moved into in 1918 are never an issue. Neither the families, nor their houses, are symbols for identification. Most people do not even know they exist. As for the Anglo-Irish big houses that dotted the landscape, they and their owners are now all gone, as utterly as if they had never existed. When the house and its magnificent grounds that gave its name to Marley Park were opened to the public, there was no attempt to appropriate their history. All that remains of the original Ballinteer are a few names, and the word "estate" itself. On a smaller theatre, this is the process that made of Trinity College in the centre of Dublin, or of the famous Georgian terraces of the city, or even St. Patrick's Cathedral, ambiguous symbols that a proper Irish nationalism could not co-opt as "really us." After all, the nationalists said in various ways, the Anglo-Irish should never have inscribed themselves on "our" landscape. In the process, as some Irish critics have argued, the nationalists alienated themselves, and the population of Ireland, from major aspects of their past.[18]

Ballinteer may have carried only one symbolic identification requiring some response from residents. It was associated with the "South" of Dublin, and thus carried, particularly among those who had little direct experience of the area, the stigmata of snobbery, superiority, middle-classness, etc., that have their uses as political weapons among the residents of other parts of Dublin. This is the area which has seen the development of an offshoot of the traditional Fianna Fail political party, the Progressive Democrats. They were particularly strong in South Dublin, and of them a columnist for the *Irish Times* once wrote

> The Progressive Democrats [is a party that] is evolving into an open and avowedly right-wing middle class party. It is the party of "I'm All-right-Jack-and-shag-you" people. It appeals to the selfish and the greedy: it is the purveyor of consumer politics, the antithesis of the rural meitheal (Healy 1987).

Some of those who bought houses in Ballinteer rather than in equivalent areas in the northern or western suburbs may indeed have done so because of the positive version of this identification (the one that would stress comfort, progress, openness to new ideas and liberalism, etc.). It may even have allowed builders to charge more for the same house. Some of our neighbours, however, were quite sensitive to the insult, and they made a major point of correcting me if I mentioned that I had come to the area to the study the "Irish middle class" -- as I initially, and naively, did. One person I had never met, but who had heard of my summary of my work, once came to me angrily to affirm that there were no people of the middle class in Ballinteer, only people of the working class. One of the local members of the Dáil (Parliament) confirmed that he would never use the word "middle class" in his speeches.[19] He had agreed that "reporters, experts" would call Ballinteer "middle class" but that it was "a horrible term":

> No way! [LAUGHTER] No way. I would never use the term in a public speech. I don't like it at all. Now the one thing about Ballinteer, you could describe it as a lot of things. It's a very settled area, a very friendly area I find, from my work as a teacher. I don't like the classification of people.

Eventually, Ballinteer in general, and Greenhill in particular, exists only in the negative. Greenhill is not a place where you might send people to find Ireland. It is the place that is never photographed for the myriad coffee table books and postcards that sell Real Ireland to the tourists and the Irish alike. Real Ireland, community, is somewhere else, in the country, in the inner city. On the negative, every one agrees: Greenhill is "not Ireland." It is no more Ireland than London or Long Island. No Saint Columbcille walked the streets making wells holy. No grandfather built the stone walls that established the family's land and identified it in relation to the other families of the parish. Ballinteer is the empty place inhabited by 15,000 people.

But Greenhill is also the place where the people are willing to sacrifice much so that they can live there. Sean Bailey, whom I discuss in greater detail later, told the story of his move in the following terms:

> I bought this house six years ago. We saved. And, we got married in 1980 and we bought a house before we got married. It was a three bedroom semi-detached out in one of the big housing estates, in a place named Clondalkin . . . Kay is originally from the area and her family lived here. We wanted to move. We liked this area. We wanted to move over here so then we just decided after a year -- we lived in the other house about a year -- we'd try and move before we had any children because we could handle the money better. So we went looking around and this came up. We didn't have the money really but the way you scrimp and save and put every penny together. So we bought this which was about twice the price of what we had paid for the other one. So we made some money on that one. Prices were really booming then. House prices were nearly doubling, you know, about a £1,000 a week. At that time there was such a boom in the building that house prices went psst. That's when we decided that if we were ever going to move, we had to do it then because when kids come along we couldn't afford to do it any later on because prices were going up. So that's how we ended up here.

Greenhill is the uncharted future. It is the place one has come to. It is also the place that one continually leaves: to go to work, to the supermarket, to the pub, to the exercise centre, to church, to school. Indeed, this is a place where few expect their children to remain after they graduate from difficult (to the children), and very expensive (to their parents), schools. To leave, one's first necessity is a car, the last is an education. These necessities, eventually, frame all aspects of one's everyday life in a place like Greenhill. Let us, then, follow my neighbours as they leave.

The view from my car

Tic, tic, tic, goes the turn signal as one leans over the steering wheel to check for incoming traffic hidden by the hedges and a high stone wall. A quick run down 100 yards of twisting rural road and then suddenly a traffic light. A line of cars on the left pushing each other. A lumbering green double decker bus screeches to a halt, drops two women and four children and then roars on shaking and heaving over pot holes and bumps. Tic, tic, tic, another turn. 'Can I pass these cyclists with this lorry coming?'

> Do you know what Dorry told me happened to her yesterday when she was driving the children to school. There were these two cyclists and . . .

Pile on the brakes; quick glance at the rear view mirror; turn signal; accelerate; pass the cyclists. Ten cars are parked in front of the small shops that house a post office, a newsagent, a pharmacy, and an off-licence. There is barely room between these cars and the oncoming traffic. Hold your breath; "if I hold the car within half a foot of the wall on the side, we should all squeeze by without having to slow down."

Another hundred yards, another turn, and the road suddenly widens. No more walls or edges but wide footpaths with strips of grass and young trees. Beyond, a vast expanse of lawns with regular and Gaelic football goal-posts. Then come the low brick and glass buildings of the local national school, and further on those of the community school, and then those of the all-Irish school. Behind all this, as a grand backdrop to this display of the munificence of the Irish State in its prosperity, are the Wicklow mountains, pine forests, fields, the square block of the Greenmount Golf course; the whole crowned by the microwave antennas that broadcast computer data to London and New York.

Another quick run and a turn into the car park of the Ballinteer shopping centre. 'A car is coming out.' 'There is parking space over there.' 'What are those children doing?' 'I wonder how crowded it's going to be?' Doors bang. 'Do I have my chequebook?'

> Hello, Mary, isn't it a lovely day? Tom was in grand form last night at the meeting, wasn't he? I really like it when he gets carried away. But do you know what he told me about Fr. Stack? It seems that, three days ago, a lady came to see him ... Well, I guess I have to go now, the boys will soon be back for lunch and they don't like it if I'm not there.

Into the bustling supermarket. Pick up a trolley, a smile at the lady at the liquor counter who is a member of the choir at the church. Shop assistants run to and fro stocking the shelves, picking up litter from the floor. "Do you need any help?" "The tomato sauce is in the next aisle over, on your right." This is Superquinn, one of the three main supermarket chains in Dublin. It is famous among the women of Greenhill for its "service." "Do you know, I saw Fergal Quinn last week in the store, he was helping an old lady that couldn't reach the cat food. He's such a nice man. Of course, the prices here are a little dearer than they are at Supercrazyprices, but the service is so much better." Another little conversation with Jennifer Hughes, from the Women's Network. Later, a quick word with the teacher who runs the boys' group over at the church. "He always says that he is late, but that never stops him from a chat!" In the queue at the checkout counter: one girl to add, one girl to pack, and one boy to push the loaded trolley to the car.

Back the car out, 'careful of that lorry.' 'I have to stop at the church to pick up this pamphlet Father Stack was talking about.' Tic, tic, tic, turn signal into the car park of the square brick block that is the parish church. Without its pyramidal roof, it would look just like the school, or the supermarket, for that matter. A cross between a warehouse and a gym that can hold 1,500 people for Mass, and more often than not does not hold them ("church attendance is dropping off, you know."). A chat with the organist and the cleaning lady. Off again, a stop at the service station for petrol, and then back home.

Unload the car, hoover the living room, call Gloria and find out what happened at Bingo last night. "Did you listen to Gaybo this morning? He had that man from Carlow that called last week about single mothers and how it's all their fault for being promiscuous and immoral. You should have heard the row!" Sandwiches for the children. "Yes David, there are clean pants in your closet. Did you get caught in the rain?" The beds. Time to get the two girls from school.

Back into the traffic. Wave at Sylvia, the crossing guard, in her white lollypopping outfit with STOP sign in hand. "You know, she hates doing this, but she says that, when she gets the money, it makes up for it. But boy, does she hate it!" A long line of cars in front of the school. A swarm of children, pushing, shoving, laughing, waving. "There is Kevin with the crutches, he broke his leg in the corridor last week. They say it could have been much worse." "Don't you think that Brandon sang beautifully at the parents' Mass, last month?" "Yes, Gregory can come and play with you tomorrow afternoon. He can stay for tea and then his parents will have to come and pick him up. We are going to your grandmother's later." "No, you can't go to David's on Thursday, I have to take Kate to Sylvia's, Niamh is coming to play with Mary and . . ." "But mom . . ." Back home with three bouncy bodies. "I almost forgot I had to drive Ann home."

Time for tea. Some spaghetti for the girls, rashers and potatoes for the boys one hour later, and then again two hours later for Sean, when he comes home from work. "Mom, is there any food in the house?" `Will they ever stop being hungry?' "Jennifer don't whine. Gregory, put on your shoes when you go out, you're tracking oil on the carpet." Move the clothes from the line outside to the stand in front of the radiator. `Is the coal fire going? Should I turn the oil burner on. I'll wait another half hour, what with the price of oil these days'. "What?! Mary, you need another copybook for the test tomorrow? why didn't you tell me earlier?! Well, I can't do it now, you'll have to ask your father when he comes home, perhaps he can run down to the shop and get it." Television, rock music, homework, bickering, laughter.

"Sean, how are we going to pay the telephone bill? Fifty five pounds, would you believe it?" "They told us at the office that we may get an £11 a week raise but we'll have to pay £5 more for the new medical insurance." "And then there are the £4 more that the mortgage is going to cost us. They said on the radio that this is what the new increase in interest rates would come to." "Mammy called this morning. We can't go over on Saturday, she is doing something with my sister. She was so sharp, I don't understand what I did to her that she should treat me like that! You would have thought we were going to take the food from her mouth. So, we'll get there next week instead." "Tonight is the night of the prayer group, I'll be going at half eight. I should be back at ten, as usual."

Back in the car. Tic, tic, tic, turn signal, the roar of first gear, traffic light, tic, tic, tic, turn signal, a bus, three cyclists. 'Why is my mother so mean? I'll have to make an intention for her tonight. Perhaps God will help. Or at least it will help me. I wonder who is bringing the biscuits tonight? Look at all the cars in front of the pub. I wonder where these young people all find the money?' Stop at the light, turn signal, another bus. Into the church car park again. An hour of prayer, 30 minutes of tea and chat. Back in the car. The turn home. Tic, tic, tic.

Constraints and actualities

There is much wisdom in the insistence by some of my informants that I think of them as "working class." Whatever else we may want to say about the people who have found themselves in Greenhill, we must say that they work very hard, and that, through their work, they find themselves dependent on a host of other people, across the country, and across the world, that they will never meet, but whose actions, in the long run, constrain what they can actually do. There is much that one cannot escape once the historical act of buying a house in any suburban estate has been made. Above all one cannot escape intimate entanglement with the very economic and cultural forces that produced the estate. Anthropologists who now talk about "world systems" have demonstrated that even the most remote of communities, in Ireland as elsewhere, are always linked, more or less directly, with groups, or institutions, whose needs and requirements resonate back to the local level, opening possibilities, and limiting others. In Greenhill, this linkage may simply be more immediate, since there are no local institutions to which the residents would be accountable, and that would shield them from the international forces that organize possibilities and constraints.

Think, for example, about the basic act that places oneself in a place like Greenhill: the act of buying a house. Most of the people of Greenhill probably first encountered it through an advertisement, say in the *Irish Property Times*. In 1986, a set of fields at the very southern edge of Ballinteer was thus being developed and advertised as "Kingston, Quality Homes at a Prestige Location, five house types with prices ranging from £38,200 to £69,300." The location is given as "Dundrum" -- thus revealing that those who accuse the buyers of "snobbery" have the same opinion of these buyers as the developer: to talk of Dundrum in this context is probably to try and conjure the image of a quaint little village on the South side. To talk of Ballinteer might either draw a blank, or be associated with the mass developments of identical houses (which it in fact is), or, worst of all, make potential buyers think of Tallaght, unemployment and lowering property values. This developer is presented as "Park Developments, (Dublin) Ltd." The company is in fact a multi-national Irish-English company that also builds in England.[20]

Simply to visit the model house confronts one with the first constraint: no public transportation will take one closer than a mile from Kingston, and it is totally impractical for a family unit to be without at least one car, though two would be better. To think seriously about buying, one then needs a bank, which implies at least one job for the family unit, and probably two. Settling in Greenhill also means taking account of the games politicians play with tax subsidies to add insulation to one's attic, or to transform a car port into an extra bedroom. It means being tied to the vagaries of the international policies determining the price of fossil fuels, and, in the past few years, to new worries about air pollution, global warming, and, always, what any of these will do to one's budget, to one's job or profession. It probably also involves delicate negotiations with parents and siblings about the possibility and extent of various kinds of help, along with the responsibilities one may gain or relinquish in the process.

And then, there is the matter of the children. When they are very young, there is the problem of caring for them during the day, dealing with them when one is tired, or looking for adult company. Later, there is the matter of deciding what school to send them to: the local public (parochial) schools, or the many private schools that dot the landscape? And then, for years, one must worry about how they are doing, and how one might help them further to make it possible for them to stay in the schools where they will work the hardest in preparation for graduating exams. All this is extremely expensive, financially and interactionally. And then there is the question of third level education: more expenses and hardships for an ambiguous prize since, at the end of the road, it is very possible that the children will leave Ireland for more or less distant shores -- just as many of their uncles and aunts have done for generations before. To help with all this, there is also the need to build a new network of neighbours, acquaintances, friends, along with continuing attempts at maintaining several older networks across Dublin, across Ireland, across the world.

Even for the middle-manager and young professional, all this is work, hard work, in all the senses of the term -- whether physical, economic, or ethnomethodological. The fact of this work, of this concrete activity in specific situations, must be played up if we, as social scientists, are not to transform the people we report on into automatons, passive cogs in impersonal machines. The machines make conditions (jobs, estates, cars, and the many narratives that link all these in conversation and symbolic representation), the people make their own lives, for themselves, the members of their households, kin and networks of friends and acquaintances.

However overwhelming the constraints that frame the people, they must still perform the rest of their days, and, in the process, produce a particularity, a difference that the casual glance may miss. Although the fifty houses that made Greenhill may have been built at the same time, with the same materials, and the same floor plan, they must still be understood as hiding fifty different lives, the product of a culturing process --what some have recently called a resistance -- that no system is so total as to defeat.

One of our neighbours in Greenhill, Sean Bailey, is a skilled mechanic in an industrial bakery. His grandparents had been small farmers in Sligo. His parents had moved to England, and then back to Dublin where he was raised. He has two brothers, one in England, where he has become a successful industrialist, one in the United States, where he is a meat inspector. The one sister is a nurse in Saudi Arabia. He himself left school at 14, drifted for a while, eventually got trained as a mechanic, and finally found his current job:

> S. B.: At the moment there we are automating the plant. We've had a lot of redundancies in that factory. New management, from the top down. They did a complete clean up, you know, sacked all the old management and things like that and now they are spending a lot of money updating the plant, new fleet of delivery trucks, new offices, everywhere. At the moment we are in there automating the plant, it's becoming computerized, which in the long run will do away with jobs. There is plenty work there at the moment. I suppose that I am more secure than a lot in there because I'm relatively young in there. I am involved in automating the plant, and I know how it works.

> H.V.: If you know how it works they may need you!

> S.B.: The way I have it done! When I leave they can forget it! There are five electricians in there. Now one of them is retiring at the end of the month. One is retiring next week, end of the month. He won't be replaced. That leaves four of us. There is one guy younger than me. So if they wanted to get rid of somebody else, he'd be the first to go.

He married a woman with a similar background to his (from the West, to Dublin, to the suburbs of the world in three generations). Together they maintain an extensive world-wide network of relatives in all sorts of positions and life conditions. For a long time, she worked at a job, then the children came and her work changed. She may go back out for a job even though "financially it's not worth it," but "she likes to get out of the house."

The Baileys, with their two young children and extensive network of kin, were optimistic, and everything seemed to be working well for them. When pipes froze in their attic, causing major damage to several rooms in the house, the network was mobilized, things were repaired in less than a month so that, along with the insurance money that they also collected, the final situation was a further improvement on what was already a comfortable life style with all the outward symbols of prosperity well displayed. At the other extreme, another household went through the last steps in a process that all in Greenhill recognized as all too possible: the husband had left a few months before we moved in, the wife closed herself in her house, and rarely ventured outside. She relied on an alcoholic son, who resided with her, for dealing with the world outside. He shopped for bare necessities and negotiated with welfare agencies. Neither of them worked. They did not tend their front garden. and thus publicised their plight in a way that left them open to further degradation. The garden had become overgrown with weeds and various detritus that the children left there as they played pranks on "the crazy lady." From time to time her ghostly figure in slippers and dressing gown would ring at someone's door, complaining about people taking drugs in her back garden, or other such stories. The mortgage had not been paid in months and, shortly before we moved out, the house was repossessed and she was committed to a mental hospital. The same month, a young gynaecologist who had moved back from Scotland to take an important position in a famous Dublin hospital moved out of the house he had been renting, and into a magnificent home in Blackrock he had bought for more than twice the price houses in Greenhill went for.

Most families fell within the range I evoke here. Some were more prosperous, some less. Some had new cars in the driveway and talked about the improvements they were going to make on their house. Some took in boarders in the summer for the few extra pounds that might help buy shoes for the too many children. Some, particularly among the women who stayed home during the day, linked themselves with neighbours for long talks over tea, biscuits, and cigarettes. Others stayed by themselves for days, and became the subject of worried talk among those who knew them. Nobody, really, had it easy, but all worked and made something that we must celebrate. The environment of semi-detached houses, cars, and shopping centres has none of the romance that social scientists and other intellectuals attach, with the tourists they claim not to be, to the thatched cottages and teeming tenements emblematic of the Real Ireland. It is now "their" environment, the environment within which they act -- what we might call the "Actual" Ireland.

In this spirit, I close this evocation of suburban life in Dublin with a sketch of another one of our neighbours, Ray Fleming. His household may have been closer to the middle of the range than the household of the Baileys I presented earlier. The Fleming household shows the wear and tear of years of labor which, when they look at it from some distance, they acknowledge as having achieved what it had to. Still, on a day to day scale, it is exhaustion that is most salient. No "success" here, just honourable survival: the

Flemings are doing their duty by themselves and their children. Ray Fleming sells advertisements for one of the major newspapers in Dublin. He was born in the Wicklow mountains. He was the son of a petty bureaucrat who moved to Galway and then to Dublin where he died. Meg Fleming is the third child of a professional from Kilkenny. She moved to Dublin as a young adult and married Ray against the wishes of her parents who all but disinherited her, the house and business going to her eldest brother. Together Ray and Meg had six children, and she is now working as a cashier in one of the local supermarkets to ensure that they all attend the private schools that will hopefully ease their way into careers. They are not in the most prestigious of schools, but it is still quite an expense. In consequence, the house is an often underheated shamble, and the car a wreck. In a few words she gives a version of the suburban dilemma in Dublin that I have tried to sketch. She talks about wanting a "house beautiful" but choosing to have six children; she talks about the work needed whether one attempts to achieve consumer perfection, or to reproduce a complex community life. Work, choices, and consequences:

Meg Fleming: But there are a lot of women that haven't time for just sitting down with a child. I find in modern day, today, in Dublin especially, of course I haven't any views of anywhere else, because I haven't lived anywhere else, that they just really concentrate on the house. They have this idea of the perfect house but, I mean, my house is just a home as far as I am concerned. But you have this perfect house, carpet, furniture, fridge, washing machine, everything has to be there and number one child arrives when all this is done. This is the new, this is definitely, I am sure it's everywhere, whereas we did it all the other way. We had six children and never thought about the consequences, absolutely never thought about it. No, we didn't. People actually have said to me, one or two people have said that we are quite irresponsible in today's age having six children. They have actually said that to me.

Susan Varenne: They have actually said that, here in Ireland?

M.F.: They said to me 'you are quite irresponsible.' You know, 'if you feel you're under money pressures, whatever, well, you just take one look at yourself, look, you've six children, you don't think that was totally irresponsible of you?' When I was having them, it never dawned on me, would it dawn on you?

[...]

M.F.: And Ray considers, which is true, when I start moaning and say 'oh, I wish I had this, and I wish I had that' you know, I don't tend to do that too much lately, I've matured that much more, but you know, when I was younger, and Ray'd say 'you know, we are very well off,' someday you are going to wake up and say, I wish I was back in the old days. You know, 'if you have your health you've your wealth,' and that's it, you have enough, you have enough food, you have enough clothes, kids are happy, that's it.

S.V.: He has a very sensible point of view. He's a sound person.

M.F.: Which would you prefer: wake up and say 'I've got a pain'. You go to hospital and they tell you you have cancer? Or would you prefer sit at home with a carpet you don't like. Which I don't like. A day will come when you can replace it. Don't rush it.

Notes

Both Susan and I want to acknowledge the welcome we received from our neighbours, the help they gave us as they opened their lives and their work for us. We pray that this report on their lives can be the return gift to which they are entitled. Intellectually, this work has benefited from many conversations, particularly with P. Friedrich, R.P. McDermott, L. Taylor, and T. Wilson.
1. My wife Susan, my three children (then aged 13, 11, and 9), and I spent 10 months in Ballinteer, Dublin 16, from September 1986 to June 1987. We all participated, Susan and I observed and recorded, in the various settings that each of us could easily enter using commonly available identifications (as man or woman, father or mother, child, and, from time to time "social scientist") to our neighbours. Thus, most of what I know about women and their lives, I learned through Susan's extra work, as she drove or accompanied friends to prayer groups, the National Housewife Association, morning teas, weddings, shopping outings, etc.
2. The construction of this paper was inspired by the recent discussions about genres of ethnographic writing (Clifford and Marcus 1986), and proceeds, partly, through what Tyler might call "evocation" (1986). As I explained elsewhere (Varenne, in press), my stance is contrary to the ironic detachment that some "post-modern" writers argue is the only possible stance anthropologists can take. Humanity does not lie in detachment but in passionate attempts at making marks that others will use.
3. In order to lighten the text, I am confining theoretical discussions to the footnotes. The theoretical framework I am using here is developed in some of my other writings (Varenne 1986; 1992). It is grounded in the conversation such critics of structuralism as Bourdieu (1977), V. Turner (1974), Giddens (1987), Garfinkel (1967), etc., have had with Durkheimian and Saussurian traditions that I still find congenial. My attempt here is to emphasize human activity while preserving the external, if not objective, facticity of the socio-cultural world within which humans always act. My "root metaphor" (Turner 1974: Chapter 1) is that of the *bricoleur* as analyzed by Lévi-Strauss (1966) who takes bits and pieces of the world around him (including pieces left for him by other human beings) to make something "different," without necessarily abolishing the properties of the objects he uses (see Weber 1986, for an account of *bricolage* in its original sense as used by the French working class).

Philosophically, *bricoler*, as a verb, may be analogised to the making of mark, to writing, to that extent there was something powerful in the initial calls for using text-writing (Boon 1982) as the root metaphor for theorising about the culture process.

The interpretive problem arose when some began telling us that this meant that we had to assume a purely hermeneutic stance. The people of suburban Dublin may be said to be writing their lives, but this life is not "literature," an empty play of surfaces mirroring each other. I respect them as I respect my own work. They, like I, are at work producing a world for themselves, their neighbours, and children, with what is given them. Culture is not fiction, it is, with due apologies, "fact-ion," the making of social facts with other social facts.

4. In order to increase the usefulness of this research, both for restudy purposes, and for historical ones, "Greenhill" is the only pseudonym in this list of place names. The names of all individuals have been changed, as well as some details of their biographies.

5. Slowly, and mostly from outside anthropology, an interest is developing in analysing the place of what might have been called "material culture" in the everyday lives of modern peoples. Traditional interests in "social structure" on the one hand, or "culture and ideology" on the other, have conspired to hide such matters as the decoration of kitchens, the choice of a car, or of a school for one's children, as somewhat irrelevant matters to report on. This is changing (Duncan 1982; Csikszentmihalyi 1981; Gullestad 1984; 1989; Miller 1984; 1986; Wallman 1984; Weber 1986). These studies still often suffer from a moralising tone inherited from earlier philosophical analyses about the inauthenticity and alienation of middle and working classes. Some, like Csikszentmihalyi (1981), are reproducing the problems associated with collapsing sociology into social psychology: they persist in looking at a person's work with an object purely as a way of getting at this person's "self" that would be somehow revealed (or constituted) in this work. Others, like Miller (1986), are deliberately struggling to liberate us from the vulgar Marxist notion that one is necessarily alienated from objects that one has not produced. What is important is the work that one produces with the object. It also reveals the object in its constraining, but not determining, presence. In many ways, the best work to build upon is still that of Herbert Gans (1967).

6. Except if otherwise noted, quoted statements are literary reconstructions of the kind of statements which I collected. They are not transcripts. Their epistemological status is the same as a third person report of the kind "the priest told me that some neighbours of people who had a child did not know what had happened." These statements should thus not be used by people working with my paper for secondary analysis of the people's own language.

7. For a nice discussion of the intellectual disdain for suburban housing see Oliver et al. (1981). They trace its development in modernist propaganda from Le Corbusier and his followers who started as iconoclasts and outsiders, and whose ideas were adopted on a large scale by state authorities, transformed into massive facts in the urban landscape, so that they eventually became that which people came to resist. See also Miller (1984; 1986).

8. These figures are for the District Electoral Divisions #3 (that grew by 45%) and #4 (that grew by 271%) of Dundrum. These DEDs are the closest census approximation to the area the people I knew referred to as Ballinteer. The figures are for the 1981 census with comparisons to the 1971 census (Central Statistics Office 1981). In that period the population of the southern suburbs of Greater Dublin increased by 67 per cent while the population of Dublin as a whole only increased by 2 per cent (the same percentage as that for the total population of Ireland).

9. See footnote 16 for a further discussion of the concept of identity.

10. "Dublin 16" is the postal code for Ballinteer and surrounding area. I have chosen this title to echo Maeve Binchy's (1982) gentle tales of "Dublin 4" -- the "middle class" area of Dublin centered on Ballsbridge in the South East.

11. The "reality" of Ireland was, of course, a central issue in the intellectual and political conversations that accompanied the movement to Irish independence, and the work that continues to be necessary to justify and reconstruct the justification for this independence. I sketched what this work has involved elsewhere (1989). "Real Ireland" is also the title of a series of "arty" postcards by Liam Blake that are for sale all over the country. Some of them were compiled in a book with the same title (Blake and Kennelly 1984). In the book, not one of close to one hundred photographs of the "people and landscape," including two dozen from Dublin itself, depicts the semi-detached houses, and estates, that now dominate. For an analysis of another interpretation of the Real Ireland, the one proposed by Jill and Leon Uris, see Torode (1984).

12. For interactional purposes, I take Ballinteer to be an ecological zone of about a quarter square mile. It is strongly defined by physical boundaries on the South (by the Wicklow mountains), on the West (by the broad expanse of Marley Park), on the East (by a series of institutional campuses preventing any direct through traffic by car). Only on the North is the boundary fluid as Ballinteer shades into Dundrum and Rathfarnham.

13. For the whole of Ireland, this dualism is also grounded in cultural interpretation of its human geography: Dublin's North is Ireland's West; Dublin's South is Ireland's East (of which Dublin is, of course, the dominant part).

14. For a polemical account of urban planning from 1960 to 1985, see McDonald (1985).

15. At the northern edge of the area, a school and church were built in the late 1970s. They may develop into the nucleus of a distinct ecological zone. In the 1980s, they mostly contributed to self-differentiation among those who had bought houses in Ballinteer. People saw subtle differences between the schools and parish priests, and did not hesitate to go out of their official parish to the "other" school or church.

16. In a recent book on ethnopsychology (White and Kirkpatrick 1985), the word "identity" is cross-referenced in the index to "Ethnicity; Person; Self; Sharing," thus revealing its semiotic structure in scholarly discourse: identity refers to something that happens within the individual, even though its roots are often made to lie in social conditions. My concern here is other. It is with the world the people I knew lived in. In this world there were many "identifications" of places, activities, people. There was not much individuals could do about these. They could, indeed they had to, deal with them, do something with them. Some people, in some situations, may also have transformed a possible identification into an overarching "identity." Marxist and Marxist inspired analysts on the one hand, and social psychologists in the tradition of G.H. Mead on the other, have assumed that this must be so. Eventually, the literature -- see for example the excellent studies in Duncan (1982) -- is more concerned with discussing possible factors determining identity than it is in discussing how an analyst is to decide what is the identity of a particular individual or group. I do not know how I could make a general statement about this without specific psychological investigation. I feel even more uncertain about talking of any

group of the people I got to know in terms of "their" identity, or what they "shared" --
particularly *ad hoc* groupings such as those I am presenting here.   As an
anthropological observer, I always encountered my neighbours in particular settings
as they were involved in action for particular local purposes. In such settings I could
observe them using certain symbols of identification, and I can now report on this
use.
17. Given the size of the windows, and the almost complete lack of insulation,
heating was indeed one of the major concerns of our neighbours.
18. This is interesting because, in the annals of European nationalism, it has been
normal practice to co-opt major symbols of an ambiguous past to one's own purposes.
Thus the Republican nationalists in France could, in the same breath, make of the
palace of Versailles, both an example of what continues to make France great, and an
example of why the Revolution was necessary to crush privilege. See also Anderson's
analysis of the transformation of the massacre of the St. Barthelemy (when a Catholic
king had a large number of Protestants massacred in Paris), into one among many
fraternal quarrels that completed the construction of France (1991: 201).
19. The sociological literature on Ireland would in fact not hesitate to call the people
of Ballinteer "middle class" (Peillon 1982; Clancy et al. 1986). Peillon refers to the
people I knew as belonging to "social categories with no project" and states that "they
affirm no vision for the future and thus fail to stamp their particular mark on the face
of modern Irish society" (1982: 78). I am not sure that he realizes how judgmental,
and eventually misleading, this analysis is. There is reason to distinguish the people
of Ballinteer from farmers and semi-skilled industrial workers (though most of my
neighbours were children of farmers, and some were skilled workers). The people,
however, achieved, maintained, and attempted to reproduce, their position through
extremely hard work.
20. The model for this housing does not appear to be very different from the one
used since the 1930s in England as presented by Oliver et al. (1981). The one
difference may be in the greater number of bedrooms in Irish semi-detached houses
(three to four on the average). Some of my informants believed that this had to do
with the Catholic Church's insistence that there be enough space in these houses for
families with large numbers of children.

References

Anderson, B. 1991 [1983]. *Imagined communities: Reflections on the origin and
    spread of nationalism*. Revised Edition. New York: Verso.
Binchy, M. 1982. *Dublin 4*. Dublin: Poolbeg Press.
Blake, L., and B. Kennelly 1984. *Real Ireland: People and landscape*. Dublin: The
    Appletree Press
Boon, J.   1982.   *Other tribes, other scribes: Symbolic anthropology in the
    comparative study of cultures, histories, religions, and texts*. Cambridge:
    Cambridge University Press.
Bourdieu, P. 1977 [1972]. *Outline of a theory of practice*. Tr. by R. Nice.
    Cambridge: Cambridge University Press.
Central Statistics Office 1981. *Census of population of Ireland*. Volume 1. Dublin:
    Published by the Stationery Office.

Clancy, P., S. Drudy, K. Lynch and L. O'Dowd, (eds.) 1986. *Ireland: A sociological profile*. Dublin: Institute of Public Administration.

Clifford, J., and G. Marcus 1986. *Writing culture: The poetics and the politics of ethnography*. Berkeley: University of California Press.

Csikszentmihalyi, M. 1981. *The meaning of things: Domestic symbols and the self*. Cambridge: Cambridge University Press.

Duncan, J., (ed.) 1982. *Housing and identity: Cross-cultural perspectives*. New York: Holmes & Meier Publishers.

Gans, H. 1967. *The Levittowners: Ways of life and politics in a new suburban community*. New York: Random House.

Garfinkel, H. 1967. *Studies in ethnomethodology*. Englewood Cliffs, N.J.: Prentice-Hall.

Giddens, A. 1987. *Social theory and modern sociology*. Stanford: Stanford University Press.

Gullestad, M. 1984. *Kitchen-table society: A case study of the family life and friendship*. Oslo: Universitetsforlaget.

_____. 1989. Small facts and large issues: The anthropology of contemporary Scandinavian society. *Annual Reviews of Anthropology* 18: 71-93.

Healy, J. 1987. The start of class politics in Ireland. Editorial column in *The Irish Times*, 23 February 1987: 10.

Lévi-Strauss, C. 1966 [1962]. *The savage mind*. Chicago: University of Chicago Press.

McDonald, F. 1985. *The destruction of Dublin*. Dublin: Gill and Macmillan.

Miller, D. 1984. Modernism and suburbia as material ideology. In *Ideology, power and prehistory*. Edited by D. Miller and C. Tilley. New York: Cambridge University Press.

_____. 1986. Appropriating the state on the council estate. *Man* 23: 353-72.

Oliver, P., I. Davis, and I. Bentley 1981. *Dunroamin*. London: Barrie & Jenkins.

Peillon, M. 1982. *Contemporary Irish society: An introduction*. Dublin: Gill and Macmillan.

Torode, B. 1984. Ireland the terrible. In *Culture and Ideology in Ireland*. Edited by C. Curtin, M. Kelly, and L. O'Dowd. Galway: Galway University Press.

Turner, V. 1974. *Dramas, fields and metaphors: Symbolic action in human society*. Ithaca, NY: Cornell University Press.

Tyler, S. 1986. Post-modern anthropology. In *Discourse and the social life of meaning*. Edited by P. Chock and J. Wyman. Washington, DC: Smithsonian Institution Press.

Varenne, H. 1986. *Symbolizing America*. Lincoln, NE: The University of Nebraska Press.

_____. 1989. A confusion of signs: The semiosis of anthropological Ireland. In *Semiotics, self and society*. Edited by B. Lee and G. Urban. New York: Mouton de Gruyter.

_____. 1992. *Ambiguous harmony: Family talk in America*. Norwood, NJ: Ablex Publishing Corp..

_____. in press. Catholic reconstructions: Reflections on an Irish priesthood. *Journal of the Steward Anthropological Society*.

Wallman, S. 1984. *Eight London households*. London: Tavistock.

Weber, F. 1986. Le travail hors de l'usine: Bricolage et double activité. *Cahiers d'Economie et Sociologie Rurales* 3: 13-36.

White, G., and J. Kirkpatrick, (eds.) 1985. *Person, self and experience*. Berkeley: University of California Press.

7 When women and men talk differently: language and policy in the Dublin deaf community

Barbara LeMaster

Anthropologists have traditionally studied exotic, marginal, and small-scale societies in rural settings. Because of this interest in the exotic, often non-Western "other", there has sometimes been an *anti*-urban attitude discernible among some anthropologists. In earlier research this resulted in a "bi-polar moralistic model", in which rural communities were associated with positive connotations, such as "community, natural, tribal society, moral, human in scale, personal, integrated, sacred"; urban communities, on the other hand, were viewed as "noncommunity, spurious, mass society, corrupt, dehumanized, anonymous, anomic, secular" (Gulick 1989: 8-10).

In spite of, or perhaps because of, this anthropological reductionism, many anthropologists have studied communities within cities. Many of these urban community studies failed to delineate the relationship between the local group and the larger society. When urban anthropology studies do not extend beyond the micro environment, little is learned about how people's local experiences affect, and are affected by, the urban context. Many urban anthropologists have made this criticism of anthropological studies, calling for a more holistic approach to the study of city life (Fox 1975; Gulick 1989; Mullings 1987).

This criticism does not negate the study of an individual community within a city as an appropriate focus for urban research. "Clearly there is no single 'correct' unit of analysis in urban anthropological research. There is always something to be learned anywhere" (Sanjek 1987: 165). What is important is what one does with the study, namely, to delineate the reciprocal relationship between the unit of analysis and macro-level structures and concerns, and to demonstrate how the "people being studied are also actors, making choices within a structure of constraints that then modify that structure" (Mullings 1987: 9). Some increasingly important arenas in cities, within which actors attempt to modify structures beyond their local communities, are neighbourhoods and school systems (Ogbu 1987).

This chapter examines the relationship between deaf people in Dublin and educational policy.[1] Many deaf people moved to the city of Dublin from throughout Ireland (since 1846 for girls, and 1855 for boys) to attend sex-segregated residential schools for the deaf. These people tended to stay in Dublin upon leaving school, which resulted in a very large deaf population residing in the city.[2] Although there has never been a census taken of the number of deaf people living in Ireland, in 1988 Niall Keane, of the National Association of the Deaf, estimated that 15,000 either partially or profoundly deaf people lived in Dublin. Of these, he estimated that 8,000 are profoundly deaf signers. Another estimate by the National Chaplaincy for the Deaf (National Association of the Deaf 1988) was significantly lower, estimating only 1,000 adult deaf people living within the Dublin diocese.

Although the precise number is unknown, there does appear to be a large number of deaf people residing in Dublin city. The residential schools for the deaf brought many deaf people to Dublin, trained them in various trades, and assisted them with finding work after graduation. Rather than return to their family homes, many deaf adults remained in Dublin. Although deaf people make their homes in various areas within the city,[3] many stay connected through their participation in the Dublin Deaf Centre, the city's deaf club. Regardless of where they live, their affiliations with other deaf organizations, their degree of deafness, or preferred style of communication, deaf Dubliners recognize and use the Dublin Deaf Centre as *their* club. It is where deaf people can and do go to meet other deaf people.[4] It is also a place where foreign deaf people go to meet other deaf people in Dublin, and it was where I met many of the people who later participated in this research. Adults who maintained connections to other deaf people through participation in the club, who were signers in school,[5] and who continued to reside in Dublin, comprised the membership of what I am calling the "Dublin deaf community".

The term "the Dublin deaf community" reflects a heterogeneous mix of people whose commonality must be understood in terms of emic interpretations of symbols.[6] In this case, language variation and changes in language over time reflect the reciprocal relationship between this group of people and macro-level processes. More specifically, educational language policies at the two Dublin residential schools for the deaf had a profound influence on the construction of deafness as a *disability*.

The two Cabra schools, St. Mary's School for Deaf Girls and St. Joseph's School for Deaf Boys, employed sign language for all face-to-face communication for approximately one hundred years. But in 1946 and 1957, respectively, the language policy changed, replacing signing with oralism (a method of speaking and lip-reading). The shift from sign language to oralism reflects more than a change in language use. It reflects a change in the kinds of symbolic behaviours deemed appropriate by deaf people, and the interpretations deemed appropriate for these behaviours (LeMaster 1990). When signing was taught as a matter of school policy, two distinct varieties emerged -- one for deaf girls, and one for deaf boys.

The emergence of distinct gender vocabularies in Irish sign language produced an unusual language situation. Very few communities exist in which men and women have different words for nearly every concept (Haas 1964; Bodine 1975), as is found in this situation. Because these signs were taught at the residential schools prior to the shift to oralism, today only men over the age of fifty, and women over the age of sixty, know these distinct vocabularies. People who attended school after the change to oralism generally do not use the gender-segregated vocabularies, and if they do, they generally do not recognize these vocabularies as having belonged to the formerly "male" and "female" school languages. This change in educational language policy created communication problems among most members of the deaf community -- between older and younger people, and within the younger generation itself.

The emergence of male and female signs among the older members of this population, and the subsequent loss of these signs by younger signers (with the shift to oralism), are indicative of the community's continuing adaptation to the wider, non-deaf society. My field research in Dublin made clear that the use of sign language in the schools by deaf and hearing people de-emphasized the disability aspect of deafness for older members of this population, whereas oralism emphasized disability (LeMaster 1990). The construction of deafness as a disability is perhaps most apparent in the current separatist movement carried on by the younger generation. One of the primary goals of this movement is to gain power over the decisions affecting their own lives, including language policy decisions.

This chapter on the Dublin deaf community examines the reciprocal relationship between micro-level and macro-level structures; that is, it considers how deaf people attempt to modify the structures that constrain them. Specifically, it explores the symbolic meanings of language variation over time by considering the effects of educational language policy on the deconstruction (among the more senior population) and later construction of disability in this culture. Further, it contextualizes the community's attempts to change gender-specific language in order to unify the language of education (thereby deconstructing not only disability but also gender), and the response to the construction of disability reflected in the more recent attempts by younger deaf people to gain power over local organizations and macro-level controls. In other words, this chapter attempts to show the process of "how symbols are used in action within [an] 'historically specific contextual approach,'" in order to demonstrate "the way in which people create history within the constraints imposed by social structures and forces" (Mullings 1987).

Deaf education in Dublin from 1846 to 1957

Unlike other groups that migrate to cities, in this instance there was no centralised Dublin deaf community prior to the establishment of the Cabra residential schools. Since the majority of deaf children were born into families with no history of deafness, many of these children arrived at school without language. It is important to note that deaf children differ from non-deaf children who attend residential schools in one extremely important and obvious way -- their deafness creates an unusual communicative isolation. The condition of "deafness" itself is, of course, not isolating. It becomes isolating within the context of a largely aural/oral society. The deaf residential school, then, became an extremely important vehicle for deaf socialisation and for the emergence of a deaf community (cf. Johnson and Erting 1989). Once deaf children were at school, they began to learn the symbolic behaviour that was important to their lives as deaf people living in Ireland, including (as Cohen said for his City men, 1974: xix-xx) "accent, manner of speech, etiquette, style of joking, play," and the "archaic norms, values, and codes" that govern this network of people.

In Ireland, the Catholic Church had not been able to respond to the educational needs of deaf children until the mid-1800s, owing primarily to the extreme poverty that characterised much of the island up to that time. There were so many needs in the community-at-large that there simply was no money, food, clothing, facilities, or energy to start a Catholic school for deaf children. Yet, in spite of these hard times, in 1846 the Order of the Dominican Sisters found a way to open a school for deaf girls. The priority of the school was to teach written English so that deaf children would be able to understand, and receive, the Sacraments. St. Mary's School for Deaf Girls was opened on convent grounds in Cabra. Children came from all parts of Ireland to attend (sometimes regardless of religious background), paving the way for the beginning of a deaf community in Dublin. A pedagogical method and a sign language were borrowed from a French school (Le Bon Saveur in Caen) for use at St. Mary's. These French signs were adapted to English morphology, and were also modified to both look more feminine and to accommodate other school concerns.

Some ten years later, in 1855, St. Joseph's School for Deaf Boys was established. The same corpus of French signs that was initially used at St. Mary's in 1846 was borrowed for use at St. Joseph's. These signs were subsequently modified according to the school's needs and interests. However, over time, the two school vocabularies became so distinctive that boys and girls could not understand each others' signs. This extensive difference in vocabularies does not have a simple explanation. Most Irish schools at this time were sex-segregated, but strong gender differences did not emerge in spoken languages. There was something peculiar about this language learning situation that led to the emergence of female and male vocabularies that were later maintained outside of the school setting. At least two sociocultural factors appear to have contributed to the emergence of sex-differentiated language in the Dublin deaf community -- residential school segregation by sex and educational language policy.

Residential school segregation by sex

Gender-segregated schools do not generally result in the emergence of strikingly different vocabularies for boys and girls, as evidenced by the general lack of sex-segregated vocabularies among non-deaf, sex-segregated Dublin schools (whether residential or not). However, in the case of the Cabra residential schools for the deaf, sex segregation led to extreme differences between the signs used at each school. As a result, the graduates from these schools had difficulty communicating with each other.

Three types of sign differences could be observed: (1) signs completely different in form, but having the same meanings, (2) signs somewhat similar in form, and having the same meanings, and (3) signs identical in form, but having completely different meanings. Analyses of male and female signs in 1986 and 1988 (LeMaster 1990) showed nearly seventy percent of the elicited vocabulary to be different for men and women. Of this seventy percent, twenty-five percent were either completely different in terms of form (#1 above) or in terms of meaning (#3 above), and approximately forty-five were similar in form, but had different meanings (#2 above).[5]

Figure 1 provides an example of male and female signs which are completely different in form but identical in meaning. As the figure illustrates for this class of sign difference, when women and men want to express the same concept, as in the concept 'green,' they employ two completely different signs. These two signs for 'green' differ in terms of three important parameters -- the shape of the hand ("handshape"), the place in which the sign is made ("place of articulation"), and the movement of the sign ("movement") -- yet they have the same meaning. Such synonymous signs differing along all three parameters are classified as morpho-phonemically 'unrelated' signs. In these cases, it is as though the deaf girls and boys had learnt two separate languages, making this a very unusual gender language situation.

Figure 1
Male and female signs GREEN differ in handshape, place of articulation, and movement.
They are unrelated in form.

In the second type of sign difference, one or two of the three parameters differ(s), while the meaning of the signs remains identical. Linguistically, these signs are said to be "related" since the sharing of at least one of the three features between the male and female signs may suggest a common or related etymology (although the commonality among the signs is not always sufficient to ensure mutual intelligibility). Figure 2 illustrates the related female and male signs for "Easter." Note that both signs use the same handshape (hence making them *related*), yet differ in terms of articulation and movement.

Figure 2
Male and female signs EASTER differ in place of articulation and movement, but with the
same handshape. They are related in form.

The third type of sign difference is observed in identical but semantically distinct signs. Figure 3 shows the example of the male sign for 'brown' and the female sign for 'red,' which are identical in form.

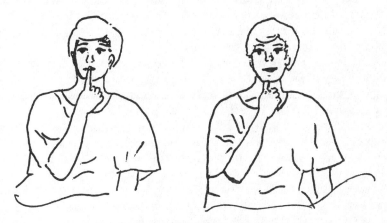

Figure 3
Male sign BROWN and female sign RED are identical.
Left start of sign action; right action completed.

Across cultures, it is rare to find this extreme difference in language used by men and women. There have been reports of gender-marked vocabulary differences among other groups of people (Bodine 1975; Harding 1975; Schieffelin 1987), but these differences generally reflect the different activities in which women and men engage (Coates 1988; Dundes et al. 1972; Edwards and Katbamna 1988; Maltz and Borker 1982; Milroy 1980; Nichols 1983; Schieffelin 1987) -- for example, discussions of child bearing for women, and circumcision for men -- rather than wholly different vocabularies. In fact, most of the language and gender research has focused on stylistic language differences (Goodwin 1980; Goodwin and Goodwin 1987; Henley in press; Lakoff 1973; 1975; Tannen 1990) rather than vocabulary differences, because it is rare to find the type of extreme vocabulary difference observed among deaf Dubliners. Even in a situation among the Kaluli in New Guinea where men and women live largely separate lives, wholly divergent vocabularies did not develop outside of vocabularies for specifically female or male oriented activities (Schieffelin 1987). Why, then, did the Dublin deaf men and women develop such widely different vocabularies as described above?

The differences in these male and female signs appear to be a product of differential opportunities to learn and use language. In the case of the Cabra schools, the signs developed as though these girls and boys grew up on separate islands. And, in essence, this is what happened. For one thing, it is known that although the schools are located near each other, boys and girls did not interact frequently. Co-educational activities were not organized during the century in which sign language was the primary school language. Also, as a result of religious practice, the Dominican Sisters (sequestered until the 1960s) were unlikely to take the girls on trips outside school grounds. Since the two schools provided little opportunity for the children to interact with each other, it was unlikely that the boys and girls had much opportunity to learn each others' signs.

During interviews with deaf adults, many reported that they did not even talk to a peer of the opposite sex until they had completed their education and begun dating. This is not to say that deaf boys and girls never saw each other before leaving school. In fact, it is highly probable that they did interact on trips home during holidays. Also, although most families had no history of deafness, I did interview some deaf adults who either had deaf parents, or deaf siblings. Therefore, it is certain that some deaf children had deaf siblings of the opposite sex, or deaf parents, or other deaf relatives of the opposite sex with whom they would interact, who also knew the Cabra school sign language. But even these deaf children (whose numbers were few) had limited opportunities to interact with their relatives, since they only saw them during holidays and other occasional visits home. The regular day-to-day interaction patterns necessary for language accommodation and assimilation did not exist for virtually all cross-gender linguistic communication.

Although some signs could have been shared between the sexes, through family and friendship ties, linguistic studies of these differences (LeMaster 1990; LeMaster and Dwyer 1991) suggest that the informal ties were insufficient to standardise signs while the children were still in school.

Educational language policy between 1846 and 1945

The Irish educational language policy also played an important role in the emergence of the sex-marked vocabularies in the Cabra schools. For at least one hundred years the language policy was to use sign language as the principal method of face-to-face communication. Oralism (lip-reading and speaking) was not used with signs, nor was it introduced into the curriculum until around 1946 at the girls' school and around 1957 at the boys' school. Both the instructional and non-instructional language was sign language. It is important to note that the entire school community -- both hearing and deaf people -- used sign language fluently for all face-to-face interactions. Sr. Nicholas, a former teacher and Principal at St. Mary's School remarked in a 1985 interview:

the deaf here in Cabra were a community -- a deaf community, . . . completely. We were like deaf people. We didn't speak either. That was lovely for the deaf. In general, teachers were primarily members of

Catholic Orders, . . . who were all hearing people. However, there were a few deaf lay teachers as well.

In order to understand the range of possible sociocultural factors that led to the emergence of distinct male and female vocabularies at the two schools for the deaf, one must focus on the language-learning opportunities that led to the eventual differentiation of boys' and girls' school signs, and on the effects of a "visual community" on deaf socialisation. It is important to remember that while the outside world gained and conveyed information primarily through auditory language, the Cabra schools created an atmosphere in which primary communication was visual, and in which deafness was the norm. Hearing people changed their primary means for communication to sign language; that is, a means of communication more suitable for deaf people's primary means for accessing information. Within these microcosm communities, all communication -- whether formal classroom instruction or idle wondering -- was easily accessed by deaf people. However, ease of communication was largely limited to each campus, meaning that boys could understand other boys, and girls could understand other girls, but boys and girls could not understand each other. Considering that the school signs were not mutually intelligible, how did boys and girls reconcile their language differences when they did interact with each other once they completed their education?

The use of gender vocabularies by deaf adults in the wider community

Not surprisingly, when deaf girls and boys left the Cabra schools and began to interact with each other, they found that they could not readily understand each others' signs. This, of course, did not stop them from dating and eventually marrying (my fieldwork indicated that many Irish deaf people marry other deaf people). Yet, in order to begin dating they had to find some way to mitigate their language differences. Learning each others' vocabulary was not an easy task considering that their lives outside of residential school were also largely segregated.

One of the most prominent meeting places for many deaf communities is the deaf club (Padden 1980; Hall 1991). At the time that male and female signs were still used in the schools, Dublin had two deaf clubs -- one for men and another for women. Also, even though men and women both typically worked once they completed their education, they tended to do different types of work. Women were often employed to do domestic work, such as knitting, or housework; whereas, deaf men were typically employed as shoe-makers and tailors.

Men and women either met at church, or during less formal encounters on the street, on a bus, at the market, and so on. Such casual meetings apparently did not provide sufficient opportunity for men and women to learn the others' signs (LeMaster and Dwyer 1991). However, once they began dating and interacting more frequently, they gained the necessary exposure to signs. Interestingly, instead of each learning the others' signs, the acquisition of signs seemed to be largely unidirectional: women learned the men's signs, but men did not learn the women's signs. This, at least, is what deaf men and women suggested to me during my research in Dublin.

The myth that exists in the community today is that once women left school and began interacting with deaf men, they completely gave up their female signs in favour of the male signs. Both women and men say this is true. Yet, research has shown that while it is true that women know more male signs than men know of the female signs, it is not true that women completely abandon their signs, nor is it wholly true that men do not know the female signs (LeMaster 1990; LeMaster and Dwyer 1991). In a 1988 study (LeMaster and Dwyer 1991), a small number of women and men were asked to provide the opposite sex's signs for one hundred and six lexical items.[7] Women were able to produce sixty-six per cent of the male signs accurately, whereas men were only able to produce twenty-four per cent of the female signs accurately.

There seem to be two occasions when the female signs are most commonly used: when only women are the intended audience, and when conversing with a woman who does not know the male signs. Because men deny knowledge of the female signs, women will occasionally use the female signs with other women in order to keep a man from understanding what is said. Yet, although men may deny knowledge of the female signs, analysis of their understanding of female signs (LeMaster and Dwyer 1991) reveals that they understand more female signs than they are able to produce. When shown female signs and asked to provide the meanings for these signs, men were able to correctly identify a majority of the female signs. Out of 148 female signs shown to eight men, on average, these men could understand nearly sixty per cent of them (LeMaster and Dwyer 1991: 382). These results of current-day knowledge suggest that men know more female signs than they claim to know, which further suggests that men have gained access to these female signs in some way.

The second situation in which women use female signs with other women is when they are talking with a woman who does not know any male signs. A small number of women who have completed their education at the Cabra residential school for the deaf have not interacted with deaf men frequently enough to have acquired the male signs. Typically these are women who have never married, and who spend most of their time with other women, rather than with men. Although these women may go to the deaf club (where most of the announcements are made in male signs, and where men are usually present), they tend to associate primarily with other women. Also, they tend to go to special events at the club which attract other women, such as "Ladies' Night" and "Bingo" night. There is usually at least one woman present at these events who will interpret the male signs into female signs for these women. These women also attend mixed-gender religious retreats (which occur at least once annually) where two interpreters are provided -- one who translates the spoken messages into female signs, and one who translates these messages into male signs. At these retreats, men certainly have greater access to female signs than they do normally.

Men who acquired male signs at the residential school for the deaf rarely use female signs. They consider these signs to be within the domain of women, and therefore effeminate. This attitude is reflected clearly by considering the community's reaction to one exception to it. There is one older man who prefers many of the female signs to the male signs, and uses these selected female signs on a regular basis. He is constantly ridiculed by other men in his age group for acting effeminately. This group's sanction of men's use of female signs is consistent with cross-gender talk in general. Women may use male language, but "men who 'talk like women' are called 'effeminate' and regarded with disdain" (Thorne and Henley 1975: 19).

For these men and women, deafness was not the focus of their lives. They did not distinguish among themselves on the basis of degrees of deafness, nor did they separate themselves from hearing people. These people willingly worked together with hearing people, as they did in the production of a dictionary, in establishing sign language teacher-training programmes, and in producing a journal about deaf people. Although deafness was a constant variable, it was not a politicised focus for these deaf people. Several factors account for this. Although a deaf identity was always present, it was not employed as often as other identities -- such as gender, age, neighbourhood, occupation, family history -- as deafness was an accepted immutable identity. Deaf people were not expected to mask their identity. Because of this cultural construction of deafness, both hearing and deaf people made accommodations in intergroup face-to-face communications. If signing was not used, then writing was employed. Consequently, the disability aspect of deafness was mitigated. In the sense that deafness was normalised for these people, disability was deconstructed.

Actors and constraints: changes in language

The reason for the shift (see Figure 4) to oralism in 1946 for girls and 1957 for boys is rather simple -- deaf adults asked the schools to provide training in speech and lip-reading. These adults were satisfied with their level of education and their written English proficiency, but when they secured work in Britain, they felt that they were at something of a disadvantage because

they were unable to speak and lip-read.[8] The cultural conception of deafness
in Britain required a different intergroup communication strategy from deaf
people, namely, oralism. Although the Irish deaf workers' written English
was superb (and they often assisted the British deaf with written work
[LeMaster 1990]), British employers would not speak directly to Irish deaf
employees through writing. Instead, the employers had the British deaf
workers interpret for the Irish deaf employees. Because of this cross-cultural
experience with deafness, some Irish deaf adults asked the Dublin schools to
add oralism to the curriculum so that they would never have to feel
disadvantaged. However, school officials felt that oralism could not simply
be *added* to the curriculum, but, instead, had to *replace* sign language since
the oralist methods of the time did not allow for joint usage of signs and
speech in the classroom.

1846 to 1946   **1855 to 1957**

FEMALE SIGNS   **MALE SIGNS**
(Saint Mary's School for Deaf Girls)   (Saint Joseph's School for Deaf Boys)

SIGNED LANGUAGE

↓

1946 to Present   **1957 to Present**
(Saint Mary's School for H-I Girls)   (Saint Joseph's School for Deaf Boys)

ORALISM*

---

*Notes
'H-I' = Hearing impaired
Signed language is currently used only in the multiply handicapped units.
Women who use female signs are approximately 60 years old today or older.
Men who use male signs are approximately 50 years old today or older.
Younger people have less access to male/female signs today.
Younger people in the Dublin schools today have less access to signed language.
At the two Cabra residential schools for the deaf in Dublin, the educational policy changed from
exclusive use of signed language for face-to-face interactions (in the mid-1800s) to exclusive use of
oralism for face-to-face interactions (in the mid-1900s).
Figure 4.
Schematic representation of change from signing to oralism in Dublin deaf schools

Coincidentally, at about this time, the Department of Education expressed an
interest in sponsoring the schools. Previously, the schools had been
successfully run by the Dominican Sisters and the Christian Brothers on
inadequate tuition fees and supplemental donations. In part because the
schools had earned an international reputation for the pupils' superb written

English proficiency, the Department of Education was eager to participate in the schools' administration. The nation-wide recognition and financial support was welcomed by the Catholic Church, and the schools became affiliated to the Department of Education in the mid-1950s.

One of the consequences of affiliation to the Department of Education was that the schools had to abide by the department's rules and regulations. Among these was a rule that all teachers must be university certified. Ironically, most deaf people could not attend university for the necessary degree since they did not speak Irish, nor had they been given appropriate pre-college coursework.

Clearly these new rules and regulations, combined with the new language policy to use oralism rather than signs, dramatically affected the availability of sign language on the campuses. Prior to these changes, there had been several deaf lay teachers at the schools. These teachers were transferred to the multiply handicapped units at the schools where sign language was still permitted. The teachers were asked to sign only within the multiply handicapped units. They were no longer permitted to sign in front of the newly oral students. Also, all new teachers brought into the schools had no knowledge of sign language. Eventually, very few remaining teachers or staff members knew or used sign language.

This change to oralism affected the signs of those who attended the schools after the mid-1900s. While students who were educated as "oral deaf" people still acquired signs, they did so covertly rather than learning them legitimately through school. Use of signing on campus would be punished, and deaf adult signers were either discouraged from visiting the campuses, or if they worked there, they were discouraged from interacting with oral deaf children. Consequently, oral students left school with a quite different knowledge of signs than that possessed by the older members of this community.

One noticeable difference between the signs of the older adults and the younger adults is in the younger adults' knowledge and use of the male and female signs. Younger deaf people do not use these signs as frequently as do the older people, and when they do, the younger signers appear to be largely unaware of the historical connection of the signs, both with regard to the deaf schools and to the signer's gender.

Another difference is that when younger people use these gender-marked signs, typically they use more male than female signs. The reason for this is straightforward. Younger people did not acquire sign vocabularies formally at the schools once oralism was introduced. These oral children either covertly acquired the signs used in the multiply handicapped sections of the schools (obtained from a dictionary of Irish sign language that was published in 1979), invented signs among their peer groups, or acquired signs through some other informal channel.

The Irish sign language dictionary attempted to neutralise the male and female sign differences by listing only one of the two varieties for each dictionary entry. The committee who compiled the dictionary consisted of deaf and hearing women and men. For each dictionary entry, this committee voted on whether to retain the male or the female sign for inclusion. By this means, male signs were the most frequently adopted, but some female signs were selected as well, and it is these that tend to continue in use among the younger generation.

When young men use female signs, they usually do not recognize them as originating from the female school for the deaf, but rather, as originating from the dictionary. During a videotaped vocabulary elicitation session, two young men in their twenties used some of the formerly female school signs in their responses for the days of the week. When I mentioned that they were using what were formerly the signs used in the girls' school, they quickly corrected me by saying that they were "using dictionary signs, not female signs," thus denying any possible implication of effeminate behaviour. The ultimate fate of female signs is uncertain at this point, but it seems that disuse of female signs and continued use of male signs is likely.

The language variation within the younger generation appears to coincide with a change in the community's sense of identity. Rather than dividing the community in terms of men and women, as the gender-marked signs did for the older people, younger signers have begun to divide their community in terms of degrees of hearing. In short, whether someone is partially deaf, profoundly deaf, hard-of-hearing, or hearing has begun to make an identity difference among Dublin's deaf people.

This coincides with the two schools' emphases on distinguishing among children with various types of hearing loss. Those who have residual hearing to aid their speech and lip-reading are separated from those who have no hearing. And both groups of oral children are separated from the multiply handicapped sections of the schools where sign language is used.

The struggles that children experience from this kind of emphasis on various degrees of hearing loss are perhaps best exemplified through the example of a deaf family currently living in Dublin. The mother of this family had attended the deaf school after the change to oralism, so she has the ability to speak *and* lip-read. The father of the family had attended the deaf school when only signs were used. He signs without lip-reading or speaking. The couple communicate primarily through the use of the husband's sign language. Most of their deaf children are in the oral programmes at school. At the time of the interview, one child was in the multiply handicapped section of school where sign language is used. According to the family, they were given instructions from one of the schools on how they should communicate within the home. They were instructed to separate their signing child from the oral children. When the children wanted to communicate with each other, they were to use the mother as an interpreter. Similarly, it was recommended that the oral children talk directly to the mother and have her interpret their comments to the father. The emphasis was on separation of oral children from signing children, because the oral children might pick up signs, thereby degrading their oral abilities.

This example embodies one of the greatest ironies of the change to oralism. Although it is believed that oralism will provide a better vehicle for the integration of deaf children into hearing society, this policy change has actually further accentuated differences between deaf and hearing people. As Cummings (1986) describes, this is not uncommon in bilingual education when a second language (in this case, oralism) is intended to be a substitute rather than a complement to existing forms of communication. By replacing sign language with oralism, deaf children are denied their deaf status. They are, in essence, instructed to mask their disability. Yet, the ineffectiveness of oralism (especially lip-reading) simply reminds these children that they are deaf, and that deafness means disadvantage in a conversation -- hence, disability. Every time a deaf person is misunderstood, or misunderstands an utterance, the disability of deafness is accentuated. In this way, disability is constructed through this educational language policy.

Along with the change in language policy has come a change in deaf group structure. Instead of a division by gender, the division among the deaf people is now more commonly based on a deaf-hearing paradigm. Perhaps the appropriate framework for this discussion is to understand the change in terms of the increasing secularisation of Ireland and of this deaf community. Nic Ghiolla Phadraig quotes Wilson's definition of secularisation as "the process whereby religious thinking, practice and institutions loose social significance" (1986: xiv). In fact, secularisation often happens as "the outcome of modernisation or development drawn out by urbanisation and industrialisation" (Nic Ghiolla Phadraig 1986: 145).

In this community, the church has decreased in importance in the *institutional* lives of deaf people over the last forty or fifty years. This declining influence began, perhaps, with the involvement of the Department of Education in the Cabra deaf schools. Although the two Catholic orders continued their presence and involvement in curriculum development, the Department of Education's rules and regulations also had to be observed. The schools' curricula became much broader, and the original religious goals of deaf education -- achievement of one's salvation through a grasp of English in order to understand and receive the sacraments (O'Dowd 1955) -- were gradually forgotten.

The church remains active in its support of the deaf community's social activities. It has contributed financially to many deaf-centred activities, including the deaf club with its many social activities, and some newsletters and journals. However, with the participation of Ireland in the European Community, deaf people have found another financial support outside of the church. The European Community has provided funds for Irish deaf people to attend conferences and other educational meetings which disseminate information on the status of deaf people in Europe. Through these contacts, deaf people have become further enabled to form organisations, write newsletters, and establish other autonomous activities.

Although the church remains a vital part of individuals' and families' lives, since the Year of the Disabled in 1980 there has been a small segment of the deaf community which has begun to seek autonomy from previous authoritative structures including, to some extent, the church. This small segment of the deaf community has embraced a Deaf-rights[9] position which seeks to empower deaf people through deaf segregation. The emphasis within this movement is to remove hearing people from deaf community decision-making positions, and to replace them with deaf people. Deaf people want the right to make all of the decisions that concern them, especially in terms of education and employment. Increasingly, deaf people seem to be involved in activities which are autonomous from the church, such as the production of newsletters, television and radio programming. More deaf people than ever before are expressing their opposition to certain school curricula and language varieties used within deaf education. The increasing globalization of this community has encouraged a more separatist attitude among younger deaf people especially.

Conclusion

Ireland adopted a policy in the 1940s to provide deaf children with the ability to lip-read and speak in the belief that it would enable them to interact more effectively with non-deaf people. This laudable effort was based on the mistaken belief that the communication strategies used by hearing people could be as effectively employed by deaf people. Instead of increasing the integration of deaf people into mainstream Irish life, this strategy not only sparked a separatist movement among younger deaf people away from hearing people, but it also divided the deaf community in terms of language and identity.

The existence of gender-segregated vocabularies among the more senior members of the Dublin deaf population underscores the importance of *gender* to them. Gender was the principal aspect of cultural identity that differentiated community members, and that appeared to be supported by the church in terms of the language policies allowing the emergence of gender-marked vocabularies. Deafness as a disability was not a central focus for these deaf people. Instead, deaf people of this era described themselves in terms of social identities other than deafness (e.g., gender, place of origin, family business, father's job, age). Whether or not someone was deaf was a given -- the degree of hearing loss was not the focus for differentiation among the more senior members of this community.

This chapter has attempted to show how these people have not simply been passive recipients of policy decisions, but instead, have had changing relationships with a number of macro-level structures, including the deaf schools, a government department, and employers. Since gender, rather than disability, was a more salient identity for the more senior segment of the population, they had a different relationship with these macro structures than do the younger generation. Because *disability* became salient for the younger generation after language policy changed, their response has been to reject traditional authority structures through a separatist movement. Both groups of people responded to these policy decisions by actively creating their own histories through the reformulation of intra-group structures and the locus of power.

Notes

1. I conducted intermittent field research in Dublin from 1984 to 1988. A variety of methods was used, including examination of documents, surveys, structured and semi-structured interviews, videotaped elicited and naturalistic language samples, and participation in the activities of the community (including residence with two community leaders). In addition to my academic research, I responded to community requests for assistance with developing interpreter training and sign language teacher training programmes, also acting on occasion as an interpreter, and delivering a lecture series on academic, applied, and advocacy issues of American deaf people in the United States. I gave similar lectures in Belfast in 1986 and 1988.
2. Until the early 1980s, nearly all deaf children in the Republic of Ireland attended the two residential schools for the deaf in Cabra. Many deaf Catholic children from Northern Ireland also attended the schools. Those who attended the Cabra schools use the gender signs and language of the Dublin schools, while other Northern Ireland deaf people of this era use Ulster sign language (more similar to the sign language used in parts of Britain). Other deaf schools have been established in Cork, Limerick, and Galway, although the Dublin schools were still the largest in 1988.
3. Deaf people live in various areas within the city of Dublin. Many, however, continued to live near the Cabra schools, and in my research I also became familiar with the large deaf community in the Tallaght section of Dublin.
4. See Hall 1991 for a discussion of the importance of deaf clubs in America.
5. All of the participants in this language study were former students of the two Dublin residential deaf schools during the time that sign language was the primary method of face-to-face communication. At the time of the videotaping of these signs in 1986 and 1988, the women were over the age of 55, and the men were over 45 years old.
6. See Cohen (1974) for a discussion of a similar type of group coherence.

7. Two women and six men participated in this part of the study. Since women exhibited their knowledge of male signs in daily interactions, the women were tested on male signs as more of a control than an exploratory effort.

8. Personal communication from Sister Nicholas.

9. As is the convention in America, I here use a capital 'D' to represent a cultural or ethnic identity, and a small 'd' to represent a hearing loss.

References

Bodine, A. 1975. Sex Differentiation in Language. In *Language and Sex: Difference and dominance.* B. Thorne and N. Henley (eds.) MA: Newbury House Publishers, Inc.

Coates, J. 1988. *Women, Men and Language: A sociolinguistic account of sex differences in language.* London: Longman.

Cohen, A. 1974. Introduction. In *Urban Ethnicity.* Abner Cohen (ed.) NY: Tavistock Publications.

Cummings, J. 1986. Empowering Minority Students: A framework for intervention. *Harvard Educational Review* 56 (1): 18-36.

Dundes, A., J. W. Leach and B. Ozkok. 1972. The strategy of Turkish boys verbal duelling rhymes. In *Directions in Sociolinguistics.* J. Gumperz and D. Hymes (eds.) New York: Holt, Rinehart and Winston.

Edwards, V. and S. Katbamna. 1988. The wedding songs of British Gujarati women. In *Women and their Speech Communities.* J. Coates and D. Cameron (eds.) London: Longman.

Fox, R. G. 1975. Rationale and Romance in Urban Anthropology. In *City Ways: A selective reader in urban anthropology.* John Friedl and Noel J. Chrisman (eds.) NY: Thomas Y. Crowell Company.

Goodwin, M. H. 1980. He-said-she-said: formal cultural procedures for the construction of a gossip dispute activity. *American Ethnologist* 7: 674-93.

____. and C. Goodwin. 1987. Children's arguing. In *Gender and Sex in Comparative Perspective.* S. Philips, S. Steele, and C. Tanz (eds.) Cambridge: Cambridge University Press.

Gulick, J. 1989. *The Humanity of Cities: An introduction to urban societies.* MA: Bergin and Garvey Publishers, Inc.

Haas, M. 1964. Men's and women's speech in Koasati. In *Language in Culture and Society.* D. Hymes (ed.) New York: Harper and Row.

Hall, S. A. 1991. Door into Deaf Culture: Folklore in an American Deaf Social Club. *Sign Language Studies* 73: 421-29.

Harding, S. 1975. Women and Words in a Spanish Village. In *Towards an Anthropology of Women.* Rayna Reiter (ed.) New York: Monthly Review Press.

Henley, N. in press. Ethnicity and Gender Issues in Language. In *Handbook of Cultural Diversity in Feminist Psychology.* H. Landrine (ed.).

Johnson, R. E. and C. Erting. 1989. Ethnicity and socialisation in a classroom for deaf children. In *The Sociolinguistics of the Deaf Community.* C. Lucas (ed.) New York: Academic Press.

Lakoff, R. 1973. Language and Woman's Place. *Language in Society* 2: 45-80.

____. 1975. *Language and Woman's Place.* New York: Harper and Row.

LeMaster, B. 1990. *The Maintenance and Loss of Female and Male Signs in the Dublin Deaf Community*. Unpublished Ph.D. Dissertation, Department of Anthropology, University of California, Los Angeles.

_____. and J. Dwyer. 1991. Knowing and Using Female and Male Signs in Dublin. *Sign Language Studies* 73: 361-96.

Maltz, D. and R. Borker. 1982. A cultural approach to male-female miscommunication. In *Language and Social Identity*. J. Gumperz (ed.) Cambridge: Cambridge University Press.

Milroy, L. 1980. *Language and Social Networks*. Oxford: Blackwell.

Mullings, L. 1987. Introduction. In *Cities of the United States: Studies in urban anthropology*. L. Mullings (ed.) New York: Columbia University Press.

National Association of the Deaf. 1986. *Hear Here*. Dublin.

Nic Ghiolla Phadraig, M. 1986. Religious Practice and Secularisation. In *Ireland: A Sociological Profile*. P. Clancy, S. Drudy, K. Lynch, L. O'Dowd (eds.) Dublin: Institute of Public Administration.

Nichols, P. C. 1983. Linguistic Options and Choices for Black Women in the Rural South. In *Language, Gender, and Society*. B. Thorne, C. Kramrarae, N. Henley (eds.) Massachusetts: Newbury House Publishers, Inc.

O'Dowd, M. 1955. *The History of the Catholic Schools for the Deaf*. Unpublished M.A. Thesis. Dublin: University College Dublin.

Ogbu, J. 1987. Ethnoecology of Urban Schooling. In *Cities of the United States: Studies in urban anthropology*. L. Mullings (ed.) New York: Columbia University Press.

Padden, C. 1980. The Deaf Community and the Culture of Deaf People. In *Sign Language and the Deaf Community: Essays in honor of William C. Stokoe*. C. Baker and R. Battison (eds.) Maryland: National Association of the Deaf.

Sanjek, R. 1987. Anthropological work at a Gray Panther health clinic: Academic, applied, and advocacy goals. In *Cities of the United States: Studies in urban anthropology*. L. Mullings (ed.) New York: Columbia University Press.

Schieffelin, B. 1987. Do different worlds mean different words? In *Language, Gender and Sex in Comparative Perspective*. S. Philips, S. Steele and C. Tanz (eds.) New York: Cambridge University Press.

Tannen, D. 1990. *You Just Don't Understand: Women and Men in Conversation*. New York: Morrow and Co. Inc.

Thorne, B. and N. Henley. 1975. Difference and Dominance: An Overview of Language, Gender, and Society. In *Language and Sex: Difference and Dominance*. B. Thorne and N. Henley (eds.) MA: Newbury House Publishers Inc.

8   Who comes first? Teenage girls, youth culture and the provision of youth services in Cork

Stephen Gaetz

> I like where I live, all right, but there's not much to do, especially if you're a girl. The lads can all go and play football, like, but it's difficult for us because there's not much organised. We can't really go out at night much because there's no place to go. We're too old for girl guides, and I wouldn't be after joining anyway . . . there's too many rules. If there was a youth club where we could go for a cup of tea and to talk, it would be grand, but there aren't any, are there? (Noelle, 16)

The degree to which patriarchal forces shape and structure the lives of women in Irish society has only in recent years become the focus of scholarly endeavours (Curtin et al. 1987; Jackson 1986; Beale 1986). Such research has demonstrated that the family, the Catholic Church, the education system and the workplace all play an important part in the process of gender socialisation, in which definitions of femininity, sexuality and "women's role" are constructed, and opportunities are structured.

There has, however, been scant treatment given to understanding the lives of teenage girls[1] in Ireland, outside of studies of education. In this chapter, I examine female public youth culture; that is, what teenage girls do away from their schools or workplace, and outside of their homes. The female teenagers who were the focus of this study[2] lived in a mixed middle class/working class parish in the city of Cork. What will be revealed is the degree to which patriarchal forces structure and limit the opportunities for female teenagers to participate in public youth culture, whether on the street or in more organized settings such as youth clubs. The marginalization of female youth culture has important consequences for the provision of youth services in Ireland. The fact that on the streets it is teenage boys who capture the attention of the police, youth workers, local residents, the mass media and indeed researchers, means that in many ways "youth needs" are defined narrowly in terms of male needs. More research on adolescent girls and youth needs should result in a youth work practice sensitive to the necessity of a female agenda in the provision of youth services.

Public youth culture and gender

The realm of "public youth culture" includes the range of activities, interrelationships and forms of expression that adolescents develop in public places such as on the streets, in youth clubs, pubs or other places where young people gather. The significance of such contexts and spaces - and what generally distinguishes them from the home environment, the school and the workplace - is that young people are less subject to the efforts of parents, agents of the state and/or the Church to supervise and control their behaviour. However, as Bell convincingly suggests, despite the tendency to see youth culture as "an external cultural influence associated with a general process of modernization transforming Irish society" (1990:34) and thus a threat to the status quo, it is worth noting that rarely is public youth culture so truly oppositional. In fact, in the Republic of Ireland, expressions of public youth culture tend to be firmly rooted in the historical traditions of the parent culture in question, in many ways reinforcing embedded cultural values relating to class, gender and ethnicity.

While there are many good ethnographies of youth culture in Britain and the United States, there have been few in Ireland (see, for example, Bell 1990; Jenkins 1983). Furthermore, until quite recently, there has been scant attention paid in the ethnographic literature of Ireland to the role of adolescent females. From early investigations of "street corner society" (Whyte 1943) to more recent accounts of British youth subcultures (Mungham and Pearson 1976), there has been an emphasis on what young males do, to the extent that the activities of young females are ignored or, at best, depicted as marginal:

> Because the most visible examples of delinquency have been found in gangs
> of boys, the concept of youth culture has been synonymous with assertive
> expressions of masculinity - hooliganism, violence etc. . . . it has attained
> another invisible prefix: (male)(delinquent) youth culture (Frith 1981:7).

Since the 1970s, there has been an effort to focus more attention on female youth culture in order to make sense of why girls are seemingly less visible in public contexts, whether in organized clubs, or more informally on the street corner (McRobbie and Garber 1976; Deem 1982; Gregory 1982; Brake 1985; Leonard 1988). A central theme has been that while at one level there can be a basis for shared experience (class and ethnicity being important contextual factors), in general teenage girls and boys experience, and participate in, youth culture quite differently. The fact that much public (working class) youth culture is "masculinist" - stressing the importance of toughness, risk-taking, male bonding, derisive attitudes towards women and homosexuals - pushes women to the margins.

Teenage girls participate less in public forms of youth culture, are less likely to be involved in so-called delinquent acts, and thus are less "visible" because, amongst other things, "they are predominantly and more scrupulously regulated in the home" (Nava 1984:11). Their domestic responsibilities tend to be more extensive, parental concerns with controlling their sexuality are greater, and thus their freedom to participate in public forms of youth culture is much more restricted. The result is that teenage girls often retreat into a "culture of femininity" that stresses romantic attachment, the importance of a small group of friends, the home, and the defence of 'sexual reputation' (McRobbie and Garber 1976; Brake 1985; Frith 1981;1983).

Female teenagers are not, then, merely marginal participants in a male dominated youth culture, whether public or private. Rather, they occupy a different space socially and structurally; one that is defined by the larger forces of patriarchy. Female teenagers are the products of a process of gender role socialisation that occurs in the home, the church, at school, in the workplace, through the mass media and within peer groups. It involves the inculcation of ideals and values (in the Republic of Ireland, strongly influenced by Catholic social teaching) that suggest significantly different roles for men and women, and which underlie a practice that organises and constructs a distinct difference in economic and political opportunities. While such patterns exist to varying degrees in all class groups, this is not the same as saying that female youth culture is classless in form. In fact, as will become clear, just as the youth culture of teenage boys must be seen through the matrix of inter- and intra-class differences, so must that of girls.

The family, sexuality and the peer group

Extensive studies of sex role differentiation in the education system and the workplace have demonstrated the pervasiveness of patriarchal values in the Republic of Ireland (Hannan et al. 1983; Breen 1984; Kellaghan 1983). It is also within the domestic sphere and within peer groups that important processes of sex-role socialisation occur, leading to the distinctive leisure practices of teenage boys and girls. The family, of course, figures centrally in this process. Historical depictions of the Irish family in rural areas suggested a strict division of labour between husband and wife (Arensberg and Kimball 1968). A woman was expected to be housewife and mother, both a care-giver and a source of emotional support, strength and understanding. While contemporary notions of the family are strongly rooted in the historical tradition of the rural family, the powerful and enduring influence of Catholicism is also significant.[3]

> The image of the Catholic mother is very strong. She is glorified as a myth and woven into the ideal of the Catholic family. Mother is a spiritual and emotional foundation for the family, the source of love and affection and of moral values. . . . She is also expected to protect and forgive her children, and display the virtues of humility, gentleness and mercy. It is an ideal which is clearly modelled on the image of Mary as mother of Jesus (Beale 1986:50).

Over the past several decades, the processes of urbanization, increasing secular influences and changing labour force demands have resulted in challenges to such traditional models of a patriarchal division of labour. There is now an increasing plurality of views on, and models of the relation between, wife, husband and family (Hannan and Katsiaouni 1977; Curtin 1986). Nevertheless, it is still a truism that women remain largely responsible for the household and social reproduction (Nic Ghiolla Phadraig 1986; Jackson 1986; Curtin 1986; Beale 1986) and that the forces of patriarchy operate in these spheres.

Within the family and the household, teenage girls are subject to a process of gender role socialisation that results in greater restrictions. First and foremost, they are socialised (not only in the family context, but through religion, education and peer groups) to aspire to the role of wife and mother. This begins at an early age and is intensified during teenage years. Second, girls are expected to perform many domestic tasks, both to ease the burden of their mother and as a form of apprenticeship for their future roles. A common complaint of the teenage girls to whom I spoke was that their domestic responsibilities were greater than those of their brothers, and few teenage boys disagreed. Third, given Irish Catholic ideals of motherhood, it should not be surprising that teenage girls are subject to their family's efforts to control their behaviour outside the home, as a means of defining and regulating their sexuality and 'reputation'.

Such limiting gender role definitions are not, of course, only defined from within the household, but are also dictated by peer groups. In public contexts, the "reputation" of a girl is socially constructed by both male and female peer groups, and by the interaction between the sexes. The moral prohibitions (largely influenced by Catholic social teaching) on sex outside the marriage and over birth control mean that girls must define their femininity in terms of contradictory expectations: they must be attractive and sexually alluring, but not "sexual". Many teenage boys to whom I spoke suggested that their bride would have to be a virgin or, if not, that her sexual experience would be limited to them (these boys held different standards for their own behaviour). Of course, this did not preclude the possibility that many teenage boys and girls were sexually active - in fact, many were - but rather, that knowledge of such behaviour was (especially for girls) to be kept discretely private. The prohibition on recognizing sexuality, however, made dealing with the potential results of such encounters more problematic.

It is clear that just as the values, behaviours and expressions of social class are defined and reproduced within the family, through youth culture and peer groups, so also is gender. The result is a much more narrow range of leisure options for teenage girls. Girls have less "free time" than boys; domestic responsibilities after school or work mean fewer hours for recreation both inside and outside the home. When they do leave the home for recreation, it is often with small children in tow, so the boundary between "work" and "leisure" becomes muddled. The fact that many parents are loath to permit teenage girls the same freedom as boys in engaging in unsupervised out-of-doors activities at night means even greater restrictions on their public activities. Teenage boys clearly have greater freedom to go out at night, stay out late, to engage in destructive acts, and to 'test' themselves by sneaking into pubs when underage, for instance. Parents often discount such behaviour with comments such as "boys will be boys". In contrast, while girls do swear, drink and smoke, they are much more subject to constraining definitions of acceptable behaviour that forces them to conduct themselves in particular ways so as to avoid damaging their reputation. Inappropriate behaviour was negatively sanctioned by peers through slagging, gossip and ostracism.

There are a number of factors, then, that lead to the marginalization of female teenagers in the sphere of public youth culture. Within the family and the peer group, Catholic values and conservative gender role expectations operate to contain and control the ability of teenage girls to participate in public youth culture on an equal footing with boys. Nevertheless teenage girls do endeavour to create "space" - both in youth clubs and on the street - to develop their own youth culture. Their activity is not merely marginal, but rather, is structurally different to that of teenage boys.

Youth culture in Ballinaclasha

Ballinaclasha is an urban Catholic parish located on the south side of the city of Cork. It consists of a mix of public and private housing estates, most of which have been built since the 1950s. While the parish does extend somewhat into the countryside, all but 100 of the population of 7450 (1984) lives in the built-up urban area, a space measuring approximately 1 kilometre wide and 1.5 kilometres long, north to south. At the geographical centre of the parish is located the Catholic Church, a primary school (for boys and girls) and two community buildings. Along Ballinaclasha Road were a small number of shops and two pubs.

While most residents referred to Ballinaclasha as a "community", it was not an area characterized by a homogeneous population, nor by extensive levels of social integration and interdependence. The dominant feature of the urban landscape was the division between the private housing in the south, and the corporation (public) housing estates in the north. In the south, 3192 residents lived in the 1091 privately owned, detached and semi-detached houses. These were generally occupied by the area's middle class residents and upwardly mobile members of the working class. According to a parish survey conducted in 1984, the 480 young people from the south were more likely to remain in school longer and less likely to be unemployed (as were their parents) than were young people from the north.

The three local authority housing estates in the northern end of the parish included 953 units of housing populated by 4360 residents, approximately 1250 of whom were between the ages of 13 and 21. Residents of this area included an additional two elements of the working class community: the so-called "respectable"[4] members of the working class (who formed the vast majority), and the "permanently outside lumpen element of the 'rough' working class" (Reynolds 1976:148). While social workers, youth workers and the police alike claimed that the levels of youth unemployment, crime and dysfunctional family situations were much greater in the north end of the parish, many of the most stable and conservative families lived there as well.

In Ballinaclasha, class division - both within and between the working class and the middle class - was not only represented spatially, it also underlay the significance of the division of the area's youth into three class-based categories. Such a tripartite scheme, similar to those described by Young and Willmott (1976), Willis (1978) and in Ireland, Jenkins (1983), reflects the emic perceptions of Ballinaclasha youth (for a more extensive description, see Gaetz 1992). Adolescents of all backgrounds recognized these three broad categories as corresponding roughly to: a) those who lived in the south (middle class and elite working class), b) the "respectable" working class and c) the area's more "rough" and aggressive young people from the north. While not all young people used the same category names, there was a common understanding of the significance of class as a factor that underlay the difference. As one fourteen year old from a northern public housing estate remarked:

> In Ballinaclasha, you're very well off, well off or not so well off. The
> different groups stick together. The not so well off aren't brought into
> things, like. They tend to form their own groups. They call the rich
> "snobs", and I suppose the rich have names for us too.

These categories not only reflected the class backgrounds of the people involved, but also defined their social networks and peer groups, leisure practices, clothing style, argot and reputation in the area generally. Such variations also reflected more significant differences in life chances, education, occupation, health, employability and availability of required youth services. These differences had an impact on the youth cultural practices of both male and female teenagers in Ballinaclasha. In the following two sections, I will discuss the youth culture of teenage girls in terms of, a) the informal street context, and b) organized youth clubs and services.

Street youth culture

The "streets of Ballinaclasha" - - that is, unsupervised public places such as street corners, at or near shops and pubs, behind buildings or in nearby parks - - were clearly important places for young people from all over the parish to interact, particularly for those from the north end. This is because their more restricted and close-knit networks (relative to young people from the south), their lack of disposable income and the centrality of the neighbourhood to the parent working class culture meant that for the most part they had fewer leisure options and were forced to spend much more of their free time in the area (Gaetz 1992). As a result, they were usually forced to create their own entertainment, and the streets became the location. A typical sight in Ballinaclasha on any night would be a group of young people congregating near the shops along Ballinaclasha Road, along the walls outside of the two community buildings, and in several prominent locations in the public housing estates in the north end of the parish.

In these various contexts, there was a significant difference between the street behaviour of teenage boys and girls. Most obvious was the fact that in general boys outnumbered girls, tended to congregate in larger groups, and in many cases were involved in activities in which girls rarely participated (including fighting, vandalism and joy-riding). The dominant perspective of teenage girls was that in these contexts they did not have the same freedom to do what boys could do. As Lisa, aged 15 said:

> For girls, it's harder, because you can't just go out and have a craic[5] with the lads. The lads are all after going out in big gangs, but girls don't do that. There aren't any big girl gangs. Girls can't do that sort of thing.

During daylight, female teenagers could be found throughout the parish in small groups, usually numbering no more than four or five (and sometimes including boys). On the way home from school or work, girls typically stopped off by the local shops to meet friends (who often attended different schools) and shared stories before heading home, in many cases to begin a round of domestic chores. It was not an uncommon sight to see teenage girls with small children or babies walking through the neighbourhood during the day. The responsibility for caring for children (their own, their parents, relatives or neighbours) acted to limit what they could do and where they could go. As one girl said about visiting a local drop-in centre for unemployed youths:

> My mum asks me to take care of Billy [her little brother] sometimes, so I stay away. Ah, sure, the lads are all right, but still you wouldn't want to be bringing the little ones down. They'd be after picking up cigarette butts off the floor and eating them, like.

At night after dark, the number of instances where one could find clusters of female teenagers became much more limited, though the sight of groups of boys was not uncommon. It was rare to find girls on the streets in the north end of the parish, except when they were en route to their homes, or going out somewhere. The shops located near the church and community buildings in the south end of the parish were often visited by middle class girls and also working class girls from the north, as well as by boys from the area. One 16 year old girl said:

> We like to go out at night sometimes for the craic. Me, Mary and Noelle, we usually go down to the posh area, down by O'Tuamas [a shop in the south end of the parish]. We don't really do much, like. We meet friends and talk . . . maybe buy some minerals. A lot of the others live down there - but they're not snobs or anything; they're sound.

At the shops as well as near the community buildings, there was often interaction between boys and girls, though clusters usually formed along gender lines. Much of the interaction between sexes took the form of "joking behaviour", with comments being shouted from one cluster to another. Such contexts did provide space for the development of relationships, though often when teenagers started dating each other, they retreated from peer group settings and spent more time at each others' homes. In spite of the fearful impressions of many adults in the area, "doing nothing", as Corrigan (1976) has described it, was perhaps the most "typical" activity of teenagers on the streets at night.

There were, however, certain areas in Ballinaclasha which, while notorious for street youth culture, were rarely frequented by girls at night. The two main places, both located in the public housing estates in the north end of the parish, were known as the Western Star (a largely disused strip shopping plaza) and "the flats" (a particularly run down section of a public housing estate), and were dominated by a relatively small but highly visible group of adolescent males who stood out from the rest of their working class counterparts. Mostly unemployed early school leavers from unskilled working class backgrounds, these young people were publicly associated with a range of illegal activities such as joy-riding, assault and vandalism, though in practice only a very small number were actually involved. Variously referred to by others in the area as "pavvies", "whackers", "blackguards" and "joy-riders" (all pejorative terms), the lads had a reputation that, on the one hand, was valued because it reinforced their self-image as being "hard", "tough" and not to be messed with, but on the other hand, was derided for the limitations it structured into their lives.

I use the term "the lads" to describe these young people, not only because this is how they refer to themselves, but also because their youth culture stresses working class masculinity, and does not (in the street setting, at least) include many females. It was not surprising to find 15 or 20 of the lads at either of these settings on any given night, yet it was rare to see more than two or three girls, and most of the time there were none at all. Most girls in Ballinaclasha - especially those considered middle class and 'respectable' working class - were unwilling to frequent these places.

> Mary (16): Those guys are crazy. They're all dangerous. They'd stab you if they could, like. I'd never go down by the Western Star and none of my friends would either. It's too dangerous. Would you be after going down there at night?

> Carmel (16): No, they're all messers. They're all into trouble at one time or another. The only reason they're excluded is because they want to be. You just have to look at them. Why do they dress that way? Why do they hang around the Western Star?

The few girls who did hang out with the lads were rarely involved in criminal activities such as joy-riding and vandalism, but often did have substance abuse problems and were themselves the victims of violence and abuse. They, like the rest of "the lads", were ostracised by many area residents young and old, and because they were fewer in numbers than males, had much weaker support networks. Girls who hung around the flats and the Western Star usually found their reputation - so important to working class girls in a strongly Catholic context - called into question. Sixteen year old Sinéad said:

> Girls can't really hang around the Western Star. Sure, some do, but they get hassled so much, like. It's easier for a guy . . . he can go down there and he won't even be noticed. He'll just be one of the gang, one of the crowd. These two girls I know used to hang around the Western Star. They used to get an awful slagging. Also, their reputations away from the Western Star

suffered. People would say things about them, like. They called them the "Western Star girls".

These girls were often derided by other girls from the area not only because they were seen to be "rough", but because their behaviour transgressed mainstream working class and middle class standards of 'respectability'. It was often assumed that such girls were more promiscuous, though this perception did not appear to be based on any real difference in behaviour. While teenage boys did split along class lines, there were certain contexts (most notably, sports teams) where such differences were played down and deemed to be unimportant. There were, however, no comparable contexts where teenage girls from particularly poor and troubled backgrounds could meet and socialise with other girls from the parish on common ground. Such girls unwittingly became a negative standard against which the behaviour of more "respectable" girls was measured.

Local youth clubs in Ballinaclasha

Ballinaclasha boasted a variety of youth clubs and services which public officials claimed compared favourably with other parishes in Cork. There were, in 1987, eight sports clubs, four youth clubs and two government youth services in the parish. However, the fact that leisure and recreation provision consisted mostly of sports (and catered to boys) and that there were few youth clubs (especially for those in their mid-teens) suggested a narrow focus, given the estimated population of over 1800 young people between the ages of 13-21 in Ballinaclasha in 1987. Young people, particularly those between the ages of 13 and 17, if they were not sports oriented and if they were not predisposed to "uniformed" groups like the Boy Scouts or Girl Guides, were certainly justified in feeling that "there was not enough to do" in the area. Girls in particular often felt left out. Muira, a fifteen year old from the north end of the parish complained:

> I have a lot of friends here, but we have nothing to do. I am bored to death of Ballinaclasha. It's a bit better if you're a boy . . . they have their sports and hurling. There should be more youth clubs, things like that. It would be grand if there was one where everybody could all get together. A coffee bar where people could chat. Have a game of table tennis. The community should be responsible for this sort of thing, but all they have is sports. Nothing for girls.

The popular perception that most organized youth activities were set up for boys was not inaccurate. Of the eight sports clubs in the area in 1987, four were exclusively for boys, including the three football clubs (consisting of twenty-one separate age graded teams, each with sixteen to eighteen players) and the boxing club. The Ballinaclasha GAA club was well known in the county, and as such only about 50% of the membership came from the parish. While it did offer sports that attracted female teenagers as members (four camogie teams as well as pitch and putt, squash and badminton), the majority of its efforts were geared towards football and hurling for boys (eleven teams for those between 11 and 21, plus street leagues for younger boys). Only three sports clubs in the parish had a significant number of females as members: the Ballinaclasha Gymnastics Club (113 of 136 members were female), the Ballinaclasha Athletic Club (a track and field club with 130 members[6]) and Community Games (approximately 250 members). It is important to note that the first two clubs attracted many members from outside the parish, and that Community Games, while organizing activities for those under 16, was more oriented to children under 13.

The two government interventions in Ballinaclasha were likewise oriented more to the needs of boys than girls. Approximately ten out of thirty of those registered in the Youth Training Workshop at any time were girls, and they were almost exclusively to be found in the catering programme. Three girls, as opposed to about thirty boys, were regulars at the Youth Development Centre, a venue for unemployed youths.

While girls were under-represented in sports clubs and government interventions, they were, curiously, over-represented in the area's two main youth clubs: the Peace Corps (sixteen females, five males) which disbanded in the summer of 1987, and Rainbow (eleven females, three males). These were the only true "teenage" clubs in the area[7], attracting members mostly between 14 and 16 years of age (the small number of members in these clubs should be compared with sports clubs). Both clubs combined community service (children's activities, hospital visits, working with the disabled) with recreation. Club members were typically from the middle class and from elite and "respectable" working-class homes. Young girls with behavioural and social problems - those considered "at risk" - were generally not involved in such clubs.

In general, the under-representation of teenage girls in the majority of Ballinaclasha sports and youth clubs and services cannot be read as an indication that they were satisfied and/or uninterested in improving the level of provision. In fact, teenage girls were very much involved in community efforts to improve the area's youth services, and two related events in 1987 highlight this point. In the summer of that year, the community association, responding to local concerns, endeavoured to initiate a community action project in order to improve youth services. Opinions were sought from young people in the area through a survey that was handed out to each household. Eighty two respondents voluntarily returned the survey, forty nine of whom were female. They clearly stated that there were insufficient leisure services in the area and advocated the establishment of more youth clubs. In particular, more sports and recreational activities geared to girls were requested.

In response to the survey, the community association elected to set up a special "youth council" that would advise the association on youth issues and formulate more specific proposals for new services. The council was organized, given space in the Community Association building, and held six meetings between October and December 1987, with attendance consistently at between twenty to twenty four young people (six of whom were males). The youth council set out to organise a disco as a trial run of their organizational abilities, with future plans to lobby the Community Association to establish a new youth club. While the council did attempt to fulfil its mandate of identifying youth needs and advising the Community Association, in many ways it functioned as another youth club. It became a place to meet and talk, to drink coffee or tea and to occupy a warm sheltered space away from home.

Gender and youth services

The relatively high level of involvement of female teenagers in local efforts to improve youth services clearly showed that there was little apathy amongst girls, and that there was a real demand for more services for teenage girls. In contrast, the low participation rates of teenage girls in existing Ballinaclasha youth clubs and services only served to emphasize the marginality of teenage girls when youth service providers define need. In this sense, Ballinaclasha is hardly unique. Though no major studies have evaluated gender differences in youth service provision in Ireland, Nava points out that a succession of reports from Britain have consistently revealed "the under-representation of girls and women and the paucity of resources available to them" (Nava 1984:10).

In the Republic of Ireland, the Catholic Church, the government, voluntary youth work organizations and community groups shape the definition of youth needs, whether through mainstream youth services (clubs, sports and recreation) or specialized services (for the disabled, unemployed or homeless, for instance). Youth needs are in many ways defined in terms of the needs of teenage boys, largely because they are more "visible" - they gather in larger numbers, and operate under fewer constraints than do teenage girls. Boys are also made conspicuous by the actions of some youths who engage in delinquent and criminal acts. When property is vandalised, cars are stolen, people are threatened and loud disturbances occur, it attracts the attention of the media, the police and local residents.

The concern with controlling the delinquency of teenage boys through youth services is hardly new, and is reflected in the history of youth provision in Ireland. Early youth club organizations, whether religious, patriotic or militaristic, were organized to control and contain the perceived threat of young, working-class male delinquents with idle time (Forde 1979; Kennedy 1984). While it is true that the youth work profession has progressed substantially in terms of objectives, methodology and the range of services provided, vestiges of this patriarchal and conservative ideology still permeate the profession today. Most youth services delivered by the State, the Catholic Church and voluntary organizations are officially intended to be utilized by young people of either sex, the implicit assumption being, however, that the needs of teenage boys and girls are essentially the same. The report by the National Youth Policy Committee (1985), for instance, identified several special categories of young people "in need" (the disadvantaged, the homeless, young travellers, the disabled, etc.), yet more or less ignored the discussion of, and establishment of policy with regards to, the needs of teenage girls. Similarly, the issue of gender was conspicuously absent from the Cork Diocese *Social Care Commission Report* (1984), which dealt at length with the issue of youth, and which resulted in the formation of the Diocesan Youth Ministry. *Ogra Chorcai*, the most prominent voluntary youth work organization in Cork in the 1970s and 1980s, had no special programmes or agenda geared to teenage girls.

A question that must then be asked is whether female teenagers do indeed have special needs? Many organisers of youth provision have argued that no real bias exists in terms of the services that they offer; that they are gender neutral and that the reason for fewer girls is that teenage girls "opt out". While female teenagers do in many cases choose not to participate, it must also be considered that they face structural limitations that boys do not, and that they do have special needs. Teenage girls become marginalized in the realm of public youth culture due to factors that operate through the education system, the mass media and the workplace, as well as within the home and the peer group. Their lack of visibility (reflecting more limited opportunities) is rarely interpreted as a problem that is in need of addressing through youth services, in the same way that the high visibility of teenage boys draws attention to the need for services.

The absence of a "female agenda" in youth work in Ireland should be seen as reflecting the larger influence of patriarchy in a class-based society. The strong influence of Irish Catholicism is a significant factor here, through the role it plays in the systematic exclusion of certain issues from debate, and practice. Such issues, dealing with the free choice of women, their bodies and their sexuality - such as abortion counselling, information and availability of contraceptives and special services for teenage mothers[8] - are not regularly and routinely part of the youth work agenda in Ireland, whether defined by dominant institutions of youth provision, or by community groups in places such as Ballinaclasha[9]. The fact that some of these special services (which are routinely part of youth work services in other countries) are illegal reflects and emphasises the degree to which religious and patriarchal control is exerted over a woman's body and her reproductive functions by societal institutions, and the limited role that can by played by youth work services.

This patriarchal bias in determining youth needs exists not only in the realm of specialized services but also, significantly, in the provision of leisure oriented youth clubs at the local level. In Ballinaclasha, while teenage girls certainly demonstrated an interest in youth clubs, most local effort went into providing sports clubs, mainly for boys. There is reason to consider the provision of youth clubs a special issue for teenage girls. The interest of female teenagers in youth clubs can and must be related to the constraints placed on young girls in terms of their ability to operate freely as part of out-of-door, unsupervised street youth culture. It is possible that such clubs were especially popular amongst teenage girls because they provided "space"; that is, a setting acceptable to parents, that allowed them to engage in a variety of public and shared activities, such as seeing friends, talking, smoking, listening to music and meeting boys. The street is, in a sense, brought "indoors" for girls, though with obvious limitations and restrictions (it must be remembered that youth clubs are usually supervised, and often by members of the clergy). Whether the interests of those girls who came from particularly poor and troubled backgrounds - the female equivalent of "the lads" - would be served by such forms of provision remains to be seen. Such girls are perhaps the most disadvantaged young people, because not only are they marginal to male youth culture, but they are also marginal to the cultures of middle class and respectable working class female teenagers.

Conclusion

For the providers of youth services in Ireland, defining youth needs has been and will continue to be a difficult task, based largely on popular understandings of "what it is like" to be an adolescent. Such renderings of the "typical" adolescent, however, rarely take fully into account the significance of gender. For instance, teenage girls do not experience the same freedom to participate in public youth culture - whether on the streets or in youth clubs - as teenage boys. This is particularly true for those from more impoverished backgrounds. Yet, the marginalization of female teenagers does not mean that they are absent or unimportant, but rather that they occupy their own "space", engage in leisure from a different perspective and to some degree have a youth culture of their own. This is not, however, a benign difference, but rather one that is shaped by the pervasiveness of patriarchal forces within the family and the peer group, and the influences of Catholic social teaching, education, the mass media and the workplace, all of which shape the way adolescents are socialised into gender roles.

A reorientation of the definition of youth needs by youth service providers - whether at the grass-roots level or within the dominant institutions of youth provision - requires a greater sensitivity to the significance of gender and an assessment of the desires, leisure patterns and the limitations that teenage girls of different class backgrounds experience. The so-called lack of visibility of female teenagers in public youth culture can no longer be used as an excuse to ignore or down-play their interests. Clubs and services must be developed that reduce the barriers of access to female teens. New services must be oriented to their special needs (based on more specific needs assessment studies). Of course, these specific strategies can only succeed as part of a broader strategy to reduce patriarchy within the home, schools, workplace and church.

Notes

1. Many young adult females in Cork to whom I spoke preferred to be called "girls" rather than women, because the latter implied a degree of sexual experience with which they did not wish to be associated.
2. The research for this project was conducted in 1987-88 in the urban parish of Ballinaclasha, in the city of Cork. It was part of a larger study on the efforts of community groups to initiate youth services in their area, and the problems they encountered. A wide range of methods were used, including participant observation, interviews with youth people and those involved in youth services, and an examination of community association records. I participated as a youth worker at the local Youth Development Centre and worked with the community association in their efforts to respond to the need for improved youth services. Pseudonyms have been used for the names of people, places and organizations.
3. Historically, since independence at least, both Church and State envisaged the family in a strongly patriarchal fashion, as evidenced, for instance, in certain passages of the constitution relating to the "family" (Article 41.1.1) and "motherhood" (Article 41.2.1).
4. I use the term "respectable working class" reluctantly, well aware of its pejorative connotations (that is, that some members of the working class are "less than respectable"). Silverman has argued that "respectable behaviour is located in five domains: language, alcohol use, religion, work and sexuality" (1987:114) To this, I would add, involvement in criminal acts (vandalism, joy-riding, etc.) and the reputation of one's family and one's peer group.
5. The term "craic" is slang for having fun, and does not refer to the use of cocaine.
6. This club did not permit me access to membership lists, but club leaders suggested that almost half of its members were female, a figure I was unable to verify.

7. The Boy Scouts (36 members) and the Girl Guides (15 members) were also prominent in Ballinaclasha, but in fact attracted few young people over the age of 12.

8. In Cork, services for unwed mothers were not integrated at all, and there were no community-based services. When a girl becomes pregnant, her first interaction with the State comes through the Southern Health Board adoption society (regardless of her intentions) and after this, she is forced to deal with a number of different government agencies. Often her first visit with a social worker doesn't occur until after the child was born.

9. The fact that in Ballinaclasha, the Catholic Church controls many of the local buildings used for clubs and the delivery of community services suggests that even if the legal prohibition against 'abortion counselling' were to be lifted, there would likely remain obstacles to the development of youth services that included this as part of its agenda.

References

Arensberg, C. and Kimball, S. 1968. *Family and Community in Ireland* Cambridge, Mass: Harvard University Press.

Beale, J. 1986. *Women in Ireland Voices of Change* London: Macmillan Education Ltd.

Bell, D. 1990. *Acts of Union* London: Macmillan Publishers.

Brake, M. 1985. *Comparative Youth Culture* London: Routledge and Kegan Paul.

Breen, R. 1984. Status attainment or job attainment? The effects of sex and class on youth unemployment. *British Journal of Sociology* 35 (3):363-386.

Corrigan, P. 1976. Doing Nothing. in *Resistance through Rituals* (eds.) Hall, S. and Jefferson, T. London: Hutchinson and Co.

Curtin, C. 1986 Marriage and Family. in *Ireland: A Sociological Profile* (eds.) Clancy, P., Drudy, S., Lynch, K., O'Dowd, L. Dublin: Institute of Public Administration.

Curtin, C., Jackson, J. and O'Connor, B. 1987. *Gender in Irish Society* Galway: Galway University Press.

Deem, R. 1982. Women, leisure and inequality. *Leisure Studies* 1:29-46.

Dillon, M. 1984. Youth Culture in Ireland. *Economic and Social Review* 15(3):153-172.

Forde, W. 1979. The Development of Youth Services in Ireland. *Social Studies* 6(3).

Frith, S. 1981. *Downtown: Young People in a City Centre* Leicester, National Youth Bureau.

_____. 1983. *Sound Effects* London: Constable.

Gaetz, S. 1992. Planning Community-Based Youth Services in Cork, Ireland: The Relevance of the Concepts, "Youth" and "Community". *Urban Anthropology* 21(1): 91-113.

Gregory, S. 1982. Women among others: another view. *Leisure Studies* 1:47-52.

Hannan, D., Breen, R., Murray, B., Hardiman, N., Watson, D., and O'Higgins, K. 1983. Schooling and Sex Roles: Sex Differences, in *Subject Provision and Student Choice in Irish Post-Primary Schools* Dublin: The Economic and Social Research Institute.

Hannan, D. and Katsianouni, L.A. 1977. *Traditional Families? From Culturally Prescribed to Negotiated Roles in Farm Families.* Dublin: Economic and Social Research Institute paper no. 87.

Jackson, P. 1986. Worlds Apart - Social Dimensions of Sex Roles, in *Ireland: A Sociological Profile* (eds.) Clancy, P., Drudy, S., Lynch, K., O'Dowd, L. Dublin: Institute of Public Administration.

Jenkins, R. 1983. *Lads, Citizens, and Ordinary Kids* London: Routledge and Kegan Paul.

Kellaghan, T. 1983. Equality in Primary Education. *Tuarascail* 9:94-96.

Kennedy, P. 1984. *The Development of Youth Work Services in Ireland.* (unpublished thesis) University College, Cork.

Leonard, D. 1988. *Families* London: Macmillan.

McRobbie, A. and Garber, J. 1976. Girls in Subcultures, in *Resistance Through Rituals* (eds.) Hall, S. and Jefferson, T. London: Hutchinson and Co.

Mungham, G. and Pearson, G. 1976. *Working Class Youth Cultures* London: Routledge and Kegan-Paul.

National Youth Policy Committee 1985. In *Partnership With Youth: The National Youth Policy* Dublin: The Stationery Office.

Nava, M. 1984. Youth Service Provision, Social Order and the Question of Girls, in *Gender and Generation* (eds.) McRobbie, A. and Nava, M. London: Macmillan.

Nic Ghiolla Phadraig, M. 1986. Religious Practice and Secularisation. in *Ireland: A Sociological Profile* (eds.) Clancy, P., Drudy, S., Lynch, K., O'Dowd, L. Dublin: Institute of Public Administration.

Reynolds, D. 1976. When Pupils and Teachers Refuse a Truce: The secondary school and the creation of delinquency, in *Working Class Youth Culture* (eds.) Mungham, G. and Pearson, G. London: Routledge and Kegan Paul.

Silverman, M. 1989. A Labouring Man's Daughter, in *Ireland From Below* (eds.) Curtin, C. and Wilson, T.M. Galway: Galway University Press.

Social Care Commission 1984. *Social Care Commission Report* Cork: Diocese of Cork.

Whyte, W.F. 1943. *Street Corner Society* Chicago: University of Chicago Press.

Willis, P. 1978. *Learning to Labour.* Farnborough: Saxon House.

Young, M. and Willmott, P. 1976. *Family and Class in a London Suburb* London: Routledge and Kegan Paul.

9   Identity and survival in a hostile environment: homeless men in Galway

Eoin O'Sullivan

This chapter provides an ethnographic account of how the homeless in the 'nightmarish postmodern landscape' (Harvey 1989: 77) view and survive their homelessness. It examines the homeless experience from the perspective of the homeless themselves, particularly those who use a night-shelter in Galway city. The men who use the shelter, especially the long term users, exist in a world of poverty, alienation, marginalisation, and rejection, where the norms of the wider society do not regulate behaviour and actions.[1] Inhabitants of this world are not voluntary members, but are individuals who, for a variety of historical and contemporary social system faults, personal inadequacies and lack of alternative facilities, are forced into this harsh environment. This chapter also explores the identity construction and social relationships of these homeless men and how the concept of distancing relates to the social ordering of shelter life and the lives of these men in the broader urban environment. It aims to highlight the complexities of life for the homeless, their internal mechanisms of control and survival, and the micro-worlds that operate among the homeless population.

There has been a noticeable shift in the social science literature regarding the aetiology of homelessness. In the late 1950s, functionalist sociology, with its assumptions of homeostasis, viewed the homeless as outsiders in the social system. Literature on homelessness focused on personality defects, utilising the concepts of disaffiliation and undersocialisation, and theories concentrated on the individual biographies of the homeless (Peterson and Maxwell 1958; Rooney 1961; Bahr 1968; Bahr and Caplow 1973). From the 1960s onwards homelessness became a concern of urban anthropologists (Spradley 1970; 1972) and symbolic interactionists (Wiseman 1971; Archard 1979). While still concentrating on the micro-level of homelessness, the symbolic interactionists integrated the role of agents and agencies of social control, in order to fully comprehend the situation of the homeless. From the early 1980s, sociology has explained homelessness as a primarily structural problem. Homelessness is now principally viewed as a consequence of deinstitutionalisation, the lack of low cost housing, unemployment and inadequate safeguards to protect the vulnerable in society (Hoch and Slayton 1989; Tucker 1990; Wright 1989; Ropers 1988; Rossi 1989; Belcher and Singer 1988; Fabricant 1987; Greve 1991).

The perception of the homeless as the middle-aged, single male transient, unkempt, reeking of alcohol, shabbily dressed and begging on the streets has been challenged, at least in the research literature. The homeless population is heterogeneous in terms of age and gender. However, it is primarily those from backgrounds characterised by low-incomes, unemployment and poverty who become homeless. As one commentator has noted, "Homelessness and wealth are mutually exclusive" (Farrell 1988: 69). It is increasingly younger people, women and children, often referred to as the hidden homeless (Kennedy 1985), and the psychiatrically ill who fill the ranks of this growing population in Ireland.[2] Missing from this contemporary analysis of homelessness is an examination of the phenomenon from the perspective of the actors themselves, their "definition of the situation" and "an understanding of the manner in which a sense of personal significance and meaning is generated and sustained" (Snow and Anderson 1987:1337).

There has been little ethnographic work on homelessness in Ireland with the result that, while the factors that can result in homelessness have been identified, little is known about the physiological and psychological strategies of survival among the homeless, their modes of adaptation and their social organisation.[3] It has become evident from numerous studies outside of anthropology that homelessness has increased dramatically in Ireland over the past ten years (Kennedy 1985; 1987; Farrell 1988; McCarthy 1988; Bell 1989; Dillon et al. 1990; Kelleher et al. 1992). Kennett identifies the "specific social and economic conditions of the present" as representing "a retreat from 'welfarism' and a reorientation of the welfare state" which "has had profound consequences in urban environments signified by the increasing disparity in enduring levels of poverty, reduction in benefit and increasing disparity in wage levels" (1992:12). The urban environment has been reshaped by this "free market populism", as the demand for unskilled labour in the inner city has been reduced and replaced by an increasing demand for professionals and managers. This results in "enclosed and protected spaces of shopping malls and atria, but it does nothing for the poor" (Harvey 1989: 77).

The bulk of the research on homelessness in Ireland has been funded by voluntary advocacy groups,[4] and it has not yet become a major concern for Irish social scientists. While research by the voluntary sector into homelessness in Ireland has increased over the past five years, it has primarily been descriptive, examining the nature, size, composition or social service needs of this population. Theoretical concerns have been neglected and as Hirschl points out, "the neglect of theoretical work imperils scientific understanding and condemns homelessness research to marginal status within the discipline of sociology" (1990: 444). Largely absent from this research has been a systematic examination of the interactions between agents of social control and the homeless population (O'Brien 1979 is a notable exception).

A Galway shelter

I conducted fieldwork on homelessness between 1986 and 1989, using one shelter for homeless men in Galway city as an example of the situation of homelessness in contemporary Ireland. This shelter is a long, single storied building located at the back of a large local authority-owned car park. Approximately 22 metres in length and 12 metres in width, it is bounded by a black painted fence over 6 feet high to the front and a large wall to the rear. Apart from a couple of signs with the name of the shelter and the organisation running it, there are no visible indications of the purpose of the building. However, regular users of the car park are aware of its purpose, since drinking gangs often congregate in a corner outside the shelter fence. A casual passer-by, on the other hand, would most likely be unaware of the purpose of the building. The shelter, which officially opened in June 1983, had its origins in the desire by a group of students and other individuals to provide accommodation for persons sleeping rough in the area. In 1979 the students, motivated by two former Simon Community[5] workers, conducted a survey of homelessness in the area and found up to 20 men sleeping rough. The group, calling itself "The Committee for the Homeless and Destitute", commenced a soup run and affiliated themselves to the Simon Community. By 1980 an office was established and two workers were employed to assist the homeless with their social welfare claims and entitlements. This group soon produced a more substantial report on homelessness in the area, identifying upwards of 25 homeless men sleeping rough in the city and highlighting the lack of facilities and support for these individuals. In November 1980, a site was found. However, local authority officials opposed this site and a local residents' group hastily established itself in opposition to the provision of the shelter. Nonetheless, the city councillors directed the local authority officials to provide a temporary shelter.

In December 1981, the Simon Community, acting on its own initiative, bought a prefabricated building and installed it at the back of a city centre car park. The facilities were basic: one small room for between 10 and 14 men, no electricity, no running water or toilet facilities. The prefab survived until August 1982, when it was destroyed in an arson attack. From August 1982 to June 1983, a temporary shelter was provided by a lay religious organisation in a residential area of the city. Objections from local residents put pressure on the local authority to provide alternative accommodation. The site on which the prefab had stood was deemed suitable as a location, and plans for a purpose built shelter went ahead, despite further objections from local residents. Funding for the shelter came from the local Health Board, channelled through the Social Service Council. The new shelter management plans did not include the Simon Community, and only after a heated dispute and the intervention of the Employment Equality Agency did the Simon Community acquire a formal role.

In June 1983, the shelter was opened. It provided accommodation for 15 men and was staffed by Social Service and Simon Community workers. By 1984 it had become apparent that the shelter was too small. On average two people had to sleep on the floor each night and there was no sleeping space for the workers. An application to extend the shelter was rejected by the Galway Corporation in March 1984. However, as a result of campaigning by Simon and the Social Service Council, the city councillors voted unanimously on 21 April 1986 against the city manager's advice to allow a planning application for an extension to go ahead. Work began on the extension in June 1988 and was completed in September of that year. With its extra facilities, it was possible to provide a greater degree of privacy for staff and residents and help alleviate the stress and tension that was evident in the smaller shelter. During the period under observation, the shelter was run jointly by two voluntary groups. There were three full-time staff employed by the local Social Service Council and three full-time volunteers from the Simon Community. In addition, there was a large group of part-time volunteers who, on average, spent one night a fortnight in the shelter assisting the full-time staff.

My familiarity with the shelter and its users developed when I worked there for a number of years as a volunteer. As a post-graduate student, an intensive period of participant observation was undertaken when I worked in the shelter on a full-time basis. My activity as a researcher was known and acknowledged by the other staff members and residents. As Bruyn has pointed out, this role may have many research advantages:

> This is the role in which the observers activities as such are made publicly known at the outset, are more or less publicly sponsored by people in the situation studied, and are intentionally not "kept under wraps". The role may provide access to a wide range of information and even secrets may be given to the fieldworker when he becomes known for keeping them, as well as for guarding confidential information. In this role the social scientist might conceivably achieve maximum freedom to gather information, but only at the price of accepting maximum constraints upon his reporting (1966: 16).

Other commentators in their examination of similar hostels have noted this situation:

> The co-operation and active assistance of the full-time staff was, however, the single most important factor in determining the type of response from the residents. This is what one would expect because the full-time staff have built up a relationship of trust and rapport with the residents over a long period of time (McCarthy 1988: 68).

> The fact I was well known in Simon probably helped many of the residents disclose information they would otherwise have not disclosed (Hart 1978: 9).

This study is not representative of all those who are homeless, as it includes only homeless males, generally over the age of 20. From July 1983 to July 1989, 1,010 different persons used the shelter for one night or more. Table 1 shows that 230 new people used the shelter between July 1983 and June 1984. This table shows a steady decline in the numbers of new users over the next four years, with a sharp increase in the period 1988-89. The figure for the period July 1983 to June 1984 is slightly exaggerated, because although the shelter had been operating in the period previous to July 1983, no statistics had been collected. Thus, all those who used the shelter in July 1983 were classified as new users. Nonetheless, those who were listed as new in July 1983 were in the main those persons who had been sleeping rough in the town prior to the opening of the shelter.

Table 1
New Admissions and Returns to the Shelter 1983-89[*]

	New Admissions	Returns	Total
1983/84	230	357	589
1984/85	182	403	585
1985/86	166	533	699
1986/87	130	474	604
1987/88	127	483	610
1988/89	175	554	729

[*]These figures must take into account that over the 72 month period of study, there were 32,936 bednights (bednights = Sum of nights spent in the shelter by 1,010 persons). This gives an average figure of 451 bednights per month and or 5,489 bednights per year.

The rates of return to the shelter are consistently high, with the overall figures showing a steady increase over the six year period. When the number of new users of the shelter is examined alongside the number of persons who were forced to return to the shelter after their initial stay, a more accurate picture of the total number of people who have used the shelter is possible. As Table 1 demonstrates, a steady increase in the number of users is apparent until the end of July 1986, from 589 in the period 1983-84 to 699 for the period 1985-86. There was a drop off in the number of users in 1986-87 and 1987-88, with a large increase for the period 1988-89.

Table 2 indicates the age groups of those who have used the shelter. The age group most represented is that between 40 and 49, wherein 32 per cent of shelter users fall. Next in order of frequency is the age group 30-39, which accounts for 26 per cent of shelter users, followed by the age group 20-29, which accounts for 21 per cent of the shelter users. Those under the age of 25 who arrive at the shelter are referred to the Youth Services who operate a drop-in centre and a residential house.

Table 2
Age of Shelter Users

Age	Number	Per cent
10-19	12	1.3
20-29	197	21.2
30-39	239	25.6
40-49	298	31.9
50-59	121	12.9
60-69	43	4.6
70-79	21	2.2
80-89	3	0.3
Total	934	100.0

Table 3 shows the total number of nights spent in the shelter by the 1,010 individuals who have used the shelter over the 72 month period. It shows that 63 per cent of the shelter users stayed in the shelter for seven nights or less. Thus for the majority of shelter users, homelessness is temporary and, with adequate support structures, need not be repeated. A breakdown of the rates of return to the shelter is presented in Table 4. After their initial stays, 54 per cent of users did not return to the shelter during the 72 month period under investigation. However, 46 per cent of those who stayed in the shelter did return, which suggests a cyclical nature of homelessness. As Blackwell has observed, "There is a continual flow of people into homelessness at different stages of the life cycle" (National Economic and Social Council 1988: 285).

Table 3
Total Nights Spent in the Shelter 1983-89

Nights	Persons	Per cent
1	316	31.3
2	103	10.2
3	67	6.6
4	52	5.1
5	45	4.5
6	35	3.5
7	21	2.1
8	23	2.3
9	21	2.1
10 - 15	75	7.4
16 - 19	33	3.3
20 - 28	61	6.0
29 - 99	98	9.7
100 - 912	53	5.2
1033 - 1495	7	0.7
Total	**1010**	**100.0**

Table 4
Rates of Return to the Shelter 1983-89*

	Number	Per cent
Never returned	542	53.7
Returned once	164	16.2
Returned twice	70	6.9
Returned three times	39	3.9
Returned four times	38	3.8
Five times	27	2.7
Between six and ten times	63	6.2
Eleven times plus	40	3.9
Twenty times plus	9	0.9
Thirty times plus	3	0.3
Forty times plus	1	0.1
Long term shelter users	11	1.1
Long term till death	3	0.3
Total	**1010**	**100.0**

* Rates of return calculated in months i.e. returned once for one month or less after the initial period of stay.

Distancing, acceptance and organisation

While certain characteristics are common to all users of the shelter, such as their common need to use the shelter facilities for both accommodation and food and their overwhelming dependence on the social welfare system, the manner in which they construct identities and associations to deal with their situation varies immensely, with the most crucial variable being the duration of the homeless career. Following on aspects of the work of Snow and Anderson (1987), I explore in this section identity and social organisation among the homeless.

A number of sub-groups can be identified within the population of the shelter. The shelter population is not an isolated or static one. As individuals enter the shelter, they soon develop links with groups of similar perspective and the group is used as the frame of reference in their social organisation and their strategies of survival. So, while membership of the individual sub-groups is fluid, entry to the groups is determined by the individuals' perceptions of their situation, constrained by loosely defined boundaries regarding appropriate behaviour and actions within the group. Sub-groups are formed primarily in order to maximise survival strategies, to support those perceived to be in a similar situation, and to maintain distinctiveness from others in the homeless population. Generating an identity through 'distancing' or 'adoption' confirms one's position in the hierarchy of relations within the shelter population.

To counteract the stigma of being homeless a number of distancing techniques are developed to overcome or 'pass' the stigma (Goffman 1963: 92; on homelessness, see Bahr 1967; Bogue 1963). Some users of the shelter distance themselves from all other users, from certain groups within the shelter population, and/or from the institution itself. Distancing manifests itself in three forms, although these are not mutually exclusive. These are associational distancing, role distancing, and institutional distancing. Distancing occurs when individuals find themselves in roles inconsistent with their perceived self-conceptions and as a result employ strategies to disassociate themselves from their new role. This is done primarily through talk, but also through physical actions. For some homeless, however, acceptance of their position takes place, especially among those who have been homeless over a long period of time. Such individuals often take a certain satisfaction from their ability to survive in this environment. These individuals are primarily the stereotypical long-term homeless with alcohol addiction, generally known as 'the winos.' Their identity is so well known that distancing offers no protection. Physical actions are an important component of identity construction among all the homeless, in that certain actions are compatible with the self-perceived social identity of a homeless person, such as public drinking, begging etc. I argue here that identities are constructed, utilising combinations of distancing and/or acceptance, to promote one's preferred role, as opposed to roles inconsistent with perceived self-conceptions.

Associational distancing

Short term users of the shelter are those who tend to adopt associational distancing. For them, the shelter is considered only as temporary accommodation, since they soon hope to obtain another dwelling. Those who need to use the shelter for short periods of time represent over half the shelter population. While no formal social organisation of this group can be established due to the temporary nature of their shelter usage, common characteristics can be identified. Unlike other groups, they do not consider themselves to be homeless and have no affinity with other shelter users. Rather, they view themselves as being temporarily out of luck, or simply needing a bed for the night. In his analysis of an American shelter, Timmer (1988:167) notes a similar situation, linking class distinctions to this lack of identification. That the ideology of the shelter includes this class distinction is sharply reflected in those shelter residents who do not want to admit their homelessness. They do not want to be identified and stigmatised as 'one of them'.

Invariably, these users of the shelter will interact together throughout their stay. This serves a number of purposes. Firstly, it disassociates them from the longer term users. Secondly, it offers physical and psychological protection from other users whom they view with fear. And thirdly, it offers the opportunity to explain to each other their reason for having to use the shelter. Comments often expressed by this group are:

> I'd never thought that I would have to use this place. I know a lot of those staying here from around the town, but I never thought that I would be here (short-term homeless).

> I'm just stuck for the night. I'll be gone in the morning. I'm not like the rest of them (short-term homeless).

These residents deny their homelessness and continuously attempt to interact with the shelter staff on the basis that they have more in common with them than with the long term homeless users. Non-resident users of the shelter, who comprise a large segment of its daily users, also adopt this pattern of behaviour. These users have generally been past residents of the shelter, but have since obtained accommodation elsewhere. However, their need to use the shelter does not end with the acquisition of accommodation. Many have difficulty in coping with living alone and surviving on social welfare and utilise the resources of the shelter to supplement their income through the procurement of food and other necessities. Long term users of the shelter, in particular the winos, dislike the presence of this group, maintaining that the shelter is for those who are homeless and not for people to come in and out for food and clothing. The shelter provides more than material assistance to non-residents. It offers them advice on rent allowances and other social welfare claims as well as providing a source of companionship. For this group the shelter also offers an alternative place to gather, other than on the streets or in their flats. Its members interact on a frequent basis but usually only within the shelter. On leaving the shelter, they revert back to their identity as someone with a home of their own.

The sub-group of the homeless population to receive the most attention, both in the popular press and in the academic journals, has been made up of those with psychiatric problems. This is a population that has increased in their need to use the shelter facilities.[6] This group tends to be fragmented in their interactions. A bond does not operate to the same extent as it does for some other groups, and the members of this group are generally regarded by the other shelter users as objects of exploitation and amusement. Those with psychiatric problems are seen as 'an easy touch' for items such as cigarettes and occasionally money. The homeless with psychiatric disorders fear verbal and physical threats if they do not produce the items required by a predatory individual. While many of them know each other from having spent time in either the major psychiatric hospital in the region, or the psychiatric unit based in the city, they display a reluctance to interact with each other. They are generally known as the 'nutters' by other users of the shelter and hostility is vented on them for what is perceived as 'mad' behaviour, such as smoking two cigarettes at the same time, or continuously walking up and down the corridors. Their social organisation reflects their experiences of institutionalisation and alienation from conventional society, as they remain distrustful of other social groups within the shelter, and suspicious of the motives of the shelter staff. They also fear the winos, because of their predatory actions towards them.

Role distancing

For some users of the shelter a more discriminating stance is adopted, in that they distance themselves only from some of those who use the shelter. 'Roadmen', for example, are individuals who are transient for the majority of their lives, who travel from hostel to hostel often sleeping rough. Their interaction with other groups is restricted because of the temporary nature of their residence in the shelter and also because they see themselves as superior to the 'one town tramps'. As one roadman put it:

> I'm a dosser and I know it and I'll always be a dosser, but I'm better than those fuckers that sit around all day drinking tea. They are not really homeless. I wouldn't call myself a man if I was like some of them.

Many of the roadmen are heavy drinkers rather than chronic alcoholics. They are on familiar terms with some subgroups such as the winos, binge alcoholics, and the Travellers. Most of them have been on the road for many years and find great difficulty in settling into a conventional lifestyle. Many follow the various race meetings and festivals around the country, and some have skills such as musicianship, card tricks etc. that can be converted into cash on such occasions. During the winter they tend to settle in one base, one of the shelters or casual wards that are available. Because of their skills, they can generate sufficient income to maintain their independence from other groups within the shelter population.

Institutional distancing

Because of the public perception of the users of the shelter as consisting primarily of winos, short term users distance themselves from being associated in any way with the shelter. They simply attempt to get out of the shelter environment as soon as possible, and make no public reference to the fact that they are staying in the hostel. However, long term users of the shelter distance themselves differently. They realise that both of the voluntary organisations running the shelter collect funds on their behalf, but they perceive that the funds are not being used solely to support the homeless. Many openly claim that the organisations do not really care about them and that they are lining their own pockets and taking ego trips at the shelter users' expense. In 1991, a charge was introduced to the shelter of £2 per night. A long term user of the shelter, in reaction to the introduction of this charge, wrote to a local paper claiming that:

> People who were living in the hostel are now sleeping out in buses. The hostel wants them to pay £2 a night and they cannot afford it as they drink and smoke their money and they cannot help it. Their own people won't help them and when they go up for a bit of food, the hostel won't provide it. Where is all the money going. The hostel was set up for people like us who are homeless.

More general comments include:

> You don't care about us, all you want is your picture in the paper so people can say how fucking great you are helping the poor homeless (roadman).

> I'm paying your fucking wages, if it wasn't for the fucking likes of me you'd have no fucking job (long-term user).

I went up to the . . . office to try and get some money to go to Dublin and get myself sorted out but the fuckers wouldn't give me a tosser. I don't get my dole for another few days so I'm broke. These are the bastards that are claiming to help the homeless (long-term homeless, but recent to the shelter in Galway).

You see them all up town every week collecting money for us, but do we get any of it, do we fuck! (short-term homeless)

Length of time spent in the shelter environment is the crucial variable in determining reaction to the shelter and the staff members. This is a situation also noted by Wiseman (1971) and Snow and Anderson (1987). As the latter concluded: "criticizing the Salvation Army. . . provided some regular users with a means of dealing with the implications of their dependence on it" (1987:1352).

Role acceptance

The group which most conspicuously accept their role of the stereotypical homeless are the winos. The most public manifestation of this role acceptance is acted out via their public drinking and begging. The winos constitute a separate entity within the overall shelter population, and their interaction on a regular basis with other shelter users is limited. They generally see other users of the shelter as not being really homeless and resent their presence in the shelter. Their definition of who is really homeless is largely based on two criteria, chronic alcoholism and complete lack of alternative accommodation. Within the framework of this chapter, the winos form only a small percentage, approximately 15 per cent at any one time, of the overall population under observation. However, they tend to be well represented among the long term residents of the shelter and are distinctive in that they view the shelter as their home and not simply a temporary abode.

The only other groups of persons the winos socialise with on a regular basis are the binge alcoholics, Travellers, and the roadmen. In all these cases alcohol provides the impetus for congregation. Binge alcoholics are those persons who in general have a place of habitation of their own or share with members of their family, but have chronic alcohol problems. They are the temporary residents of the shelter, while the winos are the permanent residents. Many have restrictions imposed on their drinking in their home environment and consequently go on an alcoholic binge in an alternative location. Their time on the binge depends on two factors, the amount of cash they have raised and their integration with the winos. The winos accept the company of the binge alcoholics because of the latter's ability to purchase good quality alcoholic beverages, while the binge alcoholic sees no stigma attached to drinking with winos because of the distance from friends and relations. It is thus a mutual relationship of sharing resources in order to maximise drinking opportunities. The forum for the procurement and consumption of the alcohol is the bottle gang. The bottle gang consists of a minimum of two participants, but rarely more than six. Otherwise, it becomes too public and may come to the attention of the Gardai.

Resources within the group are shared and this facilitates providing a drink for those without the necessary cash to buy it themselves. Abuse of this facility is not tolerated and a person who consistently abuses the bottle gang by not contributing to the 'kitty' will soon find himself excluded. The binge alcoholic will usually stay only for a short time. Having access to accommodation other than the shelter, they are not seen to be in the same chronic situation as the winos. The latter's frustration manifests itself in acts of violence towards the binge alcoholics, particularly when the binge drinker has lost his usefulness and constitutes an unwanted element in the group.

Winos also openly socialise with Travellers. Travellers are a distinct ethnic group characterised by the "classic stigmata of dispossessed peoples everywhere" (Gmelch and Bennett 1981:28). Like the binge alcoholics, alcohol procurement and consumption provide the necessary links between these individuals. A small number of Travellers share similar characteristics with the winos, such as chronic alcoholism, begging, shabby ill-fitting clothing etc. However, the relationship is a strained one, as the winos view the Travellers with suspicion and hostility. This relationship is temporary but frequent, and is facilitated when the need for alcohol is so great as to transcend feelings of hostility. The Travellers are considered to be lower on the hierarchical scale of status than any other sub-group within the overall framework of homelessness and alcoholism, and have a reputation among the users of the shelter for robbing the winos when they are drunk. Thus the interaction between both groups is limited and dictated by their alcoholic needs rather than by companionship. In fact the relationship is one of convenience.

Survival strategies

The incomes of the shelter users are not sufficient to meet their needs in terms of acquiring food, clothing, and, for some, alcohol. As a result, a network of survival strategies has been developed by the homeless to provide relief from their poverty and addiction. Begging is a common form of income supplement, in particular among the sub-group of long term homeless alcoholics. Begging is an offence under the law and carries a maximum penalty of 3 months imprisonment. Only a minority of those under study, primarily long-term chronic alcoholics, engage in begging as a means of subsistence. The main areas for begging are the car park, the railway station beside the shelter, and the public square and surrounding streets close by the shelter. As Wiseman notes, those who beg are "shrewd students of common sense psychology" (1971: 31). Those who are well groomed, appear sober and articulate, and 'spin' a good story are the most successful in obtaining money. My interviews with a number of long term homeless revealed some of their strategies:

> You see, if you're dressed all right and shaven, people don't think you're a wino, so they might feel sorry for you. If you tell them that you have to visit a sick relation urgently or you've missed your bus, they'll give you money.

> Nuns and priests are sometimes good for a few bob. If you say the right things to them like 'bless you' and all that shit they feel guilty and give you a few bob or a packet of fags. This nun saw me picking up dog ends (discarded butts of cigarettes) and she came over and gave me money for fags. I asked for the price of a bottle and she gave me that too. It was all right.

> Tourists are the best. If you talk shit to them, they think your a real character and give you money, or they might buy you a drink.

> If you get them sitting in the square, you just sit down beside them and talk to them. You don't ask them for any money straight off, you might ask them for a fag if they're smoking. After a while you give them a bit of a story and you always get money in the end, especially when the weather is good and they're sitting out.

> Women are the best for money, because they feel sorry for you or else they are scared.

Estimates vary as to how much money can be obtained from begging. Some claim that on a good day up to £10 can be begged, but most put this sum lower. "If you get the price of a bottle from begging, you're doing alright" While some of the long-term chronic alcoholics take a certain amount of pride in their begging abilities, those who do not beg dislike the labelling homeless people receive as a result of this type of activity. "I might be homeless, but I've never begged on the streets. I'll do lots of things, but I'm no beggar" is a common sentiment expressed by those who practise both associational and role distancing. As one shelter user stated:

> People think that this place (the shelter) is full of winos and beggars but it's not. I'm here because I've nowhere else to go. I'll drink the few pints like the next man, but I don't beg or drink the wine. Those fuckers give this place a bad name (short-term shelter user).

The bulk of the winos received their unemployment assistance cheque on a Wednesday morning. For those who are served in pubs, a visit to one of these pubs is the first action after receiving their cheque. For those barred from all the pubs in town, a trip to the nearest off-licence begins their day. Many are also barred from the off-licences, so a passer-by may be recruited to make the purchase. Once drink is acquired, a group of the winos will sit down in the public square and consume the bottle in classic 'bottle gang' fashion (Rubington 1968). Usually the money acquired on the Wednesday is spent by the week-end and other sources of alcohol have to be located.

> My money is always gone by the weekend, but I still have to have a drink. I don't give a fuck where I get it from, I'll drink with any cunt. Unless you're an alcoholic you can't understand (long term homeless alcoholic).

> I only drink when I get my money. I try not to drink the rest of the week, but I'm always waiting for the next day on the labour (long term homeless alcoholic).

Since Galway is a port town, smuggling can be a useful way of obtaining alcohol, cigarettes and other commodities that can be sold for a profit. The bulk of these goods come from the former Eastern Bloc countries, as coal boats from a number of these countries visit the town regularly. Bottles of spirits can be purchased at roughly half the price that the spirits are sold for in the town, and cigarettes at a quarter of their regular price. Many other items, such as electrical goods, pornographic videos and magazines, and items of clothing, can be obtained cheaply. Access to these goods is restricted, as one has to be in 'the know' to gain access to the ships. This is not an activity confined to those who are homeless, as a wide range of people avail of this service. For those who have access, however, it is a lucrative enterprise. The goods can be sold around the town with a large mark up in price, or else used by the purchaser.

Casual employment is a regular feature for some of the residents of the shelter. However, most of this employment is exploitative and short term. With nearly 300,000 unemployed in the Republic of Ireland, those who are homeless face a very competitive job market. Many have low levels of education and few skills, and with no address other than that of the shelter, employers are reluctant to take them on. Some find casual work in hotels and restaurants but this type of work is only temporary and is characterised by low wages and long hours. Many others are incapable of work because of disabilities or their age.[7] The chronic poverty of those homeless, combined for some with alcohol addiction and psychiatric problems, necessitates the discovery and exploitation of alternative sources of income.

If the price of a bottle has not been secured from begging or other sources, alcohol is usually stolen. This beer is acquired in the form of kegs stolen from a depot adjacent to the shelter. Occasionally, a full keg of beer is stolen and carried or rolled to a suitable location, usually derelict sites in isolated areas around the town. Because access to beer taps and gas is impossible, a method of extracting the beer from the kegs has been devised. The barrel is laid on its side and a small spoon is used to depress the nozzle of the keg. This results in the beer spurting out into a hand held container (usually an empty catering tin of peas or beans taken from the shelter) where it is left to settle. After a moment or two the froth is blown from the beer which is then either consumed on the spot or else poured into one gallon plastic containers (usually empty washing-up liquid or disinfectant containers taken from the shelter). By following the latter course of action, the beer can also be transported to a more suitable drinking location. The acquisition of the kegs can be a hazardous occupation. After the charge of drunk and disorderly, the most frequent charge brought against the winos is stealing kegs.

Alcohol procurement and consumption is the only bond between these people. When the bottle gang disperses upon the consumption of alcohol, the groups dissolve. If one member then goes on the 'dry', he will avoid association with other drinking members. Once the 'dry' spell is over, group bonds are resurrected with no comment on the individual's absence. According to Rooney, such relationships are "not characterised by intimacy or mutual trust and identification" (1961: 454).

Conclusion

This chapter has examined the social organisation and strategies of survival of homeless men. Utilising the concepts of distancing and adoption, it has considered homelessness as a multi-faceted, complex and differentiated socially constructed world for people who, for a variety of historical and/or contemporary social system inadequacies, or personal inadequacies, are forced to adopt new modes of social relationships and develop alternative methods of survival in a hostile environment characterised by poverty, stigmatisation, and deviance. For some of those who become homeless, the experience is brief. For others, with contacts and relationships from their previous existence lost, they enter into long term homelessness and only through collective efforts can the necessities of human existence, both physical and physiological, be met.

The adaptive strategies utilised by the majority of those in the shelter population generate a measure of self worth via identities that are inconsistent with their perceived images of homelessness. This is achieved through distancing oneself from the institutions of homelessness and other homeless individuals.

The social organisation of the homeless within and outside the shelter demonstrates clear lines of demarcation between the various sub-groups. The identity of each group is unique and patterns of behaviour are largely dictated by reference to their primary group of association. This organisation functions as a system whereby individuals align themselves with those in similar positions. As Archard notes, "The Skid Row subculture, then, functions as a social system through which homeless men are able to cushion the problems they are confronted with" (1979:176). This sub-culture functions for the individual groups of association within the overall shelter population, not for the homeless environment in general. The social organisation and identity construction of the homeless operate as mechanisms by which users of the shelter define their attitudes regarding their homeless position and their attempts to survive both physically and psychologically. Those who become homeless are not socially isolated, but weave a lacework of relationships that are socially meaningful to them. They find in others similar difficulties, associations and dependencies with which they can identify, either for the acquisition of alcohol, clothes, food and other necessities, or by indicating that they are not 'one of them'. Thus, by adoption or by distancing themselves from the popular imagery of homelessness, individuals assert their status in the shelter hierarchy and act out their strategies of survival in an increasingly hostile environment.

Notes

My thanks to Patricia Carr, Evelyn Mahon, John A. Jackson, and Roland Tormley for their comments on this essay. The results of the research upon which this chapter is based are in O'Sullivan 1990.
1. As Mair (1986: 359-60) notes, the homeless are labelled as deviant because they deviate from the norm in not having a home, many are mentally disturbed, they may abuse substances in public and they do not live in accepted family modes.
2. In 1991, there were officially 2,751 homeless individuals in Ireland (Department of Environment 1992) . Homelessness in Ireland is officially defined under the 1988 Housing Act as follows: "The person shall be regarded by a housing authority as homeless for the purposes of this act if a - There is no accommodation available which, in the opinion of the authority, he, together with any other person who normally resides with him or who might reasonably be expected to reside with him, can reasonably occupy or remain in occupation of, or, b - He is living in a hospital, county home, night shelter or other such institution, and is so living because he has no accommodation of the kind referred to in the paragraph (a) and he is, in the opinion of the authority, unable to provide accommodation from his own resources." The Department of Environment Report (1992) was the first official national survey of the extent of homelessness in Ireland since the Report of the Commission on the Relief of the Sick and Destitute Poor, Including the Insane Poor, published in 1928, which requested the Garda Siochana to carry out 'a census of homeless persons observed wandering on the public highways in a single night in November, 1925'.

The Commission arrived at a figure of 3,257 homeless persons. The 1991 figures, however, have been heavily criticised; "because of the limited, flawed definition and methodology [they] seriously underestimate the number of people who experience homelessness" (Simon Community Newsletter 1992: 5).

3. Not all of those who are homeless in Ireland are urban based, though the majority of the homeless are concentrated in urban environments. The *1991 Assessment of Homelessness* (Department of the Environment 1992) showed that 70 per cent of those defined as homeless were located in the five major urban centres.

4. For example, The Simon Community, Focus Point, The Streetwise National Coalition and The National Campaign for the Homeless.

5. Four Simon Communities operate in the Republic of Ireland, in Cork, Dublin, Dundalk and Galway. The broad aims and ideology of the Simon Communities are, that (a) Simon have a community based approach, (b) that Simon accept people as they are and not as we would like them to be, (c) that Simon show a commitment to its residents by providing long term care to them, and (d) that Simon campaign for change in society, in order to change attitudes, and to introduce legislation for a more just and equal society.

6. In the only study of its kind in Ireland, Crehan et al. (1987) found that 92 per cent of long stay patients in a psychiatric hospital had no adequate home environment to return to if discharged.

7. McCarthy (1988) has shown that 78 per cent of Simon Community residents had left school by the age of 15, and that 79 per cent of residents had no skills training.

References

Archard, P. 1979. *Vagrancy, Alcoholism and Social Control.* London: Macmillan.

Bahr, H. M. 1967. Drinking, Interaction and Identification. Notes on Socialization into Skid Row. *Journal of Health and Social Behaviour.* 8: 272-285.

———. 1968. *Homelessness and Disaffiliation.* New York: Columbia University, Bureau of Applied Social Research.

Bahr, H. M. and Caplow, T. 1973. *Old Men, Drunk and Sober.* New York: New York University Press.

Belcher, J. R. and Singer, J. 1988. Homelessness. A Cost of Capitalism. *Social Policy* 18: 44-9.

Bell, J. 1989. *Women and Children First.* A Report by the National Campaign for the Homeless on Homeless Women and their Children in Dublin. Dublin.

Bogue, D. J. 1963. *Skid Row in American Cities.* Chicago: Family and Community Study Centre, University of Chicago Press.

Bruyn, S. T. 1966. *The Human Perspective: The Methodology of Participant Observation.* Englewood Cliffs, NJ: Prentice Hall.

Commission on the Relief of the Poor. 1928. *Report.* Dublin: The Stationery Office.

Crehan, J., Lyons, N. and Laver, M. 1987. *The Effects of Self-Care Skills and Homelessness on the Independent Living Potential of Long-Stay Psychiatric Patients.* Social Sciences Research Centre, University College Galway.

Department of the Environment. 1992. *Annual Housing Statistics 1991.* Dublin: The Stationery Office.

Dillon, B., Murphy-Lawless, J. and Redmond, D. 1990. *Homelessness in Co.Louth. A Research Report.* SUS Research for Dundalk Simon Community and Drogheda Homeless Aid.

Fabricant, M. 1987. The Political Economy of Homlessness. *Catalyst* (US) 6: 11-28.

Farrell, N. 1988. *Homelessness in Galway.* Galway Social Service Council.

Gmelch, G. and Bennett, D. 1981. Interpreting the Research on Poverty in the Irish Republic. *Growth and Change* 12 (1): 27-34.

Goffman, E. 1963. *Stigma. Notes on the Management of Spoiled Identity.* Englewood Cliffs, N.J.: Prentice-Hall.

Greve, J. 1991. *Homelessness in Britain.* Joseph Rowntree Foundation.

Hart, I. 1978. *Dublin Simon Community 1971-1976: An Exploration.* Dublin: Economic and Social Research Institute.

Harvey, D. 1989. *The Condition of Postmodernity. An Enquiry into the Origins of Social Change.* Oxford: Blackwell.

Hirschl, T. A. 1990. Homelessness: A Sociological Research Agenda. *Sociological Spectrum* (10): 443-67.

Hoch, C. and Slayton, R. A. 1989. *New Homeless and Old: Community and the Skid Row Hotel.* Philadelphia: Temple University Press.

Kelleher, C., Kelleher, P. and McCarthy, P. 1992. *Patterns of Hostel Use in Dublin and the Implications for Accommodation Provision.* Dublin: A Focus Point Publication.

Kennedy, S. 1985. *But Where Can I Go. Homeless Women in Dublin.* Dublin: Arlen House.

_____. (ed) 1987. *Streetwise. Homelessness Among the Young in Ireland and Abroad.* Dublin: The Glendale Press.

Kennett, P. 1992. Homelessness: Accumulation and Regulation. In Kennett, P. (ed) *New Approaches to Homelessness.* School for Advanced Urban Studies, University of Bristol.

Mair, A. 1986. The Homeless and the Post-Industrial City. *Political Geography Quarterly* 5 (4): 351-68.

McCarthy, P. 1988. *A Study of the Work Skills, Experience and Preferences of Simon Community Residents.* Dublin: Simon Community National Office.

National Economic and Social Council. *1988. A Review of Housing Policy.* No. 87, December. Dublin: The Stationery Office.

O'Brien, J. 1979. *Criminal Neglect - Some Aspects of Law Enforcement as it Affects the Single Homeless.* A Submission from The Simon Community, National Office to The Commission of Enquiry into the Irish Penal System.

O'Sullivan, E. 1990. *Homelessness, Deviance and Social Control: The Case of a West of Ireland Shelter.* Unpublished M. A. Thesis, University of Limerick.

Peterson, W. J. and Maxwell, M. A. 1958. The Skid Row 'Wino'. *Social Problems* 5: 308-16.

Rooney, J. F. 1961. Group Processes among Skid Row Winos: A Re-evaluation of the Undersocialisation Hypothesis *Quarterly Journal of Studies on Alcohol* 22: 444-60.

Ropers, R. H. 1988 *The Invisible Homeless: A New Urban Ecology.* New York: Human Sciences Press.

Rossi, P. 1989. *Down and Out in America.* Chicago: University of Chicago Press.

Rubington, E. 1968. The Bottle Gang. *Quarterly Journal of Studies on Alcohol* 29: 943-55.

Simon Community Newsletter 1992. No. 180. Dublin.

Snow, D. A. and Anderson, L. 1987. Identity Work among the Homeless: The Verbal Construction and Avowal of Personal Identities. *American Journal of Sociology* 92 (6): 1337-70.

Spradley, J. P. 1970. *You Owe Yourself a Drunk: An Ethnography of Urban Nomads.* Lanham, MD: University Press of America.

_____. 1972. Adaptive Strategies of Urban Nomads: The Ethnoscience of Tramp Culture. In Weaver, T. and White, D. (eds) *The Anthropology of Urban Environments.* New York: Society for Applied Anthropology. Monograph Series. Monograph No.11 .

Timmer, D. A. 1988. Homelessness as Deviance: The Ideology of the Shelter. *Free Inquiry into Creative Sociology* 16 (2): 163-170.

Tucker, W. 1990. *The Excluded Americans: Homelessness and Housing Policies.* Washington, D. C.: Regency Gateway with the cooperation of the Cato Institute.

Wiseman, J. P. 1971. *Stations of the Lost: The Treatment of Skid Row Alcoholics.* Englewood Cliffs, N.J.: Prentice-Hall.

Wright, J. D. 1989. *Address Unknown: The Homeless in America.* New York: Aldine de Gruyter.

10 Traveller settlement in Galway city: politics, class and culture

Jane Helleiner

The literature on Irish Travelling People reveals a general consensus regarding their recent history. Many accounts have reviewed how post war economic changes pushed Travellers out of rural areas and into cities where they became the targets of complaints from other Irish people (Gmelch 1977: 41-51; Rottman et al. 1986: 10-13; Fay 1992: 33-4; Gmelch 1989: 304-5). The settlement programme introduced by the central government in the 1960s has been described in some detail, and a number of reports have attributed its slow and uneven implementation to resistance at the local level (Review Body 1983: 23; Rottman et al. 1986: 6). The emergence of a Travellers Rights movement, aimed at ensuring Travellers' rights to travel and to maintain a distinctive ethnic identity, has been identified as a response to ongoing harassment of camping Travellers as well as changes in Travellers' social relations brought about through urbanization (Gmelch 1989: 309-316).

While this brief sketch is familiar enough, it relies upon limited research. Moreover, most of the existing literature has focused upon, and generalised from, the experience of Dublin (Ennis 1984; Gmelch 1989; Dublin Travellers Education and Development Group 1992). In this chapter, material from another urban centre - Galway - provides an opportunity to investigate the working out of these processes "on the ground" and to generate new research questions.[1] Silverman and Gulliver (1992: 24) have recently described how "little localities" can become the context for the investigation of larger sociological and cultural problems in Ireland. In this case study, Galway city provides the focus for an examination of the links between economic growth, state policy, and class and cultural mobilisation.

Travelling people and Galway city: 1922-60

Galway city serves as the administrative, commercial and tourist centre for the western region of Ireland. For the past three decades, the city has had a high national profile in the area of Traveller-state relations. As well as being the scene of several well-publicised confrontations between Travellers and non-Travellers, it is the location of a variety of projects geared toward Traveller settlement, including a special group housing project and two training centres. Since my field research, the city has also provided a limited number of serviced campsites or "hardstands".

County Galway has a long history of Traveller presence; counts made in 1944, 1952, 1956, 1960, and 1961 revealed that Galway had more Travellers than any other county in Ireland during this period (Commission on Itinerancy 1963: 115). While this changed following the extensive migration of Travellers to the Dublin region in the 1960s and 1970s, County Galway still had the second highest number of Travellers in 1986. Moreover, unlike County Dublin, County Galway's proportion of Travellers to settled population remained relatively high (Barry and Daly 1988: 39).

Surveys of Travellers living in Galway city itself are not available before the mid-1970s, but there are references to their presence in and around the city from at least as early as 1922. Local newspaper accounts and city council minutes reveal that in the decades between independence and the introduction of the settlement programme there was growing tension between those variously labelled as tinkers, gypsies, vagrants, travellers, and the settled population. Camping Travellers were consistently described in the available reports as threats to public health, private property and/or the economic interests (especially tourism) of the city as a whole.

Complaints about Traveller camps centred upon the presence of rags, feathers, dogs and horses as well as the activity of begging - all indications of Travellers' forms of work during this period. Archival sources reveal references to various economic activities that spanned rural-urban divisions. These included tinsmithing, chimney sweeping, horse dealing, casual agricultural labour, peddling, begging and the collection and resale of recyclable goods.[2] Although Travellers were dependent upon a variety of exchanges with the settled population, they retained a high degree of control over the tools, labour and organization of the work itself. Travellers, however, lacked secure access to one of the crucial means of production: land. As with British Traveller-Gypsies, the intermittent use of land for camping and working was the major point of conflict with the settled population and the state (Okely 1983: 35-6).

In Galway city, the most vocal complaints regarding Traveller camps came from the propertied classes (i. e., landowners, private homeowners and the Chamber of Commerce). In 1923, a group of private homeowners were reported to have sent a letter to the city council claiming that there was a danger of an epidemic breaking out if the "gipsies" were not removed from a nearby camp (*Connacht Tribune* 10 March 1923: 5). In 1925, the Galway Chamber of Commerce moved unanimously that the police prevent mendicancy by "vagrants". It asked that:

> The attention of the responsible authorities be directed to the encampment of vagrants all around Galway, principally at Loughatalia. These vagrants as beggars are a perfect nuisance. In shops they worry customers to an intolerable extent. In the coming season we are expecting a large influx of tourists, and if these vagrants are around to receive them, you may expect, to the injury of our town, caricature articles will be published in British and American newspapers descriptive of beggar life in Galway (*Connacht Tribune* 18 April 1925: 5).

The local authority responded to the pressure from the propertied classes with evictions and prosecutions aimed at keeping camping Travellers out of the urban area. As early as the summer of 1922, the city council issued several orders urging the police to "have the gipsies removed from the district" (Galway Urban District Council 8 June 1922: 106). The efforts of the city council were stepped up in the 1930s. In 1937, the Town Clerk instructed solicitors to prepare bye-laws "to put itinerants out of the area" (Galway Urban District Council 3 June 1937: 269). Two years later, draft bye-laws against "tents, vans, sheds and similar structures used for human habitation" in the urban area were approved by the council (Galway Borough Council 10 October 1939: 181), but it took another four years until they were confirmed by the central government. In 1941, the council attempted, unsuccessfully, to enlist the help of the Department of Agriculture in getting "gypsies" excluded from the Borough District due to the alleged danger of their horses spreading foot and mouth disease (Galway Borough Council 11 March 1941: 375).

While camping Travellers attracted most attention, there is evidence of other Traveller families living in housing in Galway city prior to the introduction of a settlement programme. Gmelch has noted that the nation-wide slum clearances of the 1930s affected many Traveller families already established in urban areas (Gmelch 1977: 137-8). A great deal more historical research is needed on this topic but a limited examination of sources from Galway city revealed a reference to an "itinerant" living in a tenement in 1937 (Galway Urban District Council 29 April 1937: 250-1) and a report of "Gipsy vans" at one of the newly constructed terraces in 1936 (Galway Urban District Council 28 May 1936: 105). However, other early references are ambiguous. For example, squatters evicted from "shacks" in 1931 had common Traveller names and one was quoted as saying that "he had nowhere to go except the side of the road", but they were not identified by any of the labels commonly applied to Travellers (*Connacht Tribune* 7 November 1931: 7). Others with common Traveller names listed as living in tenements and condemned houses in 1933 are also not distinguished from other residents (Galway Urban District Council 25 October 1933: 82).

While the extent of housing during the 1920s and 1930s is unclear, housing files reveal that by the 1940s and 1950s there were several Traveller families living in council terraces, despite a negative housing policy on the part of the city council. City council minutes indicate that the few Traveller families who made it onto the housing lists submitted by city officials to the council were rarely appointed as tenants (even when they were classed by health officials as priority cases). As a result, many Travellers who entered housing during this period did so through informal means such as becoming lodgers or squatters.

The information on Travellers in Galway city prior to the 1950s is not extensive, but it does reveal the presence of Travellers in the urban area. It also makes clear that they were being targeted from an early date by the exclusionary practices of the local authority. This is significant, because the history of Travellers in Irish cities prior to the 1950s has been obscured by an emphasis on post-war rural to urban migration. Unfortunately the extent of this urbanization is difficult to determine at either the national or local level. The first two national counts of Travellers (undertaken in 1944 and 1952) did not include the four County Boroughs (Commission on Itinerancy 1963: 115), or the Borough of Dún Laoghaire (Dáil Éireann 23 March 1960: 873), an omission which may help explain the apparent increase in overall population in 1956. Later surveys of Travellers did include those living in the Boroughs but these jurisdictions were not separated out from the totals for each county, making it difficult to ascertain the extent of change in urban population.

Research in Britain has challenged the model of a recent rural to urban migration by pointing to historical evidence of Traveller-Gypsies (including Irish Travellers) in towns and cities during the nineteenth century (Adams et al. 1975: 172; Sibley 1981:77-88; Okely 1983: 30-31; Mayall 1988: 34-45). Further research in Ireland may also reveal a more extensive pre-war urban presence.

In the case of Galway city, Travellers were viewed as a "problem" from an early point but the 1950s saw increased efforts aimed at their removal from the city. In the autumn of 1951 the city council passed an Order for the Control of Temporary Dwellings under section 31 of the Local Government (Sanitary Services) Act 1948, and Travellers camping in Galway were successfully prosecuted despite the arguments advanced by one solicitor that "the well-fitted caravan belonging to [the individual being charged], who was a horse dealer and who was born in one of the caravans, could hardly be described as a temporary dwelling as it was the permanent abode of . . . his family" (*Connacht Tribune* 29 March 1952: 5). In the spring of 1953, the city council prohibited "temporary dwellings" from seventeen roads in the city and later the same year directed the attention of the police "to the influx of begging gypsies who were making a very bad impression on visitors" (Galway Borough Council 5 August 1953: 362). In 1955, the police were again asked "to visit Loughatalia Road [the location of a camp] frequently and endeavour to keep the tinkers on the move" (Galway Borough Council 17 February 1955: 479).

Local press reports referring to Travelling People, which increased dramatically during the 1950s, peaked in 1955 the year in which the city council began to intensify pressure on the national government through a series of resolutions calling for new legislation "for the control of itinerants" (Galway Borough Council 1 September 1955: 27). A local attack on a Traveller camp by farmers in 1956, far from generating concern for the Travellers, led a Galway politician to demand from the Minister for Justice "immediate action" against "itinerants" (Dáil Éireann 20 June 1956: 636), a call which would be repeated in subsequent years. In 1959, the Municipal Authorities Association conference, held in Galway city, supported a Galway city resolution calling on the Minister for Justice to set up a commission "to consider the problem of itinerants from all aspects" (Galway Borough Council 20 August 1959: 429; *Connacht Tribune* 19 September 1959: 9). The following year the Commission on Itinerancy was formed.[3]

The national settlement programme

National parliamentary debates reveal that the Traveller "problem" was raised by deputies earlier, but the establishment of the Commission on Itinerancy in 1960 and its report, published in 1963, marked the first systematic attempt by the central government to target Travellers (labelled as "itinerants" in the report) as a distinct category of people. The wide-ranging settlement policy that was set out in this report has remained the cornerstone of government policy toward Travelling People.

While the formation of the Commission on Itinerancy was, in part, a response to growing pressure from local authorities, the timing of government intervention in the Traveller issue, and the proposed "solution" of a comprehensive settlement programme, must be placed within the context of the national policy changes that followed the transfer of political leadership in 1957 and the adoption of the Programme for Economic Expansion in 1958.[4] The Commission on Itinerancy represented a new initiative that did more than acquiesce to calls for more exclusionary measures. Instead, its Report outlined an extensive settlement programme and promoted the argument that the "settlement" and "absorption" of "itinerants" was a necessary part of the larger project of national economic and social development.

Although the development of a settlement programme for Travellers was linked to other initiatives of the central government, implementation of the settlement programme was delegated to local authorities. The contradictions inherent in placing responsibility for the settlement of a mobile population in the hands of territorially defined local authorities became apparent almost immediately.   Corporations and county councils moved slowly in the provision of accommodation and other services to Travelling People. They claimed that any extensive provision would result in an "influx" of more Travellers into their respective jurisdictions.   At the same time, the implementation of the national Traveller settlement programme was, and continues to be, marked by political struggle at the local level. As a result, there has been considerable variation between local authorities in the extent and nature of Traveller settlement programmes.

The implementation of settlement policy in Galway city

The formation of the national Commission on Itinerancy in 1960 was accompanied by increased evictions of Traveller camps from Galway city. In the years that followed, Travellers continued to be prosecuted for camping as well as subsistence activities (e. g., begging and keeping "wandering" horses).   At the same time, they were the targets of more informal exclusionary measures. For example, city politicians urged publicans not to serve drinks to Travellers (*Connacht Tribune* 11 March 1961: 9; 6 August 1966: 1). More dramatically, Travellers were victims of vigilante attacks on their camps which included the shooting of dogs, horses and burning of caravans (*Connacht Tribune* 2 January 1960: 7; 20 February 1960: 9; 4 November 1961: 4).

While city officials and the courts, sometimes in collaboration with residents, were pushing camping Travellers outside the city boundaries (*Connacht Tribune* 23 May 1964: 9; 13 June 1964: 12), there was little relief to be found in the countryside. By 1964, the county council had also adopted bye-laws that allowed for the prosecution of camping Travellers (*Connacht Tribune* 17 October 1964: 5).   In addition, the city kept up pressure on the county council to evict those living in camps near its boundaries (Galway Borough Council 28 June 1965: 572). There is no doubt that the position of Travellers during this period was a great deal worse than it had been previously. Even the city solicitor involved in prosecuting five Traveller families for camping in 1963 acknowledged that "the [Travelling] people seemed to be suffering from a social injustice, but the law was the law. People in the locality had to be protected" (*Connacht Tribune* 16 February 1963: 6).

By 1964, the programme of Traveller settlement outlined in the Report of the Commission on Itinerancy had been adopted as government policy. Central to the settlement programme was the provision of housing for Travellers, though the Commission Report had acknowledged that a housing shortage in urban areas would make immediate implementation difficult (Commission on Itinerancy 1963: 54). Following the recommendation of the Commission, the central government advocated the construction of serviced camping sites "pending the solution of the difficulties associated with the housing of itinerants" (Review Body 1983: 16).

Local response to the new settlement policy included the formation of a Galway county-wide committee on itinerancy which began a search for locations for official camping sites (Galway Borough Council 16 December 1964: 455; 22 September 1965: 616). However, it did not take long before it was claimed that "no suitable" sites were to be found in or near Galway city (*Connacht Tribune* 2 October 1965: 1). Only after the city's designation as a regional "growth centre" and the construction of its first industrial estate at Mervue two years later (Ó Cearbhaill and Cawley 1984: 259-60) did the city council decide to "accelerate the provision of a camping site for itinerants" (Galway Borough Council 3 October 1966: 826).

The impetus for movement on the issue of Traveller settlement can be linked to changes in the local political economy during the late 1960s. The national Programme for Economic Expansion had targeted Galway city as a regional growth centre, which had the effect of generating more industrial and service jobs. The economic buoyancy of the urban area relative to the poverty of the surrounding rural region led to a dramatic increase in the urban population and a spatial expansion of the city. One result was a displacement of pre-existing Traveller camps by new industrial and housing estates. At the same time, the remaining camps were considered detrimental for a city intent on attracting and keeping international investment.

The shift toward implementation of the settlement policy was apparent when, in 1966, the city granted the Legion of Mary permission to set up a temporary school for Travellers, and when, in 1967, a local branch of the national Itinerant Settlement Council, the Galway Itinerant Settlement Council, was formed. This council was a voluntary group initially comprised of several influential and relatively wealthy citizens of Galway. Many of those involved were motivated by a concern for the economic development of the city and region, while others were inspired to social activism by Vatican II, and later by the civil rights movement in Northern Ireland. Those involved in the council shared the view that the project of Traveller settlement represented a necessary, and long overdue, national duty consistent with the goals of a modernizing Catholic country. They also shared the assumption that, given sufficient political will, this project could be accomplished in a relatively short time.

The settlement council embarked upon a campaign of public education in order to recruit support for Traveller settlement. Parallels were drawn between the Travellers and the "holy itinerant family" who had found "no room at the inn" and the camps of Travellers were described as "one of the last social blots on the fair countenance of our land" (*Connacht Tribune* 12 May 1967: 3). Despite the success of such publicity efforts, it soon became apparent that attempts to implement the settlement programme were intensifying social conflict within the city.

Traveller settlement and class

In Galway city there was a close association between neighbourhood and class which had not disappeared during the dramatic economic growth of the 1960s (Grimes 1984). While a primary goal of the industrialisation strategy in Galway city had been to provide employment to rural migrants and thereby reverse long standing patterns of emigration, many of the better-paid employment opportunities created during economic expansion were filled by well-educated migrants from other urban centres rather than by the local working class or newcomers from rural areas (Grimes 1984: 251). Thus despite an increase in the number of employment opportunities in the urban area, class-based inequalities were not eliminated.

In a class-stratified urban political economy, the implementation of the Traveller settlement programme was met with class- and neighbourhood-based resistance. For example, initial plans to provide serviced camps faltered in the face of resistance from landowners, while early attempts to house Travellers in public housing estates encountered a series of organised protests by tenants. The implications of Traveller settlement for class-based divisions within the city could not be avoided by settlement advocates. The settlement council, for example, was vulnerable to the criticism that it was comprised of relatively well-off private residents whose settlement plans, especially in the area of housing, would foist Travellers on to working class areas. Politicians were also the targets of class-based grievances. In a letter to the local press, one reader referred to rumours that residents of the Mayor's wealthy neighbourhood had "scorched" plans to build a Traveller camping site in their vicinity and accused the city council of promoting "social snobbery" and "class distinction" (*Connacht Tribune* 18 October 1968: 9).

The response of local politicians in Galway city, after an initial period of vacillation between campsites and housing, was to follow a programme of accommodating Travellers slowly and in areas where resistance was weakest. In practice this resulted in a pattern of housing Travellers in newer public estates (where there were no established neighbourhoods to oppose Traveller settlement), and, eventually, in a segregated village for Travellers. The greater reliance on housing rather than hardstands in Galway city reflected the relative weakness of public authority residents vis-a-vis private residents. While the more public protests by those living in corporation housing created the impression that resistance to Traveller settlement came solely from the working class, in fact, private residents were extremely effective at blocking proposed plans for their neighbourhoods through meetings and small deputations to city council. By the early 1980s, Galway city and county were distinguished from other areas of the country, such as County Dublin, by a high percentage of housed Travellers, and by the lack of any serviced camp provision (Rottman et al. 1986: 85-86).

While the struggle between private and public residents was an unequal one, working class protests did significantly affect the course of settlement policy implementation in Galway city. For example, some tenant groups managed to reverse or reduce settlement plans for their neighbourhoods, and/or to use the acceptance of Travellers as a bargaining chip in their struggles with the city over other grievances such as lighting and housing repairs (*Connacht Tribune* 4 November 1977: 1, 16). The slow pace of implementation, the concentration of Traveller families in newer and segregated estates, and by the mid-1980s, the reconsideration by the city of the hardstand option, revealed the political potency of public authority residents.

Discourses of settlement: class and culture

The "official discourse" (Burton and Carlen 1979) of the 1963 Report of the Commission on Itinerancy divided the Irish population into two groups, i.e. the "itinerants" and the "settled community". However, settlement efforts in Galway quickly revealed divisions within the "settled community". Many of those living in public housing estates challenged the argument found in the Report of the Commission on Itinerancy and promoted by the Galway Itinerant Settlement Council, namely, that the Travellers were the most economically deprived segment of the Irish population. The alleged "special treatment" of Travellers by settlement advocates was criticised by working class Galwegians who felt that their more legitimate claims on the state (e. g., for housing and employment) were not being met.

In one publicised incident, tenants of an estate protested the allocation of a house to a Traveller woman and her children by demonstrations, threats of a rent strike, and claims that some settled tenants were living in worse conditions than the family in question (*Connacht Tribune* 4 September 1970: 9). Settlement advocates responded by criticising the protesters for obstructing economic modernisation and displaying un-Irish and un-Catholic behaviour. The Bishop of Galway told the protesters that "it is only by . . . co-operation that the city can develop and meet all the needs of the modern age" and "to refuse shelter to one of our own people is contrary to the noblest traditions of the Irish Catholic people"(*Connacht Tribune* 4 September 1970: 9).

A few years later, when local protests led to the abandonment of plans to construct four *tigeens* (interim housing) for Travellers in the wealthiest area of the city, a letter to the editor of the local newspaper complained of discrimination against poorer, less powerful, neighbourhoods.

> Not one Corporation [city council] member ever voiced an opinion against the housing of itinerants in large numbers in a certain local authority housing estate. No! because the people of that area are poor and they had to shut their mouths and take what they got and that meant having several itinerant families as neighbours, but now in the case of Salthill, of course, this cannot be let happen.

> It is only fair that Salthill should have its share of itinerants, since its [sic] the residents of such areas that are usually over enthusiastic about settling itinerants (*Connacht Tribune* 6 April 1973: 8).

While class divisions emerged in the course of struggles over Traveller settlement, these divisions did not ultimately challenge the "itinerant" versus "settled community" distinction promoted by the settlement programme. Protesting members of the settled population also claimed superiority to Travellers by virtue of membership in the "settled community". However, the identification with the "settled community" by working class non-Travellers was problematic, for it was precisely this distinction between themselves and Travellers that they were being asked to eliminate by "integrating" Travellers as neighbours.

The Report of the Commission on Itinerancy and the Galway Settlement Council initially portrayed itinerants as poor Irish, who, if provided with houses, education and wage labour, would quickly become members of the "settled community". By the mid-1970s the rhetoric of the settlement movement was changing as the term "itinerant" was increasingly replaced by that of "Traveller" and national policy discussions began to refer to a distinctive Traveller identity and way of life (Gmelch 1989: 306). The shift toward an emphasis upon cultural rather than strictly economic divisions between Travellers and the settled population responded to working class challenges to the alleged poverty of Travellers, as well as to the apparent failure of the settlement programme to rapidly "absorb" the Travellers. The culturalist discourse would also, paradoxically, provide a framework within which Travellers in Galway city, could claim the right to pursue an alternative to housing.

The hardstand debate

During the early years of the settlement programme, housing in Galway city was in short supply and there was limited provision for Travellers. By the early 1980s the situation had changed with the construction of a number of new public estates and a special segregated "village" estate solely for Travellers. Travellers were encouraged to enter public housing and many did so. The 1986 census recorded 125 Traveller households with a total of 843 persons within the urban boundaries; two-thirds of these households (84 of 125) were living in houses or flats.[5]

While many Travellers responded to the greater availability of housing in Galway city by entering flats and houses, a minority resisted such options. The 1982 census of Travellers in the city revealed that, of forty camping households, only five expressed a desire for housing (Galway Borough Council 22 March 1982). Despite the fact that serviced campsite provision had been part of national government policy since 1964 , the lack of serviced sites or "hardstands" in Galway city and county meant that most of these camping households had an insecure access to land for parking and were living without basic services such as running water, toilets and electricity. Moreover, pressure on camping space was increasing as city workers "closed up" existing and potential parking spots in the city by placing large boulders along roadsides and other undeveloped areas. Camping Travellers, while comprising a minority of the Travellers in the city, continued to be defined as a "problem" and received a disproportionate amount of political and media attention.

During the summer of 1986, the focus upon camping Travellers intensified after the district court granted Galway Corporation an injunction for the removal of two Traveller camps located in the west side of the city on land zoned for recreational development. The city had argued that its legal obligation to the sixteen households affected had been fulfilled by offers of permanent accommodation (i.e. houses or flats). The Travellers involved had refused these offers and asked to be provided with alternative *camping* sites. Although there was an existing "agreement in principle" between the city politicians to provide hardstands in several areas of the city, the Travellers' request was not granted and they were ordered to leave.

On the advice of a city official, one group of Travellers left their camp in order to move into a nearby field recently purchased by the city. Shortly after their arrival in the new camp the Travellers were attacked by a group of settled residents who dragged their trailers out into the roadway. The incident attracted national media coverage and intensified local debate over the proposed plan for serviced sites.

The public debate over the establishment of hardstands centred upon the role that hardstands might play in facilitating the government settlement policy. A frequent argument in favour of serviced site construction was that Travellers were unable or unwilling to make a direct transition to houses and settled life. It was suggested that "feelings of claustrophobia and imprisonment" derived from "generations on the road" (*Galway Observer* 8 October 1986: 6) and "ancestral urges" to travel (*Galway Advertiser* 31 December 1986: 28) required the provision of transitional accommodation which would facilitate eventual permanent settlement in council housing. Opponents of hardstands argued that offering Travellers an alternative to housing constituted "special treatment" and would only encourage the retention of a Traveller identity. One politician stated, "I would call upon the itinerants to show more responsibility when they are offered permanent accommodation by the Local Authority and if they are offered houses they should take them and bring up their children in a settled community" (*City Tribune* 3 October 1986: 1). Another opponent of serviced sites claimed that hardstands would place undue financial burden on taxpayers, bring more Travellers to the city, encourage housed Travellers to take up camping, depreciate property values, increase petty crime, and jeopardise Galway's reputation as a tourist city (*City Tribune* 5 June 1987: 7).

While much of the public debate appeared to be focused on the merits of hardstands, the real struggle was over their proposed locations. Various residents' and tenants' associations of the city lobbied to keep hardstands out of their respective areas of the city. One residents' and tenants' association held a series of meetings to reiterate the position that it had adopted for several years: it was opposed to any serviced campsites in the area. This was accompanied by the claim that the area had already "done enough" by housing Travellers in its public estates. At meetings there was evidence of division between the residents of public and private housing. One man argued that the strong stand taken by the association against hardstands expressed the exclusive concerns of private residents and farmers. The association, he suggested, had never voiced the same opposition to housing Travellers in public estates. The suggestion that the association was not adequately representing the interests of the settled public housing tenants was quickly squelched by association executives who emphasized the need for a united neighbourhood-based, rather than class-based, opposition to hardstand provision.

Despite a city council "agreement in principle" to implement the hardstand project, any specific plans were contentious, particularly during the run-up to the 1987 general election. Some individual candidates tried to ensure voter support by not committing themselves on the serviced camping site issue, while others explicitly opposed any provision in their respective constituencies. Following a protest against hardstands by private homeowners who feared that a site would be located in their area, the city council agreement was threatened by a walk out by the members of the newly formed Progressive Democrat Party which hoped to appeal to middle class voters (*City Tribune* 17 October 1986: 1). At the same time the Workers' Party tried to ensure working class support by repeating their opposition to any further housing of Travellers in local authority estates (*Connacht Sentinel* 30 September 1986: 3).

The Traveller Committee

While the concept of the "settled community" has served to partially obscure class differences amongst the settled population in Galway, occasional references to a "Traveller community" are also problematic. Travellers in Galway city are not a homogeneous population and have never been organised into a single community. While differences between Travellers have been acknowledged by some commentators, these have tended to reflect the preoccupations of settlement policy. Thus Travellers are most frequently divided according to territorial jurisdictions, i. e., local and non-local, as well as according to accommodation, i. e., those who are housed and those who are camping ("roadside" Travellers). Frequently such categories are then wrongly equated with "settlement" and "travelling" respectively. Categorising Travellers in such terms has obscured patterns of geographical and residential mobility (movement in and out of various forms of accommodation through time) and deflected attention from other alliances and divisions amongst Travellers.

While there is a history of informal political activity on the part of Travellers in Galway, the 1986 attack on a Traveller camp led to an unprecedented attempt at organization in the form of a Traveller Committee. The composition of the Traveller Committee and its goals and strategies, however, revealed significant cleavages between Traveller households in the city and the result was fragmented rather than collective action.

Following the attack in 1986, the affected Traveller households issued a statement in which they asked for a serviced campsite. With the involvement of some settled people (members of the Galway Civil Rights Group, the Galway Unemployed Association, and some service workers), a Traveller Committee was formed and the demands of the smaller group were expanded to the larger project of lobbying the city council for the implementation of its city-wide plan for hardstands.

Several high-profile events were organized by the Galway Traveller Committee including pickets of the city council building, marches, the distribution of flyers, and public speeches. A number of months after the Committee had been formed, additional publicity was generated by the candidacy of the Committee's spokesperson, a Traveller woman named Margaret Sweeney, in the 1987 national election. This candidacy, though unsuccessful, represented the culmination of the action campaign. The emergence of a Traveller Committee and the candidacy of Margaret Sweeney in Galway city was inspired and influenced by similar events elsewhere in the country, especially Dublin (Gmelch 1989), but the strategies and goals of the Galway Committee remained locally oriented.

Spurred by the increasing difficulty of securing access to land on which to park trailers, the Committee attempted to mobilise public opinion in favour of hardstands, and win over those politicians who were delaying implementation of the existing "agreement in principle" on serviced site provision. Despite the fact that the city hardstand plan was explicitly part of a larger settlement programme, the Traveller Committee promoted the plan in the belief that serviced sites would represent an improvement, albeit imperfect, for Travellers in a situation of increased pressure on camping land.

Travellers disagreed amongst themselves over the merits of the particular hardstand plan being considered by the city. While some viewed the city proposal as ensuring access to land, others were concerned that the proposed camping sites might become "reservations" where increased state intervention would threaten crucial social relations of mobility, work, and kinship. The result was ambivalence among Travellers toward the strategy adopted by the Traveller Committee.

The decision of the Traveller Committee to lobby for the implementation of the existing city plan for hardstands involved it in a public acceptance of a number of assumptions of settlement policy. One of these was the distinction made between Galway Travellers and non-Galway Travellers. Despite the obvious contradiction involved in categorising a mobile population on the basis of jurisdictional affiliations, the Committee did not contest, indeed it promoted, the notion that hardstands should only be provided for a limited number of identifiable "long term Galway city families". The spokesperson for the Committee claimed to speak exclusively for twenty-seven to thirty of such families who had been camping in trailers in the city over a considerable period of time, and who did not want to move into permanent accommodation. The Traveller Committee also publicly advocated the provision of barriers on the sites to make the entry of "strangers" impossible and supported a city plan to provide a "pull-on/pull-off site" outside the city for "transient" Travellers.

The strategy of the Traveller Committee was largely a response to an imposed settlement agenda and discourse. The structuring of service provision to Travellers at a local level both created and encouraged the formulation of demands in terms of a localised *Galwegian* identity. At the same time, Traveller mobility had been reduced since the introduction of the settlement programme, thereby increasing the salience of a territorial affiliation. Despite a shift toward longer periods of residence in particular locations, movement both in and out of the city, as well as in and out of various forms of accommodation, remained a feature of most Travellers' lives.

Continuing patterns of geographical mobility made any exclusive calculation of "city families" problematic, and some Committee members expressed concern that any such calculation might exclude themselves or their relations. At one Traveller Committee meeting, when a man mentioned that his brother was coming back to the city after an absence, another Traveller responded that this brother would not be eligible for a site. The first man answered that if his brother was not entitled to a site, then he probably was not either, because over the course of fifteen years of camping in the city, he had often gone away for a couple of months to his in-laws, just as his brother had done.

Despite such concerns, the Committee was dominated by those who argued that hardstands would only be provided if the politicians and the public were convinced that these would be used only by "long term city families" who would remain "settled" in them, and that there would be no "influx" of Travellers into the city. One member noted: "if we are thinking of the Travellers who are coming and going to Galway that is no good. We've got to think of ourselves". The decision to limit the work of the Committee to the interests of those presently defined as "city families" worked against the development of networks with Travellers elsewhere in the country.

At the same time as the Committee downplayed the importance of mobility across urban boundaries, it also adopted and promoted another tenet of settlement policy: the categorisation of households according to type of accommodation. The Traveller Committee consistently distinguished between housed and camping Travellers within the city, insisting that it represented only the latter category. The Traveller Committee was concerned to establish that hardstands should only be provided for those *presently* living in camps, rather than for those who might wish to leave houses or flats for hardstands in the future. By representing the minority of camping households in the city, the Committee obscured the reality of movement between camps and housing by many Traveller families and limited potential support from the majority of Travellers in the city who were living in housing.

Along with concerns about possible restrictions on geographical and residential mobility, camping Travellers were divided over the impact that official campsites might have on forms of work. While some Travellers saw hardstands as providing the advantages of more flexible land-use, cheaper living costs, and security from eviction, others expressed fear that the city plan would involve increased surveillance and restrictions on various forms of work including scrap metal collection, horse dealing and trading.

Finally, many camping Travellers were reluctant to actively support the Traveller Committee because they saw the proposed hardstand plan as threatening their ability to maintain and strengthen particular kinship ties through close residence. At the time of the formation of the Traveller Committee, there were five camps within the city. Two of these camps had nine households each, another two camps had five households each, while the fifth had three households. Each of these camps was comprised of one or more clusters of households linked to one another by close kinship and/or affinal ties. In most cases, kin-based residential clusters had been established in the particular camping location for many years, although the specific composition of the cluster had changed as individual households moved in and out.

Many Travellers were concerned that their ability to choose their neighbours was threatened by the different priorities of the city. For example, political pressure to "spread" Travellers throughout the city had resulted in a plan which called for four or five hardstands of equal size, with at least one in each of the city's electoral wards. In Traveller Committee meetings, it was acknowledged that larger clusters of households might have to be divided, and smaller clusters amalgamated, in order to conform to the city plan. This compromise created tension between Travellers as different households attempted to assert their prior claims to enter specific sites.

Ambivalence amongst Travellers over the specifics of the city hardstand proposal worked against collective support for the Traveller Committee. Along with concerns about the effect that city hardstands might have on relations of mobility, work and kinship, there was also considerable scepticism about the motives of the Committee. Several Travellers suggested to me that those involved in the Traveller Committee were, in fact, only "in it for themselves" - attempting to derive benefits for their respective households rather than working on behalf of all of the camping Travellers in the city. The result was that many camping Travellers followed the activities of the Traveller Committee with interest, but remained uninvolved in any political action. At the same time, support from housed Travellers, as well as those living outside the city boundaries, was jeopardized by the exclusive focus of the Committee on the "long term city families" presently camping in trailers. The frustration involved in the attempt at collective organisation was evident in the comment of a Traveller Committee member who noted that Travellers "aren't loyal and won't come together". Most of the Committee's energy, in fact, went toward developing support among non-Travellers. The support of one non-Traveller, it was argued by another Committee member, was worth that of ten Travellers.

Much of the Committee's strategy was aimed at convincing non-Travellers of the need for hardstands. Along with approaches to city politicians and officials, the Labour Party and the Trades Council were addressed by Committee members. Invitations to attend Traveller Committee meetings were also issued to tenants' and residents' associations in the city. Such efforts had little success. One attempt at joint action between the Traveller Committee and a tenants' and residents' association dissolved when tensions between those living in the estate and Travellers in a nearby camp erupted into threats and confrontation between the two groups (*City Tribune* 28 April 1987:1).

While the Traveller Committee adopted a strategy of publicly accepting, rather than contesting, several premises of settlement policy, it did manage to develop and promote an alternative discourse of Traveller "culture". Unlike settlement advocates who presented the Traveller way of life as an obstacle to be overcome in the course of "integration", the Traveller Committee presented this as something to be retained, rather than transformed. For example, while some settlement advocates portrayed hardstands as a transitional step toward permanent settlement in houses, the Traveller Committee argued for the importance of hardstands in and of themselves. In speeches and interviews the Committee spokesperson argued that Travellers were entitled to hardstands on the basis of a distinct history and tradition. The argument was extended further in the claim that this tradition was that of the "true Ireland". Committee spokesperson, Margaret Sweeney, made the following statement during a speech at the local university:

> I think that the Travelling People are the true Irish people of Ireland and no Travelling person should be ashamed of what we are. We should be proud of it because we came from real Irish people. Our ancestors fought for this country and they had to leave their homes just the same as I'm sure some of yours had to years ago . . . Now is the time for the politicians to stand up and realise that we are Irish people. We have a right to be in this country. We have a right to say where we want to live. We have a right to live the way we want to live and it's not up to anybody else to plan how we should live (author's field notes 14 October 1986).

Some months later, when she attended a meeting of a tenants' and residents' association Margaret Sweeney stated:

> People should realise in this country we are human beings. We are the real Irish. We're as Irish as they come. I've no need to be ashamed because I'm a Traveller and I'm not going to let you or anybody else in this town take over and try to tell me how to live. I'm living right and natural and if I want a

hardstand, then I'm going to go out there and fight for it (author's field notes 10 February 1987).

The arguments made by the Galway Traveller Committee, while given impetus by the increasingly culturalist nature of dominant settlement discourse in the 1980s, nonetheless challenged the settlement agenda with an alternative discourse of legitimacy and authenticity . At the same time, the attempt to act collectively revealed the complexity of Traveller relations with one another and with the settled population. As in the case of the "settled community," the concept of a Traveller community masked significant lines of division.

While the Traveller Committee had little immediate success in pressuring the city into implementing its hardstand plan, a limited number of spaces were eventually provided a few years later. The decision to construct these official camping sites can be understood as a response to varying pressures including those emanating from the central government, the local propertied classes, local residents in public estates, and the actions of Travellers themselves.

Conclusion

This account of Traveller, settled population and state relations in Galway city conforms to, and diverges from, more general accounts of recent Traveller history. Along with increased tensions over Traveller camps during the 1950s, conflicts over the implementation of a settlement programme in the 1960s, and the emergence of a Traveller Rights movement in the 1980s, there are other aspects of the Traveller experience in Galway city that raise new questions for future work.

Evidence of a pre-war Traveller urban presence and history of local authority action against Travellers, suggests that in the case of Galway city at least, there was no "sudden" arrival of Travellers in the 1950s and that the tensions over land use were long standing. The findings from Galway would benefit from comparative work in other Irish urban centres. At the same time, a great deal more needs to be known about the relationship between local authorities and the development of Traveller policy at the national level. I have suggested that the increased attention given to "controlling" Travellers at the national level reflected changing central government priorities associated with the larger policy shifts of the late 1950s. This requires further exploration.

Examination of the implementation of the national settlement programme in Galway demonstrated the significance of the local political economy in understanding the timing and extent of Traveller settlement. An important finding was the salience of class in both the political actions and public discourses surrounding Traveller settlement within the city. Class relations, so critical in urban Ireland, have yet to be incorporated into analyses of Traveller history, settlement policy or ethnic mobilisation.

Finally, the Galway case study indicated something of the complexities of Traveller political mobilisation. In the face of continuing pressure on Traveller camps, the formation of a Traveller Committee represented an attempt by some Travellers and settled people to ensure the reproduction of a distinct way of life within the constraints of imposed state policies and local class politics. The actions and statements of the Traveller Committee revealed an increasingly self-conscious Traveller population in Galway city. The limited success of the Committee, however, also drew attention to the ways in which an imposed settlement agenda created and reproduced divisions between Travellers which worked against widespread mobilisation or sustained political action in pursuit of common goals. The experience of the Traveller Committee suggests that much more analysis of the often contradictory social relations between and amongst Travellers, settled people and the state is required if the goal of justice for Travelling People in Ireland is to be achieved.

Notes

1. While initial archival research was carried out in Galway city between January and June 1984, the major field research and additional archival work was conducted between August 1986 and June 1987 and was supported by a Doctoral Fellowship from the Social Sciences and Humanities Research Council of Canada. During this latter period, nine months were spent residing in a Traveller camp. Along with participant-observation in the camp setting, informal interviews with Travellers living in houses and members of the settled population involved in Traveller settlement were carried out. The most important archival sources consulted included local newspaper articles for the period of 1922-87, city council minutes covering the period of 1922-86, the counts of Travellers conducted by the city at varying intervals between 1975-86, minutes of the Galway Itinerant Settlement Council (1967-70) and Irish Parliamentary debates (House of Representatives) 1944-86.
2. Travellers sold goods and materials (e. g., tinware, rags, feathers, scrap metal and horsehair) to city merchants (for references to these activities see *Connacht Tribune* 29 August 1925: 5; 4 December 1926: 7; 8 June 1940: 5; 9 March 1946: 5). A reference to "tinkers" in the city market in 1938 (Galway Corporation 27 October 1938) is preceded by earlier references to "hawkers", "trading caravans", and "travelling traders" in the same area.
3. This resolution followed an earlier call made in the Dáil for the setting up of a commission (Dáil Éireann 9 April 1959: 297). Thus, the idea of a commission had been raised a number of times before the 1960 meeting of government health inspectors in Dublin which Gmelch suggests prompted the appointment of the Commission on Itinerancy (Gmelch 1989: 304).

4. I refer here to the electoral defeat of a coalition government and its replacement by a Fianna Fáil majority government in 1957. The political changes included a transfer of leadership within Fianna Fáil as Séan Lemass replaced Eamon deValera as Taoiseach. In 1960, Charles Haughey, son-in-law of Séan Lemass, was appointed to the newly created post of Parliamentary Secretary to the Minister for Justice (Oscar Traynor). One of his first tasks was to set up the Commission on Itinerancy.

5. These figures are based upon the count of Travellers taken for the Traveller Health Status Study in November of 1986. While the census takers collected data on the basis of "families", I have recalculated on the basis of "households" or co-residential units. This has resulted in some reduction of the census figures.

References

Adams, B., J. M. Okely, D. Morgan and D. Smith. 1975. *Gypsies and government policy*. London: Heineman.

Barry, J. and L. Daly. 1988. *The Travellers' health status study* . Dublin: The Health Research Board.

Burton, F. and P. Carlen. 1979. *Official discourse*. London: Routledge and Kegan Paul.

Commission on Itinerancy. 1963. *Report of the Commission on Itinerancy* . Dublin: The Stationery Office.

Dublin Travellers Education and Development Group. 1992. *Irish Travellers: New analysis and new initiatives*. Dublin: Pavee Point Publications.

Ennis, M. 1984. Twenty years of social work. Paper presented to the Irish Association of Social Workers. March 31-April 1.

Fay, R. 1992. Minorization of Travelling groups and their cultural rights- the case of the Irish Travellers. In *Irish Travellers: New analysis and new initiatives*. Dublin Travellers Education and Development Group. Dublin: Pavee Point Publications.

Gmelch, G. 1977. *The Irish tinkers: the urbanization of an itinerant people*. Menlo Park, California: Cummings Pub.

Gmelch, S. 1989. From poverty subculture to political lobby: the Traveller Rights Movement in Ireland. In *Ireland from below* (eds.) C. Curtin and T. Wilson. Galway: Galway University Press.

Grimes, S. 1984. Educational opportunities in Galway city: present trends and future prospects. In *Galway town and gown 1494-1984*. (ed.) D. Ó Cearbhaill. Dublin: Gill and Macmillan.

Mayall, D. 1988. *Gypsy-Travellers in nineteenth-century society*. Cambridge: Cambridge University Press.

Okely, J. 1983. *The Traveller-Gypsies*. Cambridge: Cambridge University Press.

Ó Cearbhaill, D. and M. Cawley. 1984. Galway city, a changing regional capital: employment and population since 1966. In *Galway town and gown 1494-1984* (ed.) D. Ó Cearbhaill. Dublin: Gill and Macmillan.

Review Body. 1983. *Report of the Travelling People Review Body*. Dublin: The Stationery Office.

Rottman, D. B., A. D. Tussing and M. M. Wiley. 1986. *The population structure and living circumstances of Irish Travellers: results from the 1981 census of Traveller families.* Paper No. 131. Dublin: The Economic and Social Research Institute.

Sibley, D. 1981. *Outsiders in urban societies.* Oxford: Basil Blackwell.

Silverman, M. and P. H. Gulliver. 1992. Historical anthropology and the ethnographic tradition: a personal, historical and intellectual account. In *Approaching the past.* (eds.) M. Silverman and P. H. Gulliver. New York: Columbia University Press.

11 An urban place in rural Ireland: an historical ethnography of domination, 1841-1989

Marilyn Silverman

For the Normans in the twelfth century, "Ireland was a colony to be settled and exploited" and its "ports provided the links, both with England and with Europe, through which this could be achieved" (Graham 1977: 39). Located at the head of navigation on the River Nore in County Kilkenny, the town of Thomastown received its foundation charter around the year 1200 - as part of the Norman conquest, as part of the outward expansion of European mercantile relations.[1] As a Norman trade centre and military-administrative stronghold, the town served as the transhipping depot for Kilkenny city, linking it and the large, productive agricultural hinterland to the ports of the southern Irish coast and to the world markets beyond. From this time until the present, international commerce has remained central, as the town continued in its functionally specialised roles linked to, and structured by, a western European "system of domination."

This notion of domination is derived from the idea that socio-economic change within Europe, and the uneven development of its various regions and states, can be analysed according to a core-periphery model. In such a model, economic differentiation reflects directly the long-term relations that emerged and persisted between regions or states which developed ("cores") as against those which did not ("peripheries").[2] In the contemporary world, "the U.S. and Central Europe" are the "'cores' to the European periphery." They are "the suppliers of capital and technology; centres of political, military and cultural dominance; providers of tourists and absorbers of migration" (Seers 1979: 8). In contrast, the periphery is where people are more "likely to be working in agriculture or tourism, to be unemployed, to see their families broken by migration, or to receive a very low income" (Seers 1979: 19). In other words, peripheries lack control over their resources and generate few innovations: new technologies and products are

imported. Their economies contain few internal linkages and generate few
multiplier effects. Migration is outward and the state often exerts great effort
to promote development (Selwyn 1979: 37-39).

This depiction points to three analytical dimensions which underlie core-
periphery relations: space, function and power. The "farther from the core a
place is, the poorer it is likely to be" and the more underdeveloped (Seers
1979: 19). This spatial relation mirrors a functional differentiation *cum*
interdependence which results in "functionally integrated regional systems"
that "interact in ways determined by power differences" (Donham 1990:
141). Ultimately, such regional systems, actualised through space, function
and power, are "hierarchically encapsulated within larger systems. Any one
region within its own core-periphery structure may be, on a higher level, a
constituent part of a more inclusive system" (Donham 1990: 142).

Ireland usually is classed as part of Europe's periphery, along "with the
countries of the Mediterranean" and the "Celtic fringe" (Seers 1979: 7;
Hechter 1975). Yet, function and power do not necessarily correspond to the
boundaries of the state, for it is seldom internally homogeneous. Given that
eastern Ireland is physically closer to the European core, and given that
places such as Thomastown, in southeastern Ireland, for centuries had
trading and administrative functions in the European system of domination,
it is not surprising that, in "Ireland, the east coast is the more dynamic"
(Seers 1979: 19). Yet, although we know this, "[t]oo little research has been
done on what might be called the geography of domination" (Donham 1990:
141). In this paper, therefore, I explore what this looks like, in the recent
past, in a town in rural Ireland - in the periphery of Europe, in the semi-
periphery of Ireland, in the core of the long-dominated and dynamic
Southeast.

The nature of domination: an 1845 portrait

In 1845, a visiting journalist described Thomastown as

> a pretty and . . . neat town with, however, . . . evidences of the want of a
> town commissionership. There are a few professional men and one or two
> large mercantile concerns. The main body of the people, however, consist
> of small shopkeepers, artisans and agricultural labourers. Of the working
> class, a hundred or so may be employed in mills, where our corn is ground
> for England's consumption and in the lime-kilns, adjacent to the town,
> which some doth say are a monopoly. Formerly, we are told, there were
> near Thomastown many small lime-burners who eked out a decent
> livelihood. Several daily labourers live in and around the town. There is
> an utter absence of . . . manufactures with the exception of one tan-yard in
> which perhaps some half dozen of persons may find employ. On the whole

as far as trade and business is to be considered, Thomastown has not much to boast (*Kilkenny Journal* 12 April 1845).

The portrait is clear in many respects, and in it can be seen how local *underdevelopment* had become particularly marked by this time. For example, the town's navigation function was not mentioned because that had been lost in the early nineteenth century - as the River Nore silted and as townspeople failed to obtain funding to remedy it, as competition from the Barrow River and Grand Canal marginalized the River Nore, and as the southeastern ports were eclipsed by Dublin and Cork (Silverman 1992).

The town also was experiencing extensive de-industrialisation and a skewing of its industrial base towards a single industry, flour milling. For apart from the small tannery and several grist mills, flour milling was all that remained of a virtual industrial revolution which had taken place after 1770: rape seed milling, starching, chandling, brewing and malting had all come and gone, the result of changing markets and competition from other centres (Cullen 1972; Halpin 1989; Gulliver and Silverman in preparation).

Finally, the "want of a town commissionership" pointed to the political domination which accompanied the deepening economic underdevelopment at the time. In 1841, the state had abolished the town's self-governing Corporation. This curtailed severely the town's administrative and political integrity. For apart from grand juries, controlled by landowners and responsible for public works, the only other local government organ was the Board of Guardians, set up by the 1838 Poor Law to collect taxes for, and to administer, poor relief in its area or "union." As of 1845, Thomastown and hinterland were contained within the Kilkenny Poor Law Union seated in Kilkenny city. Politically and administratively, Thomastown was a dependent satellite.

For all these reasons, the town "had not much to boast." Yet, the portrait of domination, typified by underdevelopment, also contained clear elements of what might be termed *modernity*. In 1845, although flour milling had become the only industry, it was modernised and export-oriented. Indeed, the town boasted two state-of-the-art mills, one of which was the fourth largest in the county. The production of lime as fertiliser, long an important export to adjacent counties, had been "rationalised" after 1820 when a modernising landlord purchased the kilns next to the town. Moreover, although its navigation had been lost, road transport had gradually improved and the town remained a small hub, for people, the post and small goods, on an inland road network which connected Dublin and Waterford. Finally, by the late 1830s, the state had eliminated agrarian violence (O'Hanrahan 1990; Gulliver and Silverman in preparation). With law and order, and with the state increasingly regulating trade (e.g. weights and measures), the town's commerce and retailing could prosper.

Such prosperity was tied to the fact that local people, labourers as well as farmers, were becoming more firmly tied to the market. Indeed, the process by which this occurred in Thomastown shows how the two aspects of peripherality - modernity and underdevelopment - can be interlinked because they form "part of a more inclusive system" of domination. In this case, European-wide economic depression had followed the end of the Napoleonic Wars in 1815. "Emigration...through Waterford" reached "an unprecedented extent" (*Kilkenny Independent* 12 May 1827) whilst, by the early 1830s, extreme distress typified the countryside around the town. Small-holders and agricultural labourers were particularly affected. The former faced declining commodity prices; the latter faced severe unemployment and falling wages. Amongst better-off farmers too, incomes had declined, credit had become expensive and, as a result, "a large increase in the quantity of every kind of agricultural produce" was being "brought to market for export to England, because the increasing poverty of farmers obliges them to live more and more upon potatoes and to sell almost the whole of the meat, corn, butter, etc. which they consumed formerly."[3] At the same time, other aspects of the wider political economy were relevant: that "more cattle, by ten to one, are now fattened for export than formerly" also arose "from the introduction of stall feeding, the general improvement of agriculture, [and] the facility of conveyance to England by steam."[4] In other words, the market flourished as living standards fell.

In this context, the town's shopkeepers did fairly well. They controlled the distribution of imported necessities (e.g. tea, coal, sugar); they held and rented out a great deal of labourers' housing in the town; they charged "exorbitant interest" (50 to 100 per cent) for credit which farmers needed for seed and provisions; they hired labour for less than subsistence wages; and they sold increasing amounts of alcohol, a commodity which was growing rapidly in popularity at the time.[5]

In all this could be seen, in Thomastown after 1815, the nature of a periphery: increasing modernity as part of increasing underdevelopment. On the one hand, law and order, flour milling, an expanding market and new technologies in transport and agriculture were associated, on the other hand, with increasing exports of labour and primary products, deepening poverty and distress, de-industrialisation, political alienation and the loss of river transport. In turn, all was part of a process by which more people were drawn into the market and by which the town reproduced itself, as did the local agents who controlled key elements of the process - commodities and capital. As the journalist noted in 1845, the town had "one or two large mercantile firms" and "small shopkeepers."

This distinction between "large" and "small" pointed in turn to a central feature at the time: the town's commercial sector was markedly stratified, as was all of urban society, with professionals, merchants, shopkeepers, artisans and labourers. Indeed, the dynamics of class differentiation in a periphery comprise an essential part of geographical domination (Blomstrom and Hettne 1984: 81-4). In Thomastown, in 1845, class - not ethnicity or politics - was fundamental. As the journalist noted:

> There are two reading rooms in the town for which papers of various shades of political opinion are taken and where Protestant and Catholic, Whig, Repealer and Tory meet . . . in goodliest fellowship. . . . [F]anaticism has no rule here - Catholics . . . scorn to interfere with the religious opinion . . . [of] . . . those of a . . . different communion and . . . a[n anti-Catholic] crusade . . . could not find supporters amongst the Protestants (*Kilkenny Journal* 12 April 1845).

The reproduction of domination, 1841-1989

The 1845 portrait of Thomastown reflected two interdependent features of its peripheral status - modernity and underdevelopment. After 1845, failure to generate "sufficient internal impetus for . . . transformation" (Berend and Ranki 1982: 13) meant that life in the town continued to reflect geographical and functional peripherality in the European system of domination. Indeed, by the late 1980s, the town's portrait was still characterised by modernity, located in consumption patterns, and by underdevelopment, typified by the structure of local production and political integration. By 1989, it had become possible, in Thomastown, to buy such imported commodities as computer programmes, designer dresses with shoulder pads and exotic foods like green peppers. At the same time, the one bed and breakfast place which had served a desultory tourist trade in 1981 had been joined by about 20 enterprises oriented to tourism. Unemployment was rampant, emigration was extensive, the effects of state intervention were everywhere apparent and local political structures were atrophied. How had the town's 1845 portrait been reproduced over time?

Spatial-physical differentiation, 1841-1989

The "class-character of capitalism incorporates international systems of centre and periphery" at the same time that "class domination is strongly influenced and reproduced by...the differentiation of neighbourhoods within cities" (Giddens 1979: 206). In Thomastown, the pattern of streets and buildings, and the class-based structuration of space, were established well before the mid-nineteenth century. After that time, the relation between class and space was continually reproduced, as a reflection of urban life in the periphery.

The town had long been divided by the River Nore. On the northern side, in the 16 acres which comprised the Corporation borough or townland of Thomastown, was a core of four short streets lined with buildings. Most buildings had two storeys but a few, backing on the river, had three. The latter had been merchant houses, built in the fifteenth century (Murtagh 1982).[6] In 1846, all but five of the town's 41 retail shops were located in these core streets. Each shopkeeping family lived in an apartment above the shop whilst, behind the buildings and beyond them, was a patchwork of outhouses, storehouses, bake houses, cow and pig sheds, yards and tiny gardens. The main commercial street was Market Street (18.5 metres wide and 107 metres long). In 1846, it contained eight private residences and 17 retail establishments (five pub-groceries, two groceries, a bakery, a hardware shop, two bootmakers' shops, two draperies, a butchery, the shops of a carpenter and of a saddler and one general shop). Market Street also was the locale for weekly, open-air pig and poultry markets.

Extending from the northeast corner of the core, and to the roads that lead to New Ross and Graiguenamanagh, was the Quay. There, river boats once had tied up near warehouses; in 1846, the Quay had a pub and a grocery. From the southwest corner, and across the bridge over the Nore, lay Mill Street, leading to the Waterford road. In that street was Grenan Mill and, off a side road, the Island Mill - the two modern flour mills. Mill Street, and the Mall leading off from it, were lined with houses occupied by mill workers. On Mill Street were three pub-groceries and the workshops of a blacksmith, a saddler and a tailor. Other streets leading out of the core to the west and north (Marshes, Ladywell and Maudlin) contained the small houses of labourers but no retail shops. Many of the labourers worked in the tannery, located on Ladywell.

Clearly the core streets comprised the commercial centre. On the roads leading to it were industrial properties and, associated with these, residential space for labourers. This patterning of streets and buildings persisted in its essentials until the late 1980s when it was possible to trace, in unbroken continuity back to the 1840s, all the buildings and their occupants in the core and feeder streets. Of course, physical changes had occurred. These, however, had reproduced and enhanced the spatial dimensions of class and domination; the space occupied by shopkeepers and labourers continued to be differentiated and two new spaces were created - one devoted to the institutions of church and state and the other to pockets of "modern"-style housing.[7]

Rising above the town in 1845, on its northeastern side, was a hill on which stood the Catholic church and cemetery, together with a National School which had opened in 1840. In contrast was a small Protestant church built in 1819 inside the ruins of a large, thirteenth century Norman church. Unlike the Catholic church which overlooked the town from the outskirts, the

Protestant church was at the centre, at the northern end of Market Street. Together they symbolised the centrality and later decline of the Ascendancy and, with it, the "devotional revolution" in Catholicism (Larkin 1972). Thus, in 1867, the Catholic church was replaced by a large, new structure and, adjacent to it in 1899, a convent and girls' primary school were opened. In 1986, the Protestant church was closed.

The state and its agents also had elaborated their physical presence in the town. As part of the town's role as a centre of commerce and coercion, the core streets had long contained a courthouse and a military (later police) barracks. In 1850, as the state expanded, a workhouse and fever hospital were built on the town's outskirts. Thus, church and state had a dramatic spatial presence: their large, imposing buildings marked the northern approaches to the town.

In the streets leading into the core, many small houses fell into ruin as the town's population declined during the second half of the nineteenth century. As well, on Mill Street and the Mall, rows of decrepit, cramped labourers' houses were demolished in the 1970s after their inhabitants had been re-housed by a state agent, the County Council. Earlier too, in 1941 and the early 1950s, the County Council had built new labourers' houses. All were located within housing estates and all estates were placed on the edges of the town. In effect, urban labourers were removed from the core as they were congregated in working class neighbourhoods.

Finally, after about 1960, new and privately built bungalows were constructed, largely in strip fashion, along the town's exit roads. Some were built by workers; others by artisans and shopkeepers. Through such mixing, these strips reflected what some chose to see as modernity - comfortable people housed in "traditional bungalows."

In these ways, and through these changes, the class-based structuration of space in the town reproduced itself over time, retaining its historical basis in class difference whilst introducing a modern variation which masked, but did not eliminate, the class differences which typify peripheral places.

Rural-urban difference and the agro-industrial economy, 1841-1925.

The "class-character of capitalism" and class domination are not only "influenced and reproduced" by spatial differentiation but also "by patterns of rural-urban difference" (Giddens 1979: 206). In Thomastown, the changing nature of rural-urban difference between 1841 and 1911 was one of the processes through which modernity and underdevelopment were linked. However, it occurred in a way which perhaps is peculiar to a periphery located so geographically close to its European core. Between 1841 and 1911, a massive export of surplus labour, both rural and urban, was accompanied by four features: a rise in living standards for all who remained, a diminution in the importance of agriculture, an expanded commercial role for the town and, by 1911, a homogenisation of living standards in both town and country.

Between 1841 and 1911, the town's population continuously declined along with the number of inhabited houses. By 1861, the 1,426 townspeople comprised 61 per cent of their 1841 number.[8] By 1881, the 1,067 town-dwellers constituted 45 per cent of the 1841 figure whilst their 223 houses were 52 per cent of the 1841 number. These decreases were accompanied by features which suggest a simultaneous rise in living standards for those who remained. First, the number of people per house declined: from 5.5 in 1841 to 4.8 in 1881. Second, housing gradually improved in a process by which the worst housing was abandoned most rapidly and by which, therefore, the overall quality of housing stock was slowly emended. Between 1841 and 1851, two-thirds of the fourth-class housing disappeared as did a quarter of the third class and about 12 per cent of the second class. By 1861, as a result, over two-thirds of town housing was first and second class quality.

A third sign of rising living standards was that servants formed an increasing proportion of the urban population. In 1841, they constituted four per cent; by 1861, six per cent. Fourth, literacy increased. In 1841, 43 per cent of the town's population (aged five and above) could, according to the census, "neither read nor write." By 1851, this had decreased to 39 per cent. By 1881, only 29 per cent was illiterate.[9] Finally, the ratio of people per retail shop gradually improved. In 1846, Thomastown Catholic parish had 181 people per town shop. In 1884, it had 93 people; by 1911, it had 67. Over time, clearly, people were buying more of what they consumed.

These demographic and lifestyle changes reflected a slow shift in the structure of the wider economy as it articulated with urban life. According to the 1841 census, almost 33 per cent of the town's population was engaged in "agricultural pursuits." By 1861, this had dropped to eight per cent. The proportion engaged in "manufacturing and trade" declined only slightly during the same period (from 49 to 41 per cent); however, the category labelled "other pursuits" increased dramatically (from 18 to 50 per cent). This suggests that the urban-based, casual or "general labourer" was less likely to be employed in agriculture and more likely, by 1861, to find work in the industrial and service sectors. Between 1841 and 1861, the town had become less agricultural and more commercial in function.

These shifts were reflected in the countryside around the town. To show this, eight rural townlands can be used.[10] In these, 532 people in 1861 comprised 56 per cent of their 1841 number. It was a decline greater than in the town. Yet, household sizes in the countryside (5.8 persons per house in 1841; 5.6 in 1861) were larger than in the town (4.9 persons per house in

1861). Thus, although population decline had been greater, it had not produced as high a living standard.

This was not because change was slower in the rural area. It was because rural living standards had been so much worse. In 1841, in contrast with the town, over three-quarters of rural housing was of the lowest standard (classes 3 and 4) and half of this was of the worst sort (class 4).[11] Yet, the quality of rural housing improved dramatically after 1841 as the poorest housing was progressively abandoned. Even so, by 1861, larger household sizes and inferior housing typified the countryside around the town: in 1861, over two-thirds of town housing was second class or better whereas, in the countryside, 60 per cent was third class or worse.

All this suggests a multi-pronged process after 1841. Massive emigration eliminated the lowest living standards in both town and country whilst, simultaneously, standards rose for those who remained. Even so, absolute standards in the countryside remained lower than in the town. However, by 1911, such rural-urban difference was eliminated - the result, after 1861, of continuing emigration, improvements in rural housing, and declining rural household sizes. By 1911, the population in the eight rural townlands was 37 per cent that of 1841. Fourth class housing had disappeared and average household size was 4.9. The town's population was 40 per cent that of 1841 but, because the size of urban households declined only slightly after 1861, household size in town and country were virtually identical by 1911. Furthermore, slightly over 70 per cent of both town and country housing was second class quality. In other words, differences in rural and urban living standards had been removed.

Such change had affected all classes; yet class differences in housing and, hence, in living standards, had been reproduced in both country and town. For example, 459 households were enumerated in the 1901 census in the District Electoral Divisions (DEDs) of Thomastown and Jerpoint Church, units which contained the town and 26 townlands (about 9,500 acres). In these, 72 per cent of "general labourers" and 69 per cent of agricultural workers lived in houses with three rooms or less; only 30 per cent of farmers did so and only 12 per cent of shopkeepers. In other words, rising living standards were, for all, connected to the reproduction of class difference.

Such demographic and lifestyle patterns between 1841 and 1911 were linked to dramatic changes in local agriculture. In 1847, labour-intensive tillage land, according to the agricultural census, formed 84 per cent of the land in use in the Thomastown area. By 1851, it comprised only 38 per cent and, by 1925, only 11 per cent. This decline lessened dramatically the need for labour. Moreover, the move away from tillage to pasture was a move towards raising beef cattle and sheep for export rather than towards labour-intensive dairying. Thus, the export of both people and animals expanded rapidly after 1841, aided by the Waterford-Kilkenny Railway which connected, at Abbeyleix, to the Dublin-Limerick line. Funded largely by English capital (Cullen 1972: 143), the line from Kilkenny reached Thomastown in 1848 (*Kilkenny Moderator* 10 May 1848). After it opened to Waterford in 1854, cattle bought at Thomastown's fair could be sold in London the next day.

The growing demand and capacity of the export market and the changing agricultural regime were reflected in the occupations of the people who remained. In the 1901 census, only 60 per cent of rural-dwellers in the parish had agricultural pursuits. In the town, the proportion employed in agriculture had declined from 33 per cent in 1841 to less than five in 1901.

This, of course, does not take into account the extent to which agriculture provided indirect employment - for artisans, such as blacksmiths, and for retailers who not only sold agricultural inputs but who also depended on the custom of farming households for non-agricultural necessities. However, it was, and had been for a long time, working class people who formed the majority of the population in both town and country. In the 1901 census, 149 people (over 13 per cent) of the 1,136 in the parish who gave their occupation were artisans; almost 52 per cent (586) were labourers and, of these, 58 per cent were non-agricultural.[12] For them, it was the vagaries in the town's industrial and service sectors which were central.

In 1845, along with the two modern, export-oriented flour mills (Grenan Mill and the Island Mill), the town's industrial sector contained three smaller flour mills (Little Mill, Dangan Mill and Jerpoint Mill) and a small tannery. Over the next decades, the milling sector inexorably declined. In 1873, Dangan Mill was turned into a woollen mill and was worked until about 1902. In 1920, the valuation records described it as "delapidated." In 1880, the modern Island Mill and the Little Mill, having been run as a single enterprise, were bankrupt - victims of an ageing owner, a lack of capital with which to invest in new technology (steel rollers to replace stone grinders), and competition from other mills, particularly those located in the major Irish ports, near the imports of durum wheat. Jerpoint Mill, by 1914, had contracted considerably. It milled only cattle feed for local farmers or sold milled wheat to dealers; in any case, it hired only a few labourers by that time. Grenan Mill though, continued. Between 1873 and 1886, an average of 29 workers were employed (Silverman 1990: 92-3).

The tannery too was doing well. Its ledgers show that its sales expanded after 1860, at first to buyers in New Ross and Waterford and then, by 1870, "to buyers well beyond the locality: thereafter, local sales were few and small" as orders went to Belfast, Cork and Sligo. In 1895, the operation was expanded and 16 labourers were employed full-time along with two artisans who did "spells of maintenance work" (Silverman and Gulliver 1986: 60).

Overall then, between 1841 and 1925, the changing nature of rural-urban difference and the local agro-industrial economy comprised a process in which modernity and underdevelopment were inextricably linked. On the one hand, modernity was evidenced in the declining importance of agriculture, in rising living standards and their homogenisation in town and country, in the tannery's expansion, and in the town's growing commercial importance. On the other hand, all this had been actualised by features typical of an underdeveloped economy: the massive export of labour and of unprocessed farm commodities, the volatility of indigenous industries and the reproduction of class differences. Most generally between 1841 and 1925, modernity and underdevelopment had been interdependent features of a singular process rooted in the peripherality of Thomastown - in the domination of capital, technology and markets located elsewhere, as part of higher order systems.

Political domination and the town, 1841-1926

Prior to 1841, the state's main concern had been law and order: its agents were the military, police, magistrates and the petty sessions. The state and its agents, however, gradually moved out from the core streets, with their barracks, court house and bridewell, into more benign methods of control, particularly the use of local administration to alleviate the disruptive potential of poverty. The 1838 Poor Law and the 1841 abolition of the town's self-governing Corporation had made Thomastown a political satellite of Kilkenny city. However, when the severity of the 1845-8 famine induced the state to create smaller administrative units, an area around the town (within, roughly, an 8 to 10 mile radius) was hived off from the Kilkenny Union to form Thomastown Union, with the town as its seat. A workhouse and fever hospital were built and a board of guardians established to administer them.

Gradually, new functions were given to these boards, as the state expanded its jurisdiction. By the mid-1870s, boards had to establish medical dispensaries; by the early 1880s, they were building rural housing for agricultural labourers. By the end of the century, they were responsible for providing potable water and medical services, financing emigrants, abating nuisances, and enforcing regulations concerning sewers, lodging houses, dairy sheds and vaccination.

Such new functions, however, did not augment the town's political integrity. This was because the town itself had no representation on the board. Instead, the town was divided between the two DEDs of Thomastown and Jerpoint Church, each of which - like all 27 DEDs making up Thomastown Union - was entitled only to two representatives on the board. Town-dwellers could never be more than a small minority. In any case, each of the two DEDs contained rural hinterland; and rural voters always outnumbered urban ones. Thus, of the 16 known guardians who resided in

Thomastown parish between 1850 and 1899, four were gentry, 11 were farmers and only one, the tanner, lived in the town. Being the seat of a Poor Law Union did not empower the town.

In 1899, a new local government act created County and Rural District Councils to be elected by all male householders. Thomastown's Union and its constituent DEDs became a Rural District, with a council and the town as its seat. Again this gave townspeople no especial say. Of the 33 parish residents who served on the District Council between 1899 and its abolition in 1926, 22 were rural-dwellers (21 farmers and one gentleman). Of the 11 townspeople who were councillors at various times, five were labourers, four were shopkeepers and two were industrialists (a flour miller and the tanner). Townsmen, of all classes, were always a small minority on the council. Thus, since the abolition of the town's Corporation in 1841, the town had been, and remained, politically dominated. Indeed, the growing modernity of local government structures (boards, councils, etc.), and their expanding functions, were all blatant signs of the town's political underdevelopment.

The Irish state and the town, 1936-1989

Until 1936, Thomastown was a net exporter of labour. In that year, however, the town began to experience a slow but consistent growth which meant that fifty years later, in 1986, its population of 1,465 was at its 1861 level. Had the geography of domination changed?

During the twentieth century, agriculture had continued to emphasise extensive systems (livestock) rather than intensive ones (tillage or dairy): average farm size increased as the number of farmers and farm labourers decreased. The slow decline in the town's industrial sector also continued. The tannery, after its brief expansion in the 1890s, succumbed to competition and government rationalisation in 1930. Jerpoint Mill continued through World War II because local wheat had to be milled for local consumption. It closed immediately after. Only Grenan Mill was left, but it too closed in 1963. It was a victim, like the town's other industrial enterprises, of competition from other centres and interests.

During the early twentieth century then, and until 1936, population decline was associated with capital-intensive agriculture and a contracting industrial base. The large number of labourers who became British soldiers during World War I was in part a reflection of high local unemployment (Silverman and Gulliver 1986: 162-5). Then, with independence and the end of the civil war in 1922, the new Irish state acted to establish control, to centralise power and to foment development. The resulting intervention proved key for the town's reproduction. For the new state not only absorbed surplus labour and kept it at home but, more importantly, it enhanced the town's role as, yet again, a centre for actualising state interests.

Thomastown's role as the seat of a Poor Law Union after 1850 and Rural District Council after 1899 had masked its political dependency. It had, however, enhanced the town's function as a formal, administrative centre and had bolstered local commerce. Provisioning both the workhouse and the officials who came to the town had given custom to many shops. However, the town's location inside wider administrative units had contributed to the hegemonic notion that regional rather than town government was appropriate, and little local reaction ensued when, in 1926, the state abolished the Rural District Council and gave its functions to the County Council. "Local government in Ireland became...county council government" (Chubb 1970: 279). The town was again a satellite of Kilkenny city. Between 1899 and 1989, only four town-dwellers served on the council - a shopkeeper and three labourers.

Thus, the "want of a town commissionership" which the journalist noted in 1845 had never altered. Indeed, the new Irish state, after 1922, exacerbated the political peripheralization begun by the British. At the same time, its interventions had important repercussions in other domains: on the local economy, on the town's urban functions and, therefore, on the town's reproduction.

The County Council particularly, as the main agent of the state, required a great deal of labour. It provided regular, pensionable work to some labourers "on the roads" and in the workhouse which, after the mid-1950s, was converted to a geriatric facility. The Council also, in replacing the worst housing, required a great deal of occasional work from the building trades. In 1981, 40 per cent of the houses in the DEDs of Jerpoint Church and Thomastown had been built by a local authority.[13] Particularly, the construction of three housing estates (123 houses) provided extensive work for artisans and labourers during the late 1930s, mid-1950s and late 1970s. State concerns had clearly contributed to the town's growth after 1936.

In addition to the County Council, labour - both permanent and casual - was required by other state agencies (e.g. post office, public works office, electricity board, the nationalised railway and transport company). Through such agencies, between 1922 and 1989, schools, houses and a community centre were built or financed; streets were paved and the post office renovated; potable water, reservoirs and sewerage were provided; electricity and telephones were installed; the courthouse and the bridge were re-built. With each addition, the town became more dependent on the state at the same time that its urban functions were enhanced. In this way, a reproductive process was engendered: by the mid-1930s, state intervention enabled the town to generate sufficient waged employment to allow it to maintain itself and, in turn, to encourage the state to intervene yet again;

this, in turn, allowed population growth which, again, required the state to provide more services that, in turn, gave jobs; and so on. Yet, part of this process was the continuing export of labour. The town's dynamism after 1936 was sufficient only to reproduce itself, not to stem the outflow. Nor did the town's growth lead to political empowerment. Although dependent on the state, townspeople had little means of affecting the state's decisions in relation to it.

Commerce in the core, 1841-1989

Although politically dependent, the town had a particular kind of independence from the state. For it was a commercial centre - a node in a hierarchical, and international, distribution system. This role had persisted over centuries. It had often induced state agents to use the town for their own purposes and, by the nineteenth and twentieth centuries, to underwrite those public works (e.g. roads, bridges) which were required to maintain trading networks and, by implication, the town.

The town's shopkeepers also contributed to the reproduction of other urban classes. Many hired at least one labourer; some of the larger ones, at times, hired more. In addition, through self-employment and casual employment, often for shopkeepers, many of the town's artisans and labourers cobbled together adequate livings. In any case, people of all classes had long been dependent on the town's shopkeepers for their consumables. Thus, the trading sector, in the core streets of the town, was integral to it; and   as commerce altered during the twentieth century, along with consumption patterns, the town grew.

Despite the massive population decline after 1841, the number of retailers in the town barely altered: 41 shops in 1846 and 45 in 1981 (see Table 1).[14] This clearly reflected increasing involvement in the market, rising living standards, changing consumption patterns and a growing penetration of commodities.

There is no extant description of the town's shops at any time. In the 1911 census, over half the retail buildings were of first class quality. Nevertheless, shopping spaces themselves were probably small. At the turn of the century, for example, a prosperous pub-grocery was about 15 to 20 feet each way. That size typified most shops in later years as well. In 1928, a long-established pub, described as "average" by the District Court judge in his licensing capacity, had a single bar room measuring eight feet by six feet, including the bar itself. There, the proprietor sold 25 gallons of whiskey a year and 12 dozen bottles of stout a week: not a large amount (*Kilkenny Journal* 15 September 1928). A larger, more prosperous pub-grocery in the 1930s occupied a room of about 30 feet by 10 in which were sold between 30 and 40 gallons of spirits a year - and a little less in the 1950s. The owner's wholesale purchases (spirits, beers, groceries and some hardware) was about £1,300 a year in the late 1930s. A successful drapery which continued for more than a hundred years measured about 150 square feet.

Table 1
Thomastown's Retailers, 1846-1981

Main Retail Specialism	1846	1856	1884	1911	1945	1981
Pub-grocery, etc.	14	17	14	11	9	3
Pub only	1	2	1	3	7	9
Grocery only	6	3	5	6	3	6
Grocery-bakery	2	2	2	2	--	--
Drapery & clothing	3	5	2	5	7	6
Bakery only	2	3	4	1	2	1
Butchery	4	2	2	3	3	2
Hardware	1	2	2	2	2	2
Saddler	3	1	1	--	--	--
Bootmaker/seller	4	3	3	3	2	--
Newsagent, etc.	--	--	--	1	4	2
Electrical goods	--	--	--	--	--	2
Garage (petrol, cars, parts)	--	--	--	--	1	3
Other	--	--	1	2	1	9
not known	1	1	--	--	--	--
TOTAL:	41	41	37	39	41	45

Despite their small sizes, the town's shops consistently supplied, at least since the mid-nineteenth century, the regular and repetitive needs of local rural and urban people: groceries, coal, liquor, bread, meat, clothing, footwear, hardware, seeds, tools, newspapers and tobacco. A few shops, catering for gentry, also held special stocks. In 1904, the account book which a small carter's household had with a baker-grocer showed regular purchases of bread, butter, milk, eggs, flour, sugar, tea, tobacco, candles, matches and, occasionally, bacon and jam. The shopkeeper baked the bread in an oven behind the shop and he blended the tea and smoked the bacon. He obtained the butter, milk and eggs from local farmers and his other commodities from Waterford and Dublin wholesalers.

The changing range of retail shops between 1846 and 1981 (Table 1) points to three alterations in the town's commerce during this period. First, a growing centralisation occurred in the retailing of staples. Until the early twentieth century, grocery shops predominated, whether on their own or linked with some other retail specialism. However, the number of groceries decreased after the middle of the twentieth century, especially when most publicans closed their grocery sections. They were unable to compete with new, self-service groceries and convenience shops which, in several cases,

were tied to regional and national chains and which were far larger than had
ever been the case. In other words, the distribution of staples became, over
time, specialised, centralised and the prerogative of fewer but larger retailers.

Second, alongside rising living standards and increasing consumption,
new commodities became available for sale in the town as new kinds of
specialist shops were opened, particularly around the turn of the century:
china and housewares, newsagents (papers, tobacco, sweets, stationery) and,
a little later, a shop specialising in factory-made footwear. Then came shops
which specialised in petrol, pharmaceuticals, electrical goods, cars and spare
parts. In addition, most local retailers gradually expanded their stock. In the
later 1960s and 1970s, factory-made bread and cakes, bottled gas, sports
goods, frozen foods and ice cream, housewares and kitchen fittings were
increasingly to be found in the town's shops. By 1981, the town's shops sold,
amongst other things, Japanese cars, German radios, Dutch flowers, tinned
English mackerel and Waterford bacon.

This pointed to a third alteration: over time, an increasing number of
commodities came from outside the local area, displacing local production
and producers. Most drastic, perhaps, was the penetration of manufactured
goods during the first half of this century: established town shops belonging
to artisan-vendors simply disappeared. Tailors, dressmakers, bootmakers,
saddlers, blacksmiths and a cooper all saw their products displaced by mass-
produced goods made elsewhere and stocked by the town's other shopkeepers.
The role of shopkeepers in processing commodities also was virtually
eliminated. Such value-added activities as blending teas, smoking bacon,
bottling beer and dressing turkeys were displaced by pre-packaged
commodities increasingly supplied by wholesalers. By the early 1970s, even
eggs, milk and butter no longer came from local producers. Victuallers no
longer butchered pigs and bread sellers no longer baked bread. People in
town and country had ceased involvement in the production or processing of
what they consumed, as had those who did the retailing.

Little information exists on early shopping habits but oral histories
indicated that local shops had a near monopoly. Although it was possible to
travel by train to Kilkenny city after 1848 and soon after to Waterford city,
this was relatively expensive and time-consuming and seems not to have
affected local shopping habits. Rather, the opposite occurred. Trains made it
easier and cheaper for shopkeepers to obtain their supplies and gave them an
advantage over shops in towns and villages in the region which were not
served by the railway.

However, at least since World War II, the town's retailers have faced
increased competition from shops in Kilkenny city and, to a lesser extent, in
Waterford. Not only were more shops and especially new kinds of shops
increasingly available there, but Thomastown people gradually acquired cars.
According to a 1981 survey,[15] two-thirds of households could drive

elsewhere to shop. Nevertheless, the town's shops appear to have retained their near monopoly. People in both town and country claimed to prefer local shops for most purposes: groceries, meats, hardware, appliances and clothes.

The history of the town's commercial sector after 1845, then, is an ironic success story. As living standards rose, the town's retailing sector expanded and, along with it, the town. Yet, this same process encouraged the consumption of non-local goods and caused local production to decline. This was associated with a world economy in which, until

> the end of the nineteenth century, . . . in spite of growing overseas competition . . ., the export opportunities of the more backward food and raw material producing countries of Europe were growing by leaps and bounds. All this . . . went hand in hand with...growing industrial exports to the markets of the periphery (Berend and Ranki 1982: 24-25).

Thomastown, at the periphery of Europe, was involved in this process. It exported people and primary goods and it imported consumables. Its increasing underdevelopment ensured its own reproduction.

Modernity and underdevelopment: a portrait from the 1980s

Economic conditions in Thomastown in the 1980s reflected clearly how modernity and underdevelopment co-existed as consumption and production increasingly diverged. Men's occupations in 1981, for example, exhibited a decided modernity: only 19 per cent in the DEDs of Thomastown and Jerpoint Church (containing the town and 9,500 acres) were in farming (54 farmers and 32 farm labourers). Instead, men were skilled (26 per cent), semi-skilled (11 per cent) or unskilled labourers (13 per cent), shopkeepers or businessmen (11 per cent), shop and clerical workers (8 per cent) and professionals or semi-professionals (12 per cent).

Educational levels too reflected modernity: all people under forty had some secondary education, the result of the vocational school built in the town in 1958. As well, about a quarter of the adults had tertiary education: apprenticeships, technical college and, occasionally, some university. In contrast, in 1911, about a quarter of the household heads enumerated could not sign their census forms.

Finally, living standards had risen dramatically. In Thomastown parish in 1981, average household size had declined to its lowest level: 3.7 people per house. Of the 507 households in the 1981 survey, virtually all had piped water, electricity and television. Nine out of ten had refrigerators: only a third had been bought before 1965. Half the households had washing machines and two-thirds had cars, but only since the 1960s. Between 1979 and 1981, sixty per cent of the households had holidayed away from home; half had left Ireland to do so.

Alongside these indices of modernity were those of underdevelopment: 21 per cent of the adult men in the two DEDs were either unemployed or retired, and over two-thirds of the adult women were homemakers. About a quarter of the working population was self-employed or, more accurately, underemployed. These were, apart from shopkeepers, people who tried to make a living using their particular skills in sales or the trades - as masons, electricians, plumbers, insurance agents, welders, carpenters or "handymen" in the case of men, or as seamstresses, hairdressers, cooks or domestics in the case of women. Others had accumulated enough capital to invest in lorries, taxis or farm equipment which they worked on short-term contracts.

Moreover, although the last flour mill closed in 1963, several town enterprises continued to absorb local labour. In 1981, apart from the state-run geriatric facility, eight enterprises each employed more than eight local people. However, the nature of these enterprises was a portrait of persisting underdevelopment: two of the eight were foreign-owned; virtually none manufactured anything; lateral spin-offs were very limited; and business histories were volatile. Thus, the two foreign factories assembled foreign-made components whilst a stud farm served an international clientele, a garage sold foreign cars, a supermarket retailed foreign foods and a heating firm installed foreign components. Only a bakery actually made bread; to do so, it used foreign flour. An abattoir, though, did process local livestock.

Lateral spin-offs from these enterprises, and others in the locality, had a late twentieth century familiarity: the vast majority of self-employed artisans in Thomastown did not make commodities but instead provided the transport, installation and maintenance services which allowed the consumption of foreign goods to continue. Also familiar was the volatility of most of the nine large enterprises: by 1989, one foreign firm was gone and the other was greatly reduced in size, as was the garage; the central heating firm and stud farm were bankrupt whilst the bakery had been bought by a Cork company. The supermarket and abattoir had expanded, however, as had the geriatric facility.

Meanwhile, class differences in the town persisted, reflected not only in space but also in the structure of local kinship networks, educational levels and consumption and emigration patterns (Silverman 1989; Gulliver and Silverman 1990: 610-614). Overall, the 1980s portrait of the town exhibited, simultaneously, persisting modernity and underdevelopment as a reflection of the European domination of a vibrant, peripheral town.

Conclusion: domination and historical ethnography

Countries of the periphery, it has been said, "all demonstrate problems of dualism, that have both historical and international roots." This dualism ostensibly occurs when a so-called modern sector, with high living standards, bureaucratic relations, etc., co-exists with an impoverished rural sector (Seers 1979: 3; Silverman 1979). However, in Thomastown, rural living standards had mirrored urban ones from early this century whilst, in any case, dualism and sectoral difference did not typify the locality. Instead, a number of other historical and structural features were key and these showed, clearly, that modernity and underdevelopment had long been mutually interdependent parts of a singular process of domination. They also showed the hierarchical organisation of that process, best illustrated perhaps by the town's changing relation to its surrounding countryside as the economies of each gradually became linked, not directly to each other, but to and through a higher order system. This was expressed in 1989 by a local farmer. "Thomastown is not a farmers' town," he said. "You don't feel welcome there. The hardware shops are concerned with builders' hardware, not farmers. ...It's also an attitude. Thomastown is not farmer-oriented. It has its own internal industries."

As part of this process of domination, class difference remained fundamental, visible in space and lifestyle. In this process, the town's political dependency was continually reproduced, as was the volatility of local productive enterprises, whether local or foreign-owned. In this process, labour remained the chief export, the economy failed to generate lateral growth and intervention from the state was ubiquitous and essential. In this process, by the late twentieth century, what was consumed was not produced, and what was produced, if at all, was sold elsewhere. All this reflected life in a periphery of Europe.

It has been argued by some, incorrectly I believe, that the period after 1961 in Ireland "marked a period of extensive social and economic change." First, according to that argument, the institutional basis of the "Irish economy was substantially altered by the augmented role of the state and the increased presence of foreign firms" (Pyle 1990: 18). Second, "Ireland changed as the proportion of employment in the agricultural sector fell and that in industry and services rose." Third, a "marked break with...the past" occurred as growth rates and manufactured exports grew, associated with the state's "export-led strategy, the influx of foreign direct investment" and membership in the EEC (Pyle 1990: 20-21).

However, this present ethnography of domination requires such conclusions to be amended, particularly in the light of its historical approach in the context of a particular locality. For, in Thomastown, the above-noted changes were neither "extensive" nor recent; they also did not constitute a "marked break." Rather, they were a continuation of an historical process of domination which was discernible in the mid-nineteenth century and which was rooted, in turn, in earlier colonial and capitalist relations. Shoulder pads and green peppers, in other words, were simply contemporary manifestations of such long-term domination and of the on-going reproduction of modernity and underdevelopment. In saying this, however, it is essential to recognise a central point: that domination - and the continuing reproduction of underdevelopment and modernity - is what had allowed the reproduction and persistence of the town itself. This, I argue, was because of the geographical and functional nature of core-periphery relations as they were manifested through time in the long-dominated, dynamic Southeast of Ireland.

What all this suggests, of course, is the simultaneous necessity and centrality of an historical approach when anthropologists "do ethnography." Such an approach not only deepens our understanding but, importantly, it addresses a question which has concerned anthropologists far more than it has other analysts: "How and why did the present come to be?" By addressing this question, either implicitly or explicitly, and by applying anthropological models, ideas and techniques to both the present *and* the past *simultaneously*, anthropologists are able to produce one kind of "historical ethnography."[16] That is, they produce analytical case studies which expand the conceptual horizons of social science itself, which go beyond the normal purview of social history, and which enhance our anthropological understandings of societies cross-culturally.

Notes

1. Field and archival research in Ireland and Thomastown was carried out by myself and P.H. Gulliver during a 14-month period in 1980-81 and for another 12 months, intermittently, during the summers of 1983, 1987, 1989 and 1992. Research was funded, at various times, by the Social Sciences and Humanities Research Council of Canada (SSHRC); the Wenner-Gren Foundation for Anthropological Research, and the Faculty of Arts, York University.
2. Numerous versions and revisions of so-called core-periphery or dependency theory exist. An excellent review is Blomstrom and Hettne (1984).
3. The descriptions were given by witnesses from Thomastown (gentry, farmers, shopkeepers, professionals) to an 1833 Parliamentary Inquiry (HC 1836).
4. *Ibid.*
5. *Ibid.*
6. It is not known when most of the buildings in the core streets were constructed. Pilsworth suggested that "a good deal of building" occurred about 1790 (1953: 26). This corresponded with the economic boom in the town as in Ireland. He also cited a "traveller, Atkinson, writing in 1815" who described the town "as being composed for the most part of tolerably good slated houses" (1953: 28). This probably referred to

the core streets and suggests that most of its buildings were extant by at least the late eighteenth century.

7. The changes to the core itself after 1845 were very minor: some improvements in amenities (lighting, heating, plumbing), the occasional amalgamation of adjacent buildings, the demolition of two, unsafe shops in the 1970s, the replacement of a shop destroyed by fire in the 1950s and the refurbishment of shop fronts. Outside the core, the distribution of shops remained virtually unchanged. In 1989, Mill Street still had its three pubs and the Quay had its pub but also a grocery built in 1950s. A small grocery had begun in 1947 on Maudlin Street and another, in the 1970s, on Ladywell.

8. Censuses of Ireland, 1841, 1851, etc. Emigration from Thomastown pre-dated 1841 (e.g. H.C. 1836). However, the 1841 census provides the first reliable statistics which can be compared with later periods.

9. The figures differed for men as compared with women, with the latter having higher illiteracy rates throughout.

10. These comprise the three "civil parishes" or census units of Ballylinch, Jerpointabbey and Pleberstown. They are not contiguous to the town but are all within Thomastown Catholic parish. They contain about 3,000 acres.

11. In the town in 1841, under seven per cent of the housing was fourth class and 36 per cent was third class.

12. These computations exclude 151 unmarried young men who enumerated themselves as "farmers' sons." This was because their adult occupations were yet to be established and, with the norm of impartible farm inheritance, only a small minority would ever become farmers in their own right. Most would emigrate and some, from the smaller farms, would become labourers.

13. Although "labourers' cottages" were built before 1926 by the Board of Guardians and Rural District Council, most state housing was built by the County Council after 1926.

14. This stability in shop numbers contrasts with a reported general increase in post-famine Ireland (Cullen 1972: 138). It is likely, though, that the increase occurred in the west and in cities. In southeastern Ireland, excluding large urban centres (e.g. Waterford and Kilkenny), Thomastown was not unusual. In the comparably sized towns of Graiguenamanagh and Callan, shop numbers were similarly stable (Gulliver and Silverman in preparation).

15. A survey of the 507 households (1,932 people) in the DEDs of Thomastown and Jerpoint Church was part of the research project (see note 1 above).

16. The idea of "historical ethnography" and its variations was elaborated in Silverman and Gulliver (1992).

References

Berend, I.T. and G. Ranki. 1982. *The European periphery and industrialization 1780-1914.* Cambridge: Cambridge University Press.

Blomstrom, M. and B. Hettne. 1984. *Development theory in transition.* London: Zed Books.

Chubb, B. 1970. *The government and politics of Ireland.* Oxford: Oxford University Press.

Cullen, L.M. 1972. *An economic history of Ireland since 1660*. London: B.T Batsford Ltd.

Donham, D.L. 1990. *History, power, ideology: Central issues in marxism and anthropology*. Cambridge: Cambridge University Press.

Giddens, A. 1979. *Central problems in social theory: Action, structure and contradiction in social analysis*. Berkeley: University of California Press.

Graham, B.J. 1977. The towns of medieval Ireland. In *The development of the Irish town* (ed.) R.A. Butlin. London: Croom Helm.

Gulliver, P.H. and M. Silverman. 1990. Social life and local meaning: "Thomastown," County Kilkenny. In *Kilkenny: History and society: Interdisciplinary essays on the history of an Irish county* (eds.) W. Nolan and K. Whelan. Dublin: Geography Publications.

_____. In preparation. *Merchants and shopkeepers: An historical anthropology of an Irish market town, 1200-1989*.

Halpin, T.B. 1989. A brief history of the brewing industry in Kilkenny. *Old Kilkenny Review* 4(1): 583-91.

Hechter, M. 1975. *Internal colonialism: The Celtic fringe in British national development, 1536-1966*. London: Routledge and Kegan Paul.

Larkin, E. 1972. The devotional revolution in Ireland: 1850-75. *American Historical Review* 77: 625-52.

Murtagh, B. 1982. *The fortified town houses of the English pale in the Later Middle Ages*. Unpublished M.A. thesis, Department of Archaeology, UCD.

O'Hanrahan, M. 1990. The tithe war in County Kilkenny 1830-1834. In *Kilkenny: History and society* (eds.) W. Nolan and K. Whelan. Dublin: Geography Publications.

Parliamentary Paper. *First report of commissioners for inquiring into the condition of the poorer classes in Ireland*. H.C. 1836, xxxi, xxxii and xxxiii.

Pilsworth, W.J. 1953. *History of Thomastown and district*. First edition. Kilkenny: Kilkenny Archaeological Society.

Pyle, J.L. 1990. *The state and women in the economy: Lessons from sex discrimination in the Republic of Ireland*. Albany: State University of New York.

Seers, D. 1979. The periphery of Europe. In *Underdeveloped Europe: Studies in core-periphery relations* (eds.) D. Seers, B. Schaffer and M-L. Kiljunen. New Jersey: Humanities Press.

Selwyn, P. 1979. Some thoughts on cores and peripheries. In *Underdeveloped Europe: Studies in core-periphery relations* (eds.) D. Seers, B. Schaffer and M-L. Kiljunen. New Jersey: Humanities Press.

Silverman, M. 1979. Dependency, mediation and class formation in rural Guyana. *American Ethnologist* 6(3): 466-90.

_____. 1989. A "labouring man's daughter": Constructing respectability in south Kilkenny. In *Ireland from below: Social change and local communities* (eds.) C. Curtin and T.M. Wilson. Galway: Galway University Press.

_____. 1990. The non-agricultural working class in 19th century Thomastown. *In the shadow of the steeple*, no. 2. Duchas: Tullaherin Heritage Society, pp. 86-104.

_____. 1992. From Kilkenny to the sea - by river, canal, tram or rail? The politics of transport in the early nineteenth century. *Old Kilkenny Review* 4(4): 988-1011.

Silverman, M. and P.H. Gulliver. 1986. *In the Valley of the Nore: A Social History of Thomastown, County Kilkenny, 1840-1983.* Dublin: Geography Publications.

_____. 1992. Historical anthropology and the ethnographic tradition: A personal, historical and intellectual account. In *Approaching the Past: Historical anthropology through Irish case studies* (eds.) M. Silverman and P.H. Gulliver. New York: Columbia University Press.

12 Urbanisation and the milieux of factory life: Gilford/Dunbarton, 1825-1914

Marilyn Cohen

Today, as in the past, the spread of industrial capitalism blurs the division between rural and urban as environmental space is restructured to meet the needs of expanding enterprises. Many urban anthropologists and sociologists agree that the city is not in itself theoretically significant in advanced capitalist societies, and that the core issue is the complex relationship between cities and the capitalist mode of production (Saunders 1981; Southall 1985: 6; Plotnicov 1985: 41; Susser 1982). However, debate continues over the degree to which urban anthropologists should maintain or relax disciplinary boundaries in their research. Plotnicov (1985: 43-52) argues that urban anthropologists should "maintain the distinctiveness of their field while not relinquishing the stimulation and instruction from other disciplines," while Susser (1982) calls for a fully interdisciplinary approach to the study of complex industrial society.

This chapter attempts an interdisciplinary historical ethnography of the urban community of Gilford/Dunbarton in County Down during the nineteenth century.[1] Silverman and Gulliver (1992: 16) define historical ethnography as "a description and analysis of a past era of the people of some particular, identifiable locality, using archival sources and, if relevant, local oral history sources." The specifically anthropological concern with locality, holism, and social change will be combined with the insights and methodologies of social historians and geographer David Harvey (1981; 1985a; 1985b). While anthropological approaches to Ireland's urban past have been few (Silverman and Gulliver 1992; 1986; Gulliver 1989; Cohen 1988; Cohen 1992a), anthropological approaches can contribute to an understanding of the differentiated nature of the urbanisation process, especially when analysing the complex intersections between change at the local level and global capitalist development.

Theoretically, in this chapter I will follow Southall's (1985:12) suggestion that urban anthropologists look to Marx's specification of a different relationship of city to society in each mode of production. Spatial forms in any society are closely linked to the overall mechanisms of its development. The production of the built environment in capitalist cities and towns is subsumed by the logic of accumulation (Harvey 1985a: xviii; 1985b: xii; 1981: 103; Gordon 1978: 28; Gottdiener 1987). This chapter will focus upon the relationship between small factory towns and the emergence of a capitalist linen industry in nineteenth century Ulster. It addresses the gap identified by Blumin (1983: 54) who argues that the neglect of smaller distinctively urban centres reduces our understanding of the complexity and diversity of the urbanisation process and urban social life.

Rural factory towns flourished in the early years of industrialisation in Ireland and Great Britain "when industrial discipline had to be imposed for the first time, and an industrial society created de novo in a rural landscape" (Joyce 1980: 146). The rapid advancement of the linen industry during this period nurtured the growth of several factory towns, which shared many characteristics of urbanism with larger towns and cities to which they were linked as part of Ulster's urban hierarchy. By the mid-nineteenth century, these local economies centred upon the linen industry were dependent upon industrial capitalism on a world scale.

I argue that factory towns in Ulster should be incorporated into a concept of urbanism as both an aspect of created environment and a way of life. Built by paternalistic employers, factory towns were artificial environments reflecting their owners' complex motivations. However, while much of the physical layout and social life were planned, many towns in east Ulster absorbed huge influxes of population during the Great Famine which greatly affected design, community structure and stability.

This case study will also explore how the convergence of several mid-Victorian socio-cultural patterns including dependency upon wages, deference, industrial paternalism, and self-help further determined the physical form of Gilford/Dunbarton, its social institutions, and the centrality of factory work. The pervasive paternal influence of the McMaster family, generated in their ownership of the large spinning mill Dunbar McMaster & Co., was felt at all levels of social life, creating a form of urbanism conceptualised by Joyce (1980) as "the culture of the factory."

The eighteenth century backdrop

Located in north-west County Down, the parish of Tullylish, in which the town of Gilford was located, formed part of the core linen triangle region in Ulster where fine linen cloth such as cambric, lawn, diaper and damask was woven. Some of the earliest bleach yards in Ulster were located along the ten mile stretch between Gilford in Tullylish and Banbridge in neighbouring

Seapatrick parish (Harris 1744: 94-106; Green 1963). By 1783, the number of bleach greens along the adjacent River Bann had grown to twenty, and by 1808, these were responsible for 67 per cent of the linen bleached in County Down (Crawford 1984: 103; Cohen 1990: 426).

The contribution of bleachers to the urbanisation process in Ulster has been less thoroughly investigated than that of drapers and landlords (Crawford 1981). Due to the time needed to bleach linen cloth, bleach greens were the first form of centralised industry in linen production. Bleachers were one of the earliest employers of wage labour, contributing to population settlements close to this source of employment. Also, as the eighteenth century progressed, more bleachers became involved in merchant activities, purchasing linens for their greens and accumulating profits both at the points of production and circulation (Crawford 1980: 116; Cohen 1990: 425-26). Finally, by the turn of the nineteenth century, powerful bleachers and drapers in the region close to Banbridge aggressively sought to overcome trade barriers and the competition posed by British mill-spun yarn by reorganising production through the putting out system.[2]

An urban experiment in a rural setting: Gilford/Dunbarton

The challenge posed by the wet spinning process in England, persuaded Irish entrepreneurs with capital (bleachers, manufacturers, cotton mill owners) to erect spinning mills or convert cotton mills to linen after 1825. Factory production of linen yarn was concentrated in the Lagan valley, Bann valley, Belfast and its hinterland. By 1850, thirty-three of sixty-eight spinning mills were situated in the Belfast region alone (Boyle 1977: 51). This region had ample sources of labour power, bleach greens, a well established system of distributing flax and semi-finished goods, and better banking and credit facilities than elsewhere in Ireland (Boyle 1977: 52).

Harvey (1985b: 12) argues that "money creates an enormous capacity to concentrate social power in space. These . . . can be put to work to realize massive but localised transformations of nature through the construction of built environments." Factory towns and hamlets along the Bann River in Tullylish such as Dunbarton, Civil Town, or Milltown were a solution to the distinct obstacles faced by capitalists attempting profitable industrial investment in rural locations during the early nineteenth century. Rural industrial capitalists needed to supply their mills and factories with adequate water power. They were also further from ports, warehouses, sources of credit, and needed to attract and control a labour force.

Gordon (1978: 40) suggests that labour control in particular was a dynamic factor. Factories were located on sites "which maximized their control over the process of production and minimized workers' resistance to that domination." Rural factory towns were ideal locations for realising these objectives, with built environments consisting minimally of houses, and, when coupled with humanitarian reform, branching out into urban experiments.

One of Ireland's earliest examples of such experiments was Dunbarton at Gilford. The growth of Gilford from a village to a town began during the 1830s. In 1824, Gilford was described as "a small post and fair town . . . famous for its bleachgrounds and manufacture of linen" (Pigot 1824: 386). By 1837, the industrialisation of Gilford was well underway with a growing population of 529 people, "a large spinning establishment, some extensive bleach greens, flour mills and chemical works all within a half mile proximity of the Newry canal" (Lewis 1837: 652). This large spinning establishment, Dunbar McMaster & Co., was completed in 1841 by local manufacturer Hugh Dunbar and his partners John W. McMaster and James Dickson. By 1846, it was one of Ireland's largest mills, employing 2000 workers.[3] Table 1 reveals the impact of this mill on the demography of Gilford. Between 1841-51, Gilford's population increased from 643 to 2814.

Table 1
Demographic Change in Gilford and Tullylish, 1831-1901

	1831	1841	1851	1861	1871	1881	1891	1901
Gilford	529	643	2814	2892	2720	1324	1276	1199
Males		300	1247	1253	1182	588	602	527
Females		343	1567	1639	1538	736	674	672
Inhab. Houses		104	333	452	502	286	288	271
Uninhab. Houses		7	21	26	57	44	25	51
People per house		6.2	8.4	6.4	5.4	4.0	4.4	4.4
Tullylish/								
Banbridge*		7049	7936	7594	6859	5285	4923	
Males		3383	3721	3563	3154	2439	2304	
Females		3661	4211	4031	3075	2846	2619	
Inhab. Houses		1232	1287	1446	1314	1110	1092	
People per house		5.7	6.2	--	--	4.8	4.5	
Tullylish/								
Lurgan*		5217	5116	4969	4295	3943	2980	
Males		2563	2531	2433	2090	1901	1450	
Females		2654	2582	2536	2205	2042	1530	
Inhab. Houses		897	914	981	852	844	673	
People per house		5.8	5.6	--	--	4.7	4.4	

Source: Cohen 1988: 307, 362.
*The parish of Tullylish was divided between Banbridge and Lurgan Poor Law Unions

To explain the extent of migration into Gilford, information about ecological characteristics at both ends of the migration stream, the nature of employment opportunities, housing stock, and the socio-economic composition of the population is required (Hershberg 1983: 437). From 1841-51, internal migration from the rural petty commodity producing townlands in northern Tullylish (included in Lurgan Poor Law Union) into settlements, such as Gilford/Dunbarton, along the River Bann was substantial. The impact of the Great Famine on these farmer/weavers was severe and many were proletarianised. Gilford's ecology was dominated by Dunbar McMaster & Co. which offered abundant employment opportunities, housing, and other amenities attracting many displaced weavers.

The link between the creation of social space and control over social relationships was well understood by paternalistic employers who built model communities (Harvey 1985a: 22-23). The provision of relatively cheap good-quality housing, and authority over the use of other aspects of social space in the effort "to reform the whole man," not only kept the cost of living down, but was a crucial means of reproducing power relations (Joyce 1980; Harvey 1985a: 50; Cohen 1992a). In the words of John Grubb Richardson (n.d.: 43), builder of the model factory town of Bessbrook in County Down, "The better the village's living standards the more contented were the people in home and factory, resulting in happier relationships between employer and employed."

The concentration of workers in factories, rather than dispersed in cottages, posed an immediate problem for those creating built environments: how to house workers in the right locations. Capitalists in Ulster and elsewhere initially sought to resolve this problem by building company-owned houses close to the factory gates (MacNeice 1981; Harvey 1985b: 22; Cohen 1992a). In the nineteenth century, the location of industry dominated the residential patterns of cities and towns and was a dynamic force shaping social relationships and life experiences (Hershberg 1983: 441; Lampard 1983: 33). In a time of limited and expensive transportation, nearly everyone needed to walk to work and lived within a mile of their employment. The location of other services such as shops, schools, churches and recreation was based on similar considerations.

Hugh Dunbar began building homes for his workforce almost immediately after leasing the necessary land. Until his death in 1847, Dunbar was the exclusive owner of the lands, mill buildings, and workers' houses. The land upon which Dunbar McMaster & Co. and the village of Dunbarton were to be built was separate from the older "Y" shaped village of Gilford. The mill itself was built on the low lying ground beside the river, and the land where the houses were built rose steeply upward from the mill gates. The earliest mill-owned houses were completed by the 1838 Valuation and arranged in terraces on the slopes above the mill. Among the earliest workers' houses owned by Dunbar were a group of terraces at Bridge Street at the base of the older part of Gilford. These homes close to the corn mill were in existence prior to the 1830s. Other early streets built by Dunbar were Ann

Street, consisting of seven houses directly up from the mill gates, and High
Street, consisting of fifty-two homes with eighteen of these back-to-back in
type. The other side of the back-to-back houses was known as Bann Street
facing the waste ground at the rear near the river. Finally, Hill Street was
built with narrower smaller homes (MacNeice 1981: 11-22).

Between 1836 and 1862, 200 houses were built at a cost of 10,000
pounds with average weekly rents at 2s. 3d.[4] During the 1860s, the firm
erected another terrace of houses at the foot of Hill Street called Sandy Row,
another three large terraces on Dunbarton Street in 1878, large terraces on
Main street in 1898, and a final six houses called New Row off Stramore
Road in 1901. After 1867, the sporadic building consisted mainly of
prestigious parlour housing which offered better accommodation (MacNeice
1981: 18-21, 23). By 1901, Dunbar McMaster & Co. owned 40.4 per cent of
the houses in Gilford/Dunbarton. All factory-owned houses were inspected
monthly by the firm owners, and annually lime washed, painted, and
repaired at the firm's expense.[5]

Dunbar's houses were more typical of urban terraces than rural cottages,
often without attached land and in some cases without rear access. About
half (51 per cent) of the total houses in Gilford/Dunbarton built by both the
mill owners and other speculative builders had no land attached for keeping
animals or growing vegetables. Mill-owned houses were less likely to have
land attached. Only 12.6 per cent of houses in Gilford/Dunbarton had
piggeries while somewhat more (19.7 per cent) had fowl houses. Factory
owned houses, such as on Hill Street, were more likely to have simple out
offices for animals such as hens. Houses owned by other landlords were
more likely to have both land and out offices such as on Castle Hill Street,
and Rutton's Row.

Dunbar and his successors, the McMasters, had a wider vision of
Dunbarton as a community which extended well beyond the provision of
workers' housing. In the mid-Victorian period, both religion and education
were central pillars in a hegemonic strategy to instil a harmony of interest
between labour and capital. To this end, Dunbar provided land rent free for
the Roman Catholic Church and the McMasters for the Church of Ireland,
Presbyterians and Methodists. Each Church had a sabbath school attached.
By 1867, the population of Gilford had grown to the point where it became a
separate parish carved out of Tullylish. The McMasters also contributed to
the cost of constructing the Church of Ireland's building in Gilford with the
parsonage erected at his expense (Bassett 1888: 263). Dunbar also built a
school which opened in 1846, consisting of three separate infant, male and
female classrooms. The cost to the firm of providing the three room school
house, teachers' salaries, heat, light, daily cleaning, repairs, annual painting
and lime washing was £104 per year (Cohen 1992a: 294). Before his death
in 1847, Dunbar built a Fever Hospital and Dispensary at the top of Hill

Street, consisting of two terrace houses under the supervision of the surgeon for the factory. Last, under the direction of the McMasters, Dunbarton included a cooperative society which offered food and clothing for sale to the workers. Participation was not obligatory and numerous other shops including grocers, fleshers, shoemakers, tailors, drapers, and blacksmiths were ready to do business with residents.

Even recreation and leisure activities were guided by the owners' commitment to progressive paternalism, self-improvement and self-help. A newsroom, library, and public lecture room were provided by the owners who contributed free rent, light and heating. A Young Men's Mutual Improvement Society was in active operation at which lectures and debates were delivered regularly by "leading and influential public men in the vicinity."[6] A Temperance Society was established and lectures were delivered to about eighteen per cent of the firm's employees. Cricket, boating, handball clubs, football clubs, and gymnastics were fostered. Finally, a penny bank was in existence since 1863 and a savings fund for workers since 1854 with McMaster allowing five per cent interest per annum on deposits.[7]

The mill owners also played a prominent role in the maintenance of the town under the Town Improvement Act (Ireland) of 1854, which set up a system of electing Town Commissioners. These Commissioners first met in 1858 with John W. McMaster J.P. in the Chair. Their responsibilities included keeping the town clean and lit, and setting rates to pay for these services. Lighting for the streets was provided by the Gilford Gas Co. owned by the McMasters. Town Commissioners continued to handle these responsibilities until 1893.[8]

Urbanism in Gilford/Dunbarton: social problems

While the paternalistic motivations of the factory owners created a relatively complex and stable community, Gilford shared with other Victorian textile towns a variety of urban problems including density, transience, sanitation, and work related health problems exacerbated by severe demographic upheaval. Although the owners of Dunbar McMaster & Co. continued to build houses throughout the period of rapid growth, they could not keep up with demand. By 1851, only a sufficient quantity of first class houses existed. In contrast, 466 families were pressing into 220 second class houses (which included most factory-owned houses); 122 families into 63 third class houses, and 49 families into 29 fourth class houses.[9] Transients and beggars were a feature of town life, as evidenced by the employment of a "scavenger" by the Gilford Town Commissioners who was responsible for removing them.[10]

Froggatt argues that it is impossible to separate the effects of industrialisation and urbanisation (Froggatt 1979: 157). In his study of byssinosis among linen textile operatives in Belfast, lungs that were damaged by inhaling flax fibres at work were worsened by squalid domestic conditions. Country mill operatives, such as those in Gilford/Dunbarton, fared better due to better quality air. However, small, cramped, overcrowded, and often poorly ventilated houses reduced this advantage. Further, health was negatively affected by discharging sewage into the Bann whose water was used for a number of domestic purposes.

Another urban problem shared by textile towns was a preponderance of females and young persons due to employment opportunities favouring these categories. Evidence suggests that in the 1860s, many single females migrated to Gilford/Dunbarton in search of work, resulting in attempts to deal with this problem by the paternalistic McMasters. Young single females "whose employment necessitates their leaving home" were "comfortably lodged with long resident and respectable families and placed under the immediate supervision of their respective clergy."[11]

In factory villages, the negative impact of an unbalanced sex ratio was intensified by the narrow employment base. Cities like Belfast with a more diversified labor market had proportionately fewer men employed in linen mills and factories than in Gilford/Dunbarton. Employment opportunities for females in Dunbar McMaster & Co. resulted in a higher proportion of female-headed households in Gilford/Dunbarton (31.3 per cent) than in Belfast (20 per cent) (Hepburn and Collins 1981: 216-217; Collins 1982: 4; Cohen 1992b: 306). Due to their smaller size and scarcity of resident males, female-headed households often faced poverty since females in all categories in the linen industry earned a maximum of 11 or 12 shillings per week in 1906 (about two thirds that of an unskilled labouring man). To cope with poverty, female-headed households lived in lower class houses, shared residences with other households, and relied more heavily on the wages of resident children resulting in fewer years in school and higher rates of illiteracy (Cohen 1992b: 307-12).

A third problem characteristic of urban life in Gilford/Dunbarton was residential segregation. In Belfast, "residential segregation was clearly a dominant feature of life" with a Dissimilarity Index of 65.7 (Taeuber and Taeuber 1972: 29-30; Hepburn and Collins 1981: 215).[12] In Tullylish, most of the Roman Catholic population lived either in Gilford/Dunbarton or in Lawrencetown. Gilford/Dunbarton was the only community large enough to have named streets, which allows for the calculation of a comparative statistic. The Dissimilarity Index for Gilford/Dunbarton was 46.6, a figure considerably lower than Belfast.

While this is not surprising in a small factory town composed of only eighteen streets, more fine-grained analysis reveals considerable variation in segregation from one street to another. Seven streets in Gilford/Dunbarton were entirely Catholic or Protestant, accounting for 8.0 per cent of Catholic households and 12.9 per cent of Protestant households. Catholic households were in the majority on only five streets. Sixty-one per cent of all Catholic households lived on these streets with 48.8 per cent living on Castle Hill Street in Gilford and Hill Street (Keady Row) in Dunbarton. Protestant households formed the majority on the remaining thirteen streets. On only five of these did the proportion of Catholic households approximate the proportion of Catholics (21.6 per cent) in the town.

Oral evidence sheds further light on differing perceptions of how religion structured residence patterns within Gilford/Dunbarton. For example, the existence of "little ghettos" was recognised by most Catholics interviewed. They named the two Catholic ghettos: Castle Hill Street and Hill Street (Keady Row), and stated further that it was difficult for Catholics to get a house on the "Main Row" (High Street) closer to the mill gates. Protestants, in contrast, tended to under-emphasize ghettos, stressing instead the closeness of community life in the past, summarised in the following way: "They would have lived more closely then they do now...there wasn't so much politics."[13]

One Protestant street, "Mechanics Row" in Dunbarton, directly reflected the relationship between religion and the local division of labour. Harvey (1985a: 109) has argued that the analysis of residential segregation needs to move beyond explanations which focus on preferences toward those specifying the necessary relationships between segregation and social structure. In this regard, census evidence suggests that social class and occupational status were more important variables than religion in determining the class of house in which one lived (except in first class houses where class and religion were interchangeable).

At the level of social structure, religion was an essential component in the composition of social classes and of strata within the working class. The small upper class of landowners, capitalists and professionals in Gilford/Dunbarton was exclusively Protestant. The middle class of shop owners was also predominantly Protestant with Catholics filling certain niches such as publicans. Among the working class, most of the highly skilled male occupations such as flax dressers, mechanics, and craftsmen were Protestants. Semi-skilled occupations and women's occupations reflected the proportions of both faiths in the community, and unskilled occupations such as labourers were predominantly Catholic. These strata within the working class were associated with differences in material strategies, with skilled workers better able to keep wives at home and children in school.

Urbanism in Gilford/Dunbarton: popular memory

Oral evidence relating to town life prior to World War I was obtained from fifteen residents of Gilford/Dunbarton in 1983-84.[14] What emerged was a picture dominated by work at Dunbar McMaster & Co and the long arm of influence extended by the McMaster family. Earning wages at the mill provided material resources for the household, structured household routine, determined the duration of children's schooling, and provided a setting for friendships and camaraderie among co-workers.

In Gilford/Dunbarton, the physical presence of the paternalistic McMasters and their imprint on the built environment was intensified by deep class divisions. During the "Linen Boom" of the 1860s, several of the owners of Dunbar McMaster & Company built large mansion houses for themselves in Gilford. This upper class of capitalists and property owners did not mix socially with the working class. Rather they lived above, physically and symbolically, often on a hill in a large mansion with substantial surrounding property, staffed with servants and other accoutrements of wealth and status. The deep social division between the upper and working class was mentioned by everyone I interviewed:

> yes that's where Mr. McMaster lived and he was lord of the manor, if you know what I mean . . . Everybody was bowing and scraping to him if they saw him coming. They just had to get their hats off immediately.[15]

Local upper class families formed a distinct subculture with gender divided activities characteristic of a rural gentry.[16] Owners would talk to and take a friendly interest in their workers' lives, and workers could turn to their employers in times of financial need for small loans. Nevertheless, a worker's experience of his/her factory owner was as a distinct gentleman. "He was always up high. You were just a poor thing."[17]

Within the rather rigid constraints generated by the workplace and low wages, a distinct working class culture evolved in Gilford/Dunbarton centred upon social relationships with kin, neighbours and co-workers. In small factory towns, the overlap between these groups was great and kinship served as a basis for obtaining employment, residential preferences, leisure activities and self-help efforts (Clarkson 1983: 156; Collins 1982: 3). The factory itself was the source of considerable social life which was divided along gender lines. Co-workers formed strong ties rooted in camaraderie which carried over into community life. Male co-workers frequently drank together after work at one of the local pubs. While women did not frequent pubs, single women would often take walks together on long summer evenings. Married women who did not work outside the home led more private domestic lives centred around visiting, church, and shops.

Working class activities which were non-sectarian often bore the imprint of factory work. One example was a local ten-member dramatic company which was composed mostly of working men and women who met to rehearse after hours. Another was dances which were held in various venues such as Catch-My-Pal Hall in Gilford. Originally a corn mill owned by the mill, it was turned into a hall by a temperance organisation where meetings, dances, and "wee concerts" were held in the winter months. Another dance was organised by spinning mill employees called the "spinners' ball." A former employee at Dunbar McMaster & Co. recalled how it began:

> I was on that committee. We formed that one time at work. These people was always saying like ach, we should run a dance . . . so we got in touch with the manager and the bosses and all and we asked them like could we get the hall? You see, the hall belonged to them. So then they said like what about us puttin' in and gettin' a band and we would run it as a spinners' and we done that yearly. You had a committee like, but then you hada make tea and the pastry and all. It was great fun.[18]

While residential segregation coupled with religious endogamy largely structured the formation of intragroup social networks along which services and to some extent resources were shared, the need for self-help among the working class, and close interaction among Catholics and Protestants at work and in the community resulted in a considerable degree of interdependence which often crossed religious lines. Although men were involved in these self-help networks, married women were at their core since they relied upon them daily to stretch tight budgets and meet their need for social interaction. The vernacular term used to describe such interdependence was "neigh-bourliness" and there was a broad consensus relating to its value. Nearly everyone agreed that neighbourliness was in part a strategy for coping with poverty and that it was stronger in the past due to the lack of state aid to the poor. A Protestant man emphasised the strength of this norm in the following way:

> Everybody was neighbourly. Nobody asked you any questions. You were a neighbour. You worked in the mill beside them. You were there beside them everyday in the week. You'd go home at night, you were mixin' with 'em and all the rest of that. Lived together, worked together, helped each other. If there was any trouble with your Roman Catholic friends next door you were in just the same as the other side, the Roman Catholic, was in to you. Would sit up with you all night if you were ill or anything.[19]

Conclusion

Silverman and Gulliver (1992: 22) argue that anthropologists analyse localities comprehensively, yielding "expertise in the problem at a manageable and contextualized local level." However, the boundaries of the locality remain "permeable," forming "a context within which 'big' sociological and cultural problems can be investigated" (Silverman and Gulliver 1992: 23-26). In this chapter, the value of this anthropological focus was explored. Gilford/Dunbarton was approached holistically, including where possible the voices of real people, to explore the intersections between capitalism, social class, cultural hegemony, and a specific urban form: factory towns.

Problems related to urbanisation and urbanism in Gilford/Dunbarton cannot be isolated from "big" questions related to the social organisation of work under capitalism. Production in any community is intimately connected with a variety of structures, both physical and social, which shape its organisation and meaning (Joyce 1987: 2). In rural factory towns such as Gilford/Dunbarton, the links between the imperatives of factory work, the organisation of social life, and the logic of accumulation were quite transparent since the total built environment bore the controlling imprint of the paternalistic mill owners. The influence of the McMaster family was as much about deference and cultural hegemony as benevolence; the owners attempted to promote class harmony through meeting workers' material, spiritual, and recreational needs while encouraging the growing value placed upon independence among the working class. Thus, factory culture in Gilford/Dunbarton was successful to the extent that it pervaded "quotidian life" in its totality (Joyce 1980: 192).

The centrality of capital accumulation compromised even the most humane intentions, especially in circumstances where the social dislocation associated with primitive accumulation was compounded by the Great Famine. Under these extreme circumstances, dependence upon wage labour caused enormous internal migration into many industrialising regions in east Ulster. Small factory towns dominated by large mills, exemplified by Gilford/Dunbarton, bulged at the seams, causing a number of social problems characteristic of Victorian textile towns generally.

Gilford/Dunbarton was characteristic of Ulster towns with economies solely based upon the linen industry. Once the years of expansion were over, there was not enough economic diversification to sustain continued growth. In the 1880s, many Gilford residents emigrated to Greenwich, New York, to work in the newly opened Dunbarton Mill. After Dunbar McMaster & Co. joined the Linen Thread Combine at the turn of the century, the era of factory culture ended in Gilford. While World War I provided a temporary lift, most of the factories and mills along the Bann in Tullylish closed their doors soon after the end of World War II. A disappearing economic base resulted in a familiar pattern of out-migration with migrants contributing to the urbanisation of larger, more economically diverse towns and cities in Ireland such as Portadown, Belfast or those overseas.

Notes

This research received support from the Joint Committee on the International Doctoral Research Fellowship Program for Western Europe of the Social Science Research Council, the Board of Foreign Scholarships under the Fulbright-Hays Act, and the Wenner Gren Foundation for Anthropological Research. I acknowledge this support with thanks, and also thank the residents of Tullylish who graciously gave of their time.
1. The methodology employed in this chapter is typical of historical ethnography (Silverman and Gulliver 1992: 16). I combined a variety of archival sources including British Parliamentary Papers, the 1901 Census Enumerator's Schedules for the parish of Tullylish, the Census of Ireland 1841-1901, the Minutes of the Meetings of Gilford's Town Commissioners, and oral histories conducted with thirty-five elderly residents of Tullylish during July and September of 1983.
2. S. Lewis, A Topographical Dictionary of Ireland (1837: 177); Report from the Select Committee on the Linen Trade of Ireland, Vol. 5 (1825:. 104); Reports of Assistant Commissioners on Handloom Weavers, Industrial Revolution: Textiles, IUP ser., Vol. 9 (1839-40: 659).
3. Reports by Inspectors of Factories, IUP ser., Industrial Revolution: Factories, Vol. 7, 1842-47, Report by James Stewart, p. 24.
4. Reports from Commissioners, Paris Universal Exhibition, Vol. 20, Part III (1867-68: 60-61).
5. Paris Universal Exhibition (1867-8: 60-63).
6. Paris Universal Exhibition (1867-8: 65).
7. Paris Universal Exhibition (1867-8: 65-69, 83, 87-92).
8. Public Record Office of Northern Ireland (P.R.O.N.I.) D.2714/3A, Minutes of Meeting of Ratepayers, Gilford Town Commissioners, 1859-1915.
9. (P.R.O.N.I.), 1851 Census of Ireland.
10. (P.R.O.N.I.), D.2714/3A, Minutes of Meeting of Ratepayers, Gilford Town Commissioners, 1859-1915.
11. Paris Universal Exhibition (1867-8: 28, 47).
12. The Dissimilarity Index is a measure of residential segregation. Its use in this context expresses the percentage of Catholic households in Gilford/Dunbarton that would have to shift from one street to another to effect an even or unsegregated distribution. The higher the value the higher the degree of residential segregation.
13. Oral interviews, Catholic male resident of Gilford, July, 1983; Protestant female resident of Gilford, July, 1983.
14. The oral histories covered a wide range of topics including working conditions in the various mills and factories, family strategies, gender roles, women-centered networks, self-help, schooling, and leisure activities. While my main focus was work-

ing class individuals, one middle class shopkeeper and two factory owners were also interviewed.

15. Oral interview, Protestant female, former reeler and resident of Gilford, July, 1983.
16. Oral interview, Protestant male, former bleach green owner and resident of Halls Mill, July, 1983.
17. Oral interview, Protestant female, former reeler and resident of Gilford, July, 1983.
18. Oral interview, Protestant female, former spinner and hemstitcher, resident of Banford, July, 1983.
19. Oral interview, Protestant male, former flaxdresser and resident of Gilford, July, 1983.

References - Primary Sources

Census of Ireland, 1841-1901 (Public Record Office of Northern Ireland).
D.2714/3A Minutes of the Meeting of Ratepayers, Gilford Town Commissioners, 1859-1915 (Public Record Office of Northern Ireland).
1901 Census Enumerators' Schedules for Gilford Town (Public Record Office of Ireland).
Report from the Select Committee on the Linen Trade of Ireland. Vol. 5, 1825.
Reports of Assistant Commissioners on Handloom Weavers. Industrial Revolution: Textiles. I.U.P. ser., Vol. 9, 1839-40.
Reports from Commissioners, Paris Universal Exhibition. Vol. 20, Part III, 1867-68.
Reports by Inspectors of Factories. Industrial Revolution: Factories. I.U.P. ser., Vol. 7, 1842-47.

References - Secondary Sources

Bassett, G.H. 1888. *The Book of County Armagh.* Dublin: Sealy, Bryer and Walker.
Blumin, S.M. 1983. When Villages Become Towns. In *The Pursuit of Urban History.* (eds.) D. Fraser and A. Sutcliffe. London: Edward Arnold.
Boyle, E.J. 1977. *The Economic Development of the Irish Linen Industry, 1825-1914.* Ph.D. dissertation, The Queen's University of Belfast.
Clarkson, L. 1983. The City and the Country. In *Belfast: The Making of the City.* Appletree Press.
Cohen, M. 1988. *Proietarianization and Family Strategies in the Parish of Tullylish, County Down, Ireland, 1690-1914.* Ph.D. dissertation, The New School for Social Research.
_____. 1990. Peasant Differentiation and Proto-industrialisation in the Ulster Countryside, 1690-1824. *Journal of Peasant Studies.* 17(3): 413-32.
_____. 1992a. Paternalism and Poverty: Contradictions in the Schooling of Working Class Children in Tullylish, 1825-1914. *History of Education.* 21(3): 291-306.
_____. 1992b. Survival Strategies in Female-Headed Households: Linen Industry Workers in Tullylish, County Down, 1901. *Journal of Family History.* 17(3): 303-18.

Collins, B. 1982. Families in Edwardian Belfast. Unpublished paper presented to the Urban History Group of the Economic History Society annual meeting, University of Aberdeen.

Crawford, W.H. 1980. Drapers and Bleachers in the Early Ulster Linen Industry. In *Negoce et Industrie en France et en Irlande aux XVIIIe et XIXe Siècles*. (eds.) L.M. Cullen and P. Butel. Paris: Center National de la Recherche Scientifique.

_____. 1981. The Evolution of Ulster Towns. In *Plantation to Partition: Essays in Honour of J. L. McCracken*. (ed.) P. Roebuck. Belfast: Blackstaff Press.

_____. 1984. *Economy and Society in Eighteenth Century Ulster*. Ph.D. dissertation, The Queen's University of Belfast.

Froggatt, P. 1979. Industrialisation and Health in Belfast in the Early Nineteenth Century. In *The Town in Ireland*. (eds.) M. O'Dowd and D. Harkness. Belfast: Appletree Press.

Gordon, D. 1978. Capitalist Development and the History of American Cities. In *Marxism and the Metropolis*. (eds.) W.K. Tabb and L. Sawers. New York: Oxford University Press.

Gottdiener, M. 1987. Space as a Force of Production: Contribution to the Debate on Realism, Capitalism and Space. *International Journal of Urban and Regional Research*. 11(3): 405-16.

Green, E.R.R. 1963. *The Industrial Archaeology of County Down*. Belfast: H.M.S.O.

Gulliver, P.H. 1989. Doing Anthropological Research in Rural Ireland: Methods and Sources for Linking the Past and the Present. In *Ireland From Below*. (eds.) C. Curtin and T.M. Wilson. Galway: Galway University Press.

Harris, W. 1744. *The Ancient and Present State of the County of Down*. Dublin: Edward Exshaw at the Bible on Corkhill.

Harvey, D. 1981. The Urban Process Under Capitalism: A Framework for Analysis. In *Urbanization and Urban Planning in Capitalist Society*. (eds.) M. Dear and A.J. Scott. London: Methuen Inc.

_____. 1985a. *The Urbanization of Capital*. Baltimore: Johns Hopkins University Press.

_____. 1985b. *Consciousness and the Urban Experience*. Baltimore: Johns Hopkins University Press.

Hepburn, A.C. and B. Collins. 1981. The Structure of Belfast, 1901. In *Plantation to Partition: Essays in Honour of J.L. McCracken*. (ed.) P. Roebuck. Belfast: Blackstaff Press.

Hershberg, T. 1983. The Future of Urban History. In *The Pursuit of Urban History*. (eds.) D. Fraser and A. Sutcliffe. London: Edward Arnold.

Joyce, P. 1980. *Work, Society and Politics*. New Brunswick: Rutgers University Press.

_____. 1987. The Historical Meanings of Work: An Introduction. In *The Historical Meanings of Work*. (ed.) P. Joyce. Cambridge: Cambridge University Press.

Lampard, E. E. 1983. The Nature of Urbanization. In *The Pursuit of Urban History*. (eds.) D. Fraser and A. Sutcliffe. London: Edward Arnold.

Lewis, S. A. 1837. *A Topographical Dictionary of Ireland*. London: S. Lewis & Co.

MacNeice, D.S. 1981. Industrial Villages of Ulster: 1800-1900. In *Plantation to Partition: Essays in Honour of J. L. McCracken* (ed.) P. Roebuck. Belfast: Blackstaff Press.

Pigot, J. 1824. *Pigot's Provincial Directory*. London: J. Pigot & Co.

Plotnicov, L. 1985. Back to Basics, Forward to Fundamentals: The Search for Urban Anthropology's Mission. In *City and Society*. A. Southall, P.J.M. Nas, and G. Ansari (eds.). Leiden: Leiden Developmental Studies No. 7.

Richardson, J. N. Sons, and Owden, Ltd. n.d. *Bessbrook: A Record of Industry in a Northern Ireland Village Community and a Social Experiment, 1845-1945*. Belfast.

Saunders, P. 1981. *Social Theory and the Urban Question*. New York: Holmes & Meier Publishers, Inc.

Silverman, M. and P.H. Gulliver. 1986. *In the Valley of the Nore*. Dublin: Geography Publications.

_____. 1992. Historical Anthropology and the Ethnographic Tradition: A Personal, Historical, and Intellectual Account. In *Approaching the Past*. M. Silverman and P.H. Gulliver (eds.) New York: Columbia University Press.

Southall, A. 1985. Introduction. In *City and Society*. (eds.) A. Southall, P.M.J. Nas, G. Ansari. London: Institute of Cultural and Social Studies.

Susser, I. 1982. Urban Anthropology in the U.S.A. *Royal Anthropological Institute News*. 52: 6-8.

Taeuber, T. and A.F. Taeuber. 1972. *Negroes in Cities: Residential Segregation and Neighborhood Change*. New York: Atheneum.

13 Beyond ethnography: primary data sources in the urban anthropology of Northern Ireland

Richard Jenkins

The implicit offer which I make in this chapter's subtitle of a characteristically anthropological perspective on urban life prompts a question. What distinguishes urban anthropology from, say, urban geography or sociology, its most obvious academic and intellectual rivals? One plausible answer might be to point to social anthropology's reliance upon long-term participant observation. The anthropologist's immersion in daily life is the discipline's principal source of data and the basis for its distinctive epistemological claims (Holy 1984). It is also an initiatory *rite de passage*. For most social anthropologists, whether they work in urban settings or in more traditionally anthropological village locations, ethnographic data, collected largely during face-to-face interaction in the community which is the subject of the research, is the bedrock of the disciplinary enterprise. Certainly, urban anthropologists see themselves, and are seen by others, very much as ethnographers, "urbanologists with a particular set of tools" (Hannerz 1980: 4).

I do not want to suggest that this should change (or, at least, not change very much). Collecting and writing ethnography is too valuable a research strategy to abandon or devalue, no matter the context, and its place at the heart of social anthropological research practice is secure. Participant observation does, however, have some limitations as a research approach - it may be asking too much to describe it as a method - which become particularly apparent in the course of urban fieldwork. *Inter alia*, these are: the uneven access which one has, as a researcher, to a range of areas of community life which are private or semi-private; the complexity and scale of urban life in a modern, industrial society, which render anything other than limited and partial empirical coverage an unrealistic objective; the capacity of the (relatively) powerful to hinder one's attempts to examine their lives;

and the ubiquity of more or less severe social conflict in many urban situations, which places particular strains on participant observation. I have discussed these problems elsewhere, in the course of reflecting upon the experience of fieldwork in Belfast (Jenkins 1984: 157-161), and I will not dwell further on them here.

Rather than emphasise differences of method as a boundary criterion for the discipline, I want to suggest here that social anthropology is, perhaps more than anything else, a constellation of specific interests: kinship and the family, religion and symbolism and social identity, all set within a context of local-level daily life. These, in turn, have led to the development of a distinctive body of theoretical frameworks and concerns. To return to Hannerz's characterisation of urban anthropology, the tools which I want to emphasise are concepts rather than methods. If anthropology is not to restrict itself in urban research to an unacceptably narrow range of situations within which its interests are approachable - something which may be unavoidable if participant observation remains the sole or primary research strategy - then kinds of data other than face-to-face ethnography may, on occasions, need to be brought into the foreground of the enterprise. Rather than, as is typically the case at the moment, drawing upon archival or documentary sources to provide supporting or background material for the "real" data of conventional ethnography, anthropologists should be more ready to consider these sources as their main or primary datum when circumstances require or permit.

First-hand ethnography might in such a situation provide, at best, contextual information, interpretive support or apt illustration, a hierarchy of relevance which is, perhaps, to turn the anthropological world upside down. To further underline this (admittedly mild) subversion, I think it can also be suggested that, although the inadequacies of participant observation are, for the reasons suggested above, at their most visible in urban settings, many of the approach's limitations are apparent in rural research as well. The nature and viability of the trade-off between the epistemological authority of ethnography, and its limited horizons and scope, ought, therefore, to be considered, whatever the context.

And there is a further point to make: over and above the limitations of participant observation which have already been mentioned, some situations or subjects are, with the best will in the world and regardless of the urban or rural nature of the work, not amenable to ethnographic research via "traditional" fieldwork. They are, however, distinctively anthropological or, to put it better perhaps, well within the range of interests which anthropology recognises as its own. For the purposes of this chapter I have in mind three kinds of social situation, although one could doubtless think of others.

First, there is the *dangerous*, a category which, on the face of things, speaks for itself. Of course, many anthropologists have undertaken field research in difficult circumstances. It can be argued that much anthropological fieldwork is inherently more dangerous than other forms of social science research (and this may be part of its romantic allure). However, I am talking about a more specific category of threat. Some topics are intrinsically more dangerous than others, whether because of the risk of a stray bullet - - real or metaphorical - - or the possibility of more personally-focused violence. Constraints of personal safety may limit the kinds of questions which may be asked or the subjects which may be investigated. It may not be sensible to participate in or observe some situations at all.

Second, there are *extraordinary* events, which do not routinely arise in the context of the daily life of any community. Extraordinary happenings - - the various "moving Virgins" which manifest themselves in Ireland during the 1980s (Ryan and Kirakowski 1985; Tóibín 1985) are a good example - - are only likely to be accessible to ethnographic research either as a consequence of extreme serendipity, or *ex post facto*.

Third, there is the *non-local*: events or social phenomena which might be common or routine enough within a particular context, but not easily approachable or properly understandable within a strictly local setting. A suitable example here might be regional or national "moral panics" (Cohen 1972), such as African witch-cleansing movements (Marwick 1982; Richards 1982; Willis 1982) or the current anxieties in the United States, the United Kingdom and elsewhere concerning the sexual abuse of children (Howitt 1992; Jenkins, P. 1992; La Fontaine 1990).

At this point, the suggestion that I am reinventing the wheel might be thought to have some merit. A diversity of methods in social anthropology is, of course, nothing new. For many researchers, participant observation and ethnography have always taken their appropriate place alongside other data-gathering approaches and other kinds of data (Epstein 1967; Pelto and Pelto 1978). However, ethnography in the Malinowskian tradition continues to be accorded pre-eminence. Although methodological and epistemological pluralism has made some inroads into the anthropological collective consciousness, there is still a long way to go before the discipline embraces a range of methods as broad as that which, for example, characterises sociology.

Nevertheless, it would be misleading to suggest that anthropologists in Ireland (and, indeed, elsewhere) have never used data from documentary sources. Examples such as the Thomastown research of Silverman and Gulliver (1986), Harris's study of Rathlin (1974), Vincent's work in Fermanagh (1989) and the recent collection edited by Silverman and Gulliver (1992) are not to be ignored. However, in these cases the authors are either writing an anthropological analogue of local history, or are concerned to construct an account of the here-and-now which is firmly located within a historical perspective (see Gulliver 1989). Historical anthropology or anthropological history is a useful and worthwhile enterprise, increasingly established as a specialism in its own right. But it remains a specialism - and a fairly unusual one at that - that is something rather different to the use of documentary evidence which I am advocating.

To reiterate, I am proposing two arguments for the anthropological use of documentary sources as primary, rather than secondary, data. First, since participant observation is particularly constrained in its scope in urban contexts, documentary research is a useful alternative of which more use could be made by anthropologists. Second, there are certain kinds of subject - the dangerous, the extraordinary and the non-local, for example - which may frustrate or defy participant observation. In cases such as these, documentary sources are likely to prove indispensable if research is to be undertaken at all.

In order to clarify and support these arguments I will now describe briefly two such cases, each deriving from urban Northern Ireland in the early 1970s. The first illustrates the general limitations of urban participant observation and the particular constraints imposed by danger. The second, which does not focus upon a peculiarly urban topic (although most of the material comes from small-town Northern Ireland), is an example of the extraordinary and the non-local.

The local genesis of paramilitary organisations in Belfast

The Northern Irish "troubles" have been the subject of a great deal of attention from social scientists. Some of these have been social anthropologists. Until relatively recently the anthropological tradition in Northern Ireland has tended to concentrate, however, on the countryside and small towns of the six counties, emphasising the persistence of relatively harmonious local social life in the face of violence, conflict and the sectarian divide (Buckley 1982, 1984; Bufwack 1982; Glassie 1982; Harris 1972; Larsen 1982a, 1982b; Leyton 1975).[1] In part, this emphasis reflects the continuing, albeit somewhat weakened, persistence of a view of the social world as basically benign which derives, on the one hand, from anthropology's romantic streak and, on the other, from Radcliffe-Brown's structural-functionalism. In part, however, it must also be recognised as an accurate reflection of the relative "normality" - and I am aware of the problematic status of this notion - of most of the Province, most of the time. It may also be due in some measure to the location and timing of the fieldwork in question. More recent field studies, particularly in border areas - "bandit country" - might suggest a less peaceful reality (e.g. Hamilton et al. 1990; Vincent 1989).

There are only a few studies by anthropologists of urban politics or violence in Northern Ireland (Feldman 1991; Jenkins 1982; Sluka 1989), although anthropology does offer urban studies of unemployment and the labour market (Howe 1990; Jenkins 1983) and sociologists have produced some good ethnographies (Bell 1990; Brewer and Magee 1991; Burton 1978; Gillespie et al., 1992). Although there are two useful books about militant loyalism (Bruce 1992; Nelson 1984) neither claims to be ethnographic. The characteristic and interesting features of the books by Feldman and Sluka - referred to above and focusing upon nothing other than political violence - are (1) the superficiality or "thin-ness" of the ethnography in Sluka's case, or its problematic status as evidence in Feldman's, and (2) their focus upon the normative or cultural world of attitudes and discourse - practices and events in historical time and space are largely overlooked.[2] Much the same could be said for Burton's earlier study of support for the IRA in a north Belfast Republican enclave. These comments, particularly with respect to Burton and Sluka, should not, however, be read as damning criticism: in both cases I believe the authors' arguments and conclusions to be essentially correct with respect to the shifting and conditional nature of communal support for Republican paramilitary violence. However, if my comments are justified, they raise the linked issues of the constraints upon what it is possible to learn about a dangerous topic such as political violence from participant-observer fieldwork, and the kind of evidence to which one is in general limited by adopting this approach in urban research.

To look at the first of these issues, the works of Burton, Feldman and Sluka seem to suggest that face-to-face ethnographic research limits the researcher who is interested in political violence to looking at what people say about it: i.e., attitudes and discourse. Unless the researcher is in the right place at the right time, and needless to say many researchers, in a case such as this, might not want to be, anything else is unlikely. Oral history of a kind is possible - and here an example might be Billy's tale from my own research (Jenkins 1982: 77-86) - but there are problems with this kind of material: faulty memory, the role of "story-telling", etc. (Thompson 1978: 91-37; Vansina 1965: 40-46, 76-113). It certainly cannot be used on its own as a record of "what happened"; even when triangulated against other kinds of data, its status as evidence about anything other than the cultural or normative sphere remains problematic. At best, informants may be able to offer reliable data about their own histories.

An important consideration which is likely to constrain informants is simply the wish to avoid self-incrimination or the incrimination of others. Further, important ethical issues aside, as Polsky once remarked in a discussion of sociological field research looking at crime or deviance:

> most of the danger for the field worker comes not from the cannibals and
> head-hunters but from the colonial officials. The criminologist studying
> uncaught criminals in the open finds sooner or later that law enforcers try to
> put him on the spot (Polsky 1971: 145).

This point holds good in every respect for the study of political violence in
Northern Ireland (see also, Sluka 1990). The researcher is limited in terms
of what people are prepared to divulge, on the one hand, and what it is
sensible to know, on the other.

These problems are also connected to the second issue, the sort of
evidence which urban participant observation produces. This is typically of
two kinds: first, statements and utterances, whether these be gathered in
interviews or in a less structured fashion, and second, other items of
behaviour, as observed and recorded by the fieldworker. These can both
produce accurately "factual" data about events, but they are likely to do so in
an even more uneven and limited fashion than, say, in a small rural
community. Insofar as the anthropological tradition emphasises the
epistemological authority of the eye witness, all other sources of data are
treated, generally, as of secondary importance. In the case of urban political
violence, these "other" kinds of data must become more central to the
research enterprise if social anthropology is to expand the scope of its interest
beyond the kinds of studies which have so far been undertaken.

At this point, it may perhaps be helpful to look at a concrete example.
Northern Irish paramilitary organisations did not appear overnight and, in
their present forms, they are the historical products of complex processes of
development. The loyalist paramilitary organisations with which I am
concerned here have their immediate roots in the local politics of particular
ethnic enclaves in the greater Belfast area during the late 1960s and early
1970s. Local politics are, of course, something about which social
anthropology has had much to say (e.g. Bailey 1969; Swartz 1969). There
are, what is more, specific examples of anthropological analyses of violent
politics at the local level which may shed useful light on the genesis of
paramilitary organisations within urban Northern Irish communities: in
particular, there are studies of the development of the Sicilian mafia (e.g.
Blok 1974; Schneider and Schneider 1986)[3] and of the institution of
caciquismo in central America (e.g. Friedrich 1965, 1969). Each of these
examples provides us with an analysis of a situation in which: (a) the nation
state fails in its modernising task of securing the monopolisation of violence,
and (b) local-level informal responses to the resultant social control vacuum
become, after a fashion, institutionalised into (violent) political
organisations. In both respects, the parallels with Northern Ireland are
obvious.

The details of such an analysis belong, however, in another paper. What
is important here is the recognition of the topic as appropriately

anthropological.[4] How might the interested anthropologist proceed, then, to investigate the local formation and subsequent development of paramilitary political organisations? Let us take my own case, and look at "Ballyhightown", a large, Protestant, public housing estate on the northern fringes of the Belfast urban area (Jenkins 1982, 1983). I undertook fieldwork there, as a community worker and as a postgraduate student, for 22 months between 1976 and 1979, the avowed research topic being youth unemployment and the transition to adulthood, the linked experiences of "growing up" and "coming of age" (with due apologies to Margaret Mead).

As is often the way with social anthropological fieldwork, the avowed topic was not all that I became interested in. Paramilitary politics were impossible to ignore, for four reasons. First, some of the young people I was studying were "involved", or had been in the past. Second, the loyalist paramilitary organisations existing in Ballyhightown were visibly active and hard to overlook as an aspect of the wider social context which provided the study with its backdrop. Third, in as much as the experience of field research was for me, as for many others, personally transformative, coming to terms with violence and, most particularly, Protestant violence - given that I grew up a Protestant in Northern Ireland - was imperative. Finally, as an undergraduate I had acquired an interest in local level politics and political violence and was, hence, sensitised to the topic. As a result, while my central interest remained the transition to adulthood, I also collected data about the period in the early nineteen-seventies when the "troubles" first really impinged upon the estate - between 1970 and 1973 the population of Ballyhightown changed from 40 per cent Catholic to effectively 100 per cent Protestant and the area acquired a reputation for intimidation and violence which it had yet to lose by the late 'seventies - and the local development of paramilitary organisations, particularly the (at that time legal) Ulster Defence Association (UDA).

What kind of data did I collect? In the first place, my field notes are full of small items which are relevant to the subject of "paramilitaries". Most of this material, however, relates either to events which were current at the time of the fieldwork, or to attitudes towards the UDA or the (illegal) Ulster Volunteer Force (UVF), and most of it does not come from members of either organisation. Some of it does, however, and some of it relates to recent local history. Some of the autobiographies I collected, whether oral or written, are also of relevance in this respect. A second source of data was a few highly focused conversations/interviews, with members or ex-members of paramilitary organisations, journalists, community activists etc. This is the point at which problems begin to arise with respect to the material's delicacy and confidentiality. I shall return to these issues below. For the moment, suffice it to say that this delicacy was usually recognised by the interviewee as well as by me, and sensible limits to what could and should be discussed were negotiated. Without these limits the material would simply not be usable at all.

The question now arises of the source of the focus in the interviews: how did I know which questions to ask? My basic "factual" knowledge of what had happened derived from four sources. First, there were the official or other reports about intimidation in housing in Belfast which discussed Ballyhightown (e.g. Darby and Morris 1974). Second, I combed the incomparable collection of printed ephemera concerned with the "troubles" (mainly paramilitary and community organisation publications) which has been assembled by Belfast's Linenhall Library, for references to the estate and its environs.[5] Third, I systematically went through the encyclopaedic chronology of events related to the "troubles" compiled by Deutsch and Magowan for the years 1970-74 (Deutsch and Magowan 1973-75). Fourth, I collected references to the area in other books about the "troubles" by journalists, politicians and academics.

These sources provided a useful baseline. Of the four sources, the Linenhall Library collection deserves a special mention. In particular, the *WDA News* (published by the Woodvale Defence Association), the *Loyalist News,* and the *UDA News* (initially published as *UDA*) provide a fascinating, if not always easily interpretable, window on the social climate within loyalist communities during the dark years of the early 1970s. There are many references to Ballyhightown and the surrounding area in these publications. As the voice, albeit perhaps a distorted and distorting voice, of loyalists themselves they are especially valuable. They are also a much under-used research resource.

In addition, the importance of newspapers cannot be underestimated. Both local newspapers and the Belfast dailies are a mine of information about urban communities. So far, I have in this context only used them for the period in question via the scrapbooks of a friendly local journalist. A more systematic piece of research would involve submitting the Belfast Central Library's superb newspaper collection to the same thorough treatment which I gave the Linenhall Library archive. Even the limited resource of the scrapbooks, however provided a large amount of material.

There is, of course, a fairly obvious problem with newspapers as sources: they are written by journalists who, as individuals and as an occupational community, have their own variable agendas, standards and degrees of competence and honesty, and who are working under a set of legal, commercial and proprietorial constraints. This necessitates that what one reads in newspapers should be treated with caution (much the same as the anthropologist must exercise care in the interpretation and authorisation of the testimony of any informant).

Allowing for considerations of this kind, the point remains that, in any analysis of the rise of the "Ballyhightown Defence Association" (and its subsequent incorporation into the UDA, together with other local Defence Associations in the Belfast area) printed material, of one kind or another, would necessarily take precedence as research evidence. This is so for three major reasons.

First, there are the problems which are generally associated with retrospective research of any kind. Memory is a tricky and unpredictable repository of information: some things are remembered accurately, some half-remembered, some forgotten, others are embroidered and, in other cases, a narrative is constructed which is more about the justification or rationalisation of a present state of affairs than anything else. To use Bourdieu's terminology, retrospective accounts are, almost by definition, likely to be "official accounts" (Bourdieu 1977: 18-19). More straightforwardly, and for a variety of "good" and "bad" reasons, lies may be told. While the documentary evidence which has been discussed above is not always "true" (regardless for the moment of the epistemological issues raised by that word, even when it is placed within cautionary inverted commas), it is at least contemporary with the events to which it refers or relates. More than that, the material is an integral dimension of those events. It is primary rather than secondary material. If it is justificatory, part of a political strategy, this is so much more to the good from the researchers' point of view (provided, of course, that the strategy can be discerned). More than "just" a record, it becomes another aspect of the "action", to be analysed accordingly.

At this point, the possibility of having been in Ballyhightown during these early years of the 1970s, at the time of the intimidation and the formation of the local Defence Association, should, perhaps, be briefly considered. Certainly the problems of retrospective work would not have arisen. Would this have made research any easier? The short answer is that research into political violence would probably have been both unavoidable and impossible: unavoidable in that the ferocity and pace of events during this period were such that they would have rapidly dwarfed any other research interests which a fieldworker might have had; impossible because it would not have been a good time to ask questions, take notes and pay too close attention. I may be overstating the problems, but I do not think so. At best, one would have been limited in the same way as Burton, Sluka and Feldman to a study of attitudes and discourse.

This brings me, second, to the unavoidable problems of sensitivity and confidentiality which have been mentioned briefly above. Oral testimony has a number of problems in this respect: it is essentially private, it may be incriminatory, it is confidential (yet offered to be used, in an anonymous fashion), etc. In the context of a study of violent politics - as opposed to a study of attitudes to violent politics - oral testimony is potentially compromising and may put ethnographer, informant or, indeed, others at risk. In this respect, documentary evidence of the kind to which I am referring has the very great virtue of being already in the public domain. There is, therefore, much less danger of exposing that which discretion might suggest should be left hidden (although there may be a danger of inadvertently drawing attention to things hitherto unnoticed).[6] If it is already public, it should be usable. It does not, however, mean that this is the end of the problem: the issue then arises of how one should use it. In my own case, for example, it would necessitate a decision about whether or not to persist with the legal fiction of "Ballyhightown" or to identify the estate by its real name. Doing this raises the further problem of how one is to write about real and identifiable individuals. At this stage I remain uncertain about this last point, although a number of fictionalising or anonymising strategies suggest themselves (the construction of composite characters, for example).

Third, even allowing for the problems of retrospective research and specific considerations of safety and sensitivity, there are the limitations of participant observation with respect to research into any topic in an urban context which have already been discussed. Access to all relevant areas of Ballyhightown life would simply not have been possible: in particular, tensions between paramilitary organisations themselves, and between them and other sections of the community, would have made life difficult (at the least) and access to a wide enough range of opinion and experience problematic. Ballyhightown is also very big: there are more than 3,500 dwellings and more than 14,000 people. The problems of size and scale are more severe than these figures indicate, however. Many of the people who were active in various aspects of life on the estate during the early 1970s had moved or were otherwise unavailable (some were in prison, for example) by the time of the research. Many more had never lived on the estate at all, their role in Ballyhightown being occupational or organisational. They would have been very difficult to locate. Furthermore, forty per cent of the population at that time - and a very important 40 per cent - had been intimidated out. For a researcher dealing with Protestant paramilitaries, the cooperation of these Catholic ex-residents would have been difficult, and probably impossible, to obtain. Partiality, in both senses of the word, would have been a handicap too severe to address by participant observation alone.

Short of actually carrying this piece of research further, there is little more to be said. To do so would entail the rigorous search of the newspaper records suggested earlier. It would also be sensible to seek out further public documentary sources: transcripts of relevant court cases might be one such. Following this renewed primary data gathering, further interviewing would be necessary, to fill in gaps and shed light on problematic areas, with a range of people inside and outside the estate. Without the framework and focus provided by the documentary sources, this interviewing would be potentially unproductive, insofar as it would be amorphous and too wide-ranging, unreliable, inasmuch as there would be little or nothing to test its "truth" against, and dangerous, because of the risk of lack of direction and ignorance leading to an inadvertent and unwelcome initiation into knowledge about serious crime.

A legitimate objection at this point might be that it is naive to expect to undertake research of this kind without running the last, and very serious, risk mentioned above. I am not sure. However, I am sufficiently unsure about it to have so far done nothing more than contemplate the prospect. Discretion might suggest that the situation stays like this. I will now turn, therefore, to my second case, in which progress has been rather more concrete.

Witchcraft panics in Northern Ireland, 1973-74

Even more than violent politics at the local level, "witchcraft"[7] is a recognisably anthropological research topic. The belief in witches in tribal and pre-literate societies is, in fact, one of the anthropological interests *par excellence*. Recently, there have been a number of participant-observation studies by social anthropologists of modern "witches" (Luhrmann 1989; Moody 1974) or of "traditional" witchcraft beliefs in contemporary European societies (Favret-Saada 1980, 1989; Sachs 1983).

Modern witchcraft or satanism, and traditional folk beliefs (for Ireland, see Jenkins 1977), are only parts of the picture, however. Recent years have seen a wave of social anxiety about satanism in Britain, particularly as it is connected with ritualised forms of sexual abuse.[8] Arising out of fundamentalist Christian propaganda, on the one hand, and developments in social work practice, on the other, there have been a number of what may best be described as ritual abuse "moral panics", the most notorious of which have been in Nottingham and the Orkneys. Comparisons with "witch-cleansing" movements in tribal societies or the witchcraft persecutions of early-modern Europe do not seem inappropriate.[9] In as much as it is possible to judge from the news media, these public concerns have yet to have much impact in Ireland, north or south. There was, however, a collective panic about satanism in Northern Ireland in the early 1970s. At the time of writing I am still collecting material relating to these events, so what I have to say is, of necessity, tentative. The case does serve, however, to illustrate nicely my argument in this paper.

Put briefly, what happened was this. A full-page feature article appeared in the *Sunday News* (published in Belfast) on 5 August 1973, describing a find of dead sheep, which had apparently been ritually-slaughtered, on the Copeland Islands, off the north Down coast. Witchcraft was rumoured. A month later, on Sunday, 9 September, the mutilated body of a child, Brian

McDermott, was found in Belfast in the River Lagan. By 11 September the newspapers were speculating about a "witchcraft" connection.

There was then a brief period of relative silence in the press on the subject of witchcraft. Beginning in late September, however, and stretching on into early December (with the intensity of interest diminishing gradually) the local newspapers of the Province - in Dungannon, Ballymena, Banbridge, Enniskillen, Larne and elsewhere - were full of reports of rumours about the sacrifice of animals, the threatened abduction and sacrifice of children, and other related items. There were also persistent public statements by the Royal Ulster Constabulary (RUC) emphasising the absence of any evidence to support the rumours. Here is an example of the newspaper coverage:

WITCHCRAFT RUMOURS DISTRESS PARENTS
Rumours about witchcraft, now rife in mid-Ulster, are terrifying children and causing grave concern to parents. Stories circulating all over the country claim that witchcraft is being practised in some areas and that a blonde, blue-eyed girl, aged from between three and eleven is to be abducted this weekend for use in a black magic ritual.[10]

Three points should be made here about the newspaper coverage of these stories. First, hardly any of it dealt with anything more substantial than rumour. Second, following some reports in the Belfast daily newspapers in late September, it proceeded as an identifiable wave of press reports in an area south of a line Dungannon-Lurgan-Downpatrick (i.e. south Down, south Armagh and south-east Tyrone) from mid-October 1973. From here, it spread north and west over the following weeks. Third, it clustered around Halloween (October 31), a calendrical festival long associated with ghosts and witches. At the time we are concerned with, adults and children alike were having to accustom themselves to a new and much less spectacular celebration of Halloween, the traditional fireworks having been banned in 1970.

It was not only in conventional newsprint that rumours of witchcraft surfaced, however. Various news-sheets associated with loyalist paramilitary groups also discussed these issues. In fact, one of the earliest appearances of the rumours was in the *WDA News*, vol. 1 no. 32, datable approximately to the end of September 1973, [11] in a story about Catholic teenagers attempting to contact the spirits of dead IRA men. This story also mentioned the McDermott murder and advised parents (in this context, Protestant parents, of course) that the best defence was to send their children to Sunday School and generally bring them up in the faith of the reformation. The consistent theme in these publications, is that "witchcraft" is a problem in Catholic areas:

Fear of the dreaded Black Magic is rapidly spreading through many R.C. areas of Belfast. According to reprots (sic.) received from local residents many cats and dogs are being used as sacrifices in rituals. The priests and the people now fear that these devil worshippers may soon turn their attention to young children. Reports were also received that the children in many of these areas were forbidden to wear Halloween masks, in fact after dusk parents did not allow their children out of doors.[12]

There was, therefore, a general awareness - at various levels, in various degrees, and from various perspectives - of "witchcraft" and "black magic". There was also, it seems fair to say, a fear of "witches". Indeed, my own interest in all of this was first aroused, as a student in Belfast at the time, by a combination of the press reports and the things that people were talking about. As I was an undergraduate erstwhile anthropologist, it was obviously of interest. Some of my material - and indeed some minor ethnography from my home town of Larne and elsewhere - was collected at this time. Most of what I have drawn upon for the brief account above, however, derives from the Belfast Central library's newspaper archive and The Linenhall library's political ephemera collection.

My memory of what it was like to be in Northern Ireland at that time - participant observation of a sort - has, however, suggested further lines of inquiry. In particular, the context in which the rumours grew and spread is worthy of further attention. Anyone who was in and around Belfast during the period 1972-73 will remember the atmosphere of fear and insecurity generated by the loyalist assassination campaign. In particular, as is well-documented in Dillon and Lehane's *Political Murder in Northern Ireland* (1973), some of the most grisly of these murders - typically involving the use of knives and probably carried out by more than one hand[13] - were characterised in the press and elsewhere at the time as "ritualised" killings. Not only, therefore, was the psycho-social ground prepared in a general sense, so to speak, but there were also available specific examples of "ritual murder" to help the fear of witchcraft along. The McDermott tragedy fits into place as the most extreme case - the "ritual" murder and mutilation of a child - around which anxiety could be expected to accrete. A significant boundary - in terms of acceptable violence - had been transgressed.

Nor is this all. At least two urban ethnographers - Burton and Feldman - provide us with first-hand material about "troubles"-related supernatural fears and mythologies. The "black man", ghosts, and banshees were all other-worldly inhabitants of the north Belfast Catholic enclave of "Anro" during Burton's fieldwork (1978:23-8). Significantly for my research, Burton was in Belfast between September 1972 and April 1973; the "black man" rumours, which were in part about black magic and animal sacrifice, were thus current in Belfast some time before they appeared in the newspapers. Burton's material serves to further underline my earlier point about

ethnographic serendipity and extraordinary events; his presence in north
Belfast at the right time must, for my purposes, be regarded as an extreme
stroke of luck. More recent stories about the "black man" have also been
documented in Feldman's study of discourse about political violence in
Northern Ireland, which also includes an account of the McDermott murder
as a "black magic" sacrifice (1991: 81-4). In this context, however, the
stories are very much in the oral history or "contemporary legend" category,
having only limited value for an attempt to understand the events of the
witchcraft panic itself.

Feldman argues that the "black man" stories have their factual basis in
the counter-insurgency tactics of the Parachute Regiment and other British
Army units (the killing of dogs, in particular). This interpretation of
witchcraft-related rumour in Northern Ireland is not new. The only
significant reference to the witchcraft scare which I have so far been able to
identify in the Republican publications in the Linenhall library's collection,
in *Republican News* dated 24 November 1973, makes the connection even
more explicit, and from a somewhat different perspective. Under the heading
"Black Magic - Black Propaganda!", the article opens with a discussion of
the use of accusations of "black magic" against the Mau-Mau in Kenya, and
goes on to say:

> It is not surprising that the same trick should be played on Irish people
> during their struggle. The British counter-insurgency team has been
> working hard on the black magic theme for some time now . . . their
> purpose is clear. It is first to suggest that diabolical influences are at work
> behind the freedom struggle . . . secondly, it is an attempt to impose a
> voluntary curfew on the anti-imperialist population and make them live in
> fear.[14]

The article also makes considerable play of the fact that Brigadier Frank
Kitson, recently in command in Belfast, had been the British Army officer
responsible for devising and implementing the black propaganda counter-
insurgency tactics in Kenya (as he had himself revealed in a recent book on
the subject).

With respect to Belfast, the sensible caveat must be entered that,
particularly in the early 1970's, conspiracy theories were two-a-penny. All
the more interesting, therefore, to discover, in journalist Paul Foot's
investigation of the case of Colin Wallace (an Army intelligence officer, from
Northern Ireland, who was apparently involved in Army "black propaganda"
operations in the Province, left the Army under a cloud and claims to have
been subsequently framed for murder) that Wallace claims responsibility for
creation and spread of the witchcraft rumours. Their purpose? First, to keep
certain areas free of people for security purposes, and second, "to smear the

paramilitary organisations, particularly on the Republican side, with a bit of anti-Christ" (Foot 1990:146).

Apart from a couple of brief flurries of activity in the newspapers in March and November 1974 - one of them involving the discovery of crude "black magic" regalia in a cave in Islandmagee, Co. Antrim - that seems to have been that. There is, however, a considerable amount of research still to be done. I have, as yet, only scratched the surface of the newspaper archives for 1974. There is also some interviewing to be done. Colin Wallace has, at the final time of writing, just been interviewed, but there are other people of varying degrees of significance who appear in the press coverage who may also have useful perspectives upon what was going on. Community and other organisations and the Churches may also be a source of information.

The point, in the context of this discussion, is that here is a topic of conspicuously anthropological interest which simply could not have been researched using traditional participant-observation fieldwork. In the first place, it would have required good fortune of the highest degree for a fieldworker to have been in the right place at the right time: the events were, in their context, truly extraordinary. In this respect, as already suggested, we are thrice blessed to have Burton's ethnographic account of the "black man" stories.

Second, the witchcraft panic was a diffuse, non-local phenomenon in terms of its geography. In this sense, there was no "right place" to be. In addition to Belfast I have collected newspaper coverage from locations as far apart as Armagh, Ballymena, Banbridge, Bangor, Carrickfergus, Cookstown, Downpatrick, Dungannon, Enniskillen, Larne, Lisburn, Lurgan, Newcastle, Portadown and Strabane. Obviously, no fieldworker could have covered all of these locations (and these references are all to one short period of a few weeks in late 1973). Nor is the problem simply one of pragmatics. There is also a conceptual issue here of some importance. Burton's ethnography can be used to make the point. What he interpreted as mainly a pre-occupation of young people, an excuse for lads to escort the girls of their fancy home at night (1978:26), becomes something quite different when viewed in its wider context, which is the six counties as a whole. It is not a strictly local phenomenon; any purely local viewpoint might, at best, trivialise the matter.

Third, the documentary evidence itself - the newspapers and political publications, in particular - is among the most important data anyway. Nor is it simply a record of something that happened (and, indeed, in many of the instances with I am here concerned, it seems likely that it is almost a record of something that didn't happen). The newspapers are an integral aspect of the scare in their own right: they spread it and they helped to create it. Nor could the connection with the Army - in particular the Colin Wallace angle - have been easily elicited by an ethnographer, other than as another rumour.

This is a social phenomenon which was manifest at a level other than the local community and this dimension cannot be ignored in any analysis.

Conclusion

In this chapter I offer a view of anthropology which emphasises its subject matter and conceptual frameworks, rather than its dominant method or research approach, as the discipline's defining feature. I argue that if urban anthropology - in Ireland or elsewhere - is not to overly restrict itself in terms of research topics, a pluralism of method which is something other than "participant observation plus a bit of background documentary research" is required. Specifically, I suggest that we should explore the use of documentary evidence of one sort or another as the primary datum of contemporary social anthropological research, an approach which is quite different to the use of archival material in historically-oriented research.

There are two justifications for advocating modest innovation of this kind. One derives explicitly from the urban context (although it may have further resonance) and one is more general. First, the scale and complexity of social life in towns and cities are major constraints upon the scope and usefulness of conventional participant observation. This is by no means an original argument, but it still deserves attention. It may also increasingly apply to all social life in modern, industrialised societies, whether rural or urban. This is, of course, not an argument for abandoning ethnography, merely a suggestion that we should be aware of its limitations and be ready to consider alternatives where appropriate.

Second, there are some social phenomena or situations for which alternative research strategies are not only appropriate but necessary if research is to be carried out at all. In this paper I have begun to explore three of these, the dangerous, the extraordinary and the non-local. There are likely to be others which I have not considered.

If my arguments are correct, they call for the learning of new research skills and approaches and, perhaps, the consideration of a subtly new perspective on social anthropology's view of itself. They may also lead to the opening up of new avenues of empirical inquiry and conceptual development. That, as much as anything else, is both the challenge and the opportunity provided by urban anthropology.

Notes

The University College of Swansea Research Support Fund and my own Department in Swansea have made resources available for the witchcraft research. The Department of Education (NI) provided a postgraduate award which funded the research in "Ballyhightown" all those years ago. May McCann and Geraldine and Liam O'Dowd deserve more than my thanks for their hospitality during recent research trips in connection with the witchcraft project.

1. For a dated but still useful overview of anthropological analyses of the "troubles" and their social context, see Donnan and McFarlane 1983.

2. See my reviews of these books: R. Jenkins 1991; 1992.

3. This remark should not be misunderstood as a facile characterisation of paramilitary organisations and their members as "gangsters".

4. Although, in my consideration of this topic, non-anthropological sources of analytical insight (e.g. Brown 1975) have been as important as the works cited in the text.

5. This is now available on microfiche at both the Linenhall Library and the Belfast Central Library.

6. And here it should, perhaps, be pointed out that simply finding out about certain things - serious crimes of one sort or another - is problematic enough without the issue of their exposure coming up for consideration.

7. The word is in inverted commas, because of the range of beliefs and practices which are subsumed under its umbrella.

8. See Boyd (1991) for a journalistic and somewhat partisan discussion; at the time of writing, Jean la Fontaine is engaged on a study of ritual abuse on behalf of the British Department of Health (see also, P. Jenkins 1992).

9. This should not be understood, however, as a suggestion that all allegations of ritual abuse are without foundation.

10. *Ballymena Chronicle and Antrim Observer,* 8 November 1973.

11. There are problems with the precise dating of some loyalist publications; this date is my own best approximation on the basis of internal evidence and cross-referencing to events of known date.

12. *Ulster Loyalist*, 15 November 1973.

13. Some of these killings, from July 1972 onwards, marked the beginnings of the activities of the notorious "Shankill Butchers" (Dillon 1990).

14. *Republican News*, vol. 3 no. 13, 24 November 1973.

References

Bailey, F G. 1969. *Stratagems and Spoils: A social anthropology of politics.* Oxford: Basil Blackwell.

Bell, D. 1990. *Acts of Union: Youth culture and sectarianism in Northern Ireland.* London: Macmillan.

Blok, A. 1974. *The Mafia of a Sicilian village 1860-1960.* Oxford: Basil Blackwell

Bourdieu, P. 1977. *Outline of a Theory of Practice.* Cambridge: Cambridge University Press

Boyd, A. 1991. *Blasphemous Rumours: Is satanic ritual abuse fact or fantasy?* London: Fount.

Brewer, J and Magee, K. 1991. *Inside the RUC: Routine policing in a divided society.* Oxford: Clarendon Press.

Brown, R. 1975. *Strain of Violence: Historical studies of American violence and vigilantism.* New York: Oxford University Press.

Bruce, S. 1992. *The Red Hand: Protestant paramilitaries in Northern Ireland.* Oxford: Oxford University Press.

Buckley, A D. 1982. *A Gentle People: A study of a peaceful community in Ulster.* Cultra: Ulster Folk and Transport Museum.

_____. 1984. Walls within walls: Religion and Rough Behaviour in an Ulster Community. *Sociology* 18: 19-32.

Bufwack, M. S. 1982. *Village without Violence.* Cambridge, Mass.: Schenkman.

Burton, F. 1978. *The Politics of Legitimacy: Struggles in a Belfast community.* London: Routledge and Kegan Paul.

Cohen, S. 1972. *Folk Devils and Moral Panics: The creation of the mods and rockers.* London: MacGibbon and Kee

Darby, J. and Morris, G. 1974. *Intimidation in Housing.* Belfast: NI Community Relation Commission.

Dillon, M. 1990. *The Shankill Butchers: A study in mass murder.* London: Arrow.

Dillon, M. and Lehane, D. 1973. *Political Murder in Northern Ireland.* Harmondsworth: Penguin.

Deutsch, R and Magowan, V. 1973-75. *Northern Ireland 1968-74: A chronology of events.* 3 vols. Belfast: Blackstaff.

Donnan, H. and McFarlane, G. 1983. Informal social organisation. In J Darby (ed.) *Northern Ireland: The background to the conflict.* Belfast: Appletree.

Epstein, A L. (ed) 1967. *The Craft of Social Anthropology,* London: Tavistock.

Favret-Saada, J. 1980. *Deadly Words: Witchcraft in the Bocage.* Cambridge: Cambridge University Press.

_____. 1989. Unbewitching as therapy. *American Ethnologist* 16: 40-56.

Feldman, A. 1991. *Formations of Violence: The narrative of the body and political terror in Northern Ireland.* Chicago: University of Chicago Press.

Foot, P. 1990. *Who framed Colin Wallace?* revised ed London: Pan.

Friedrich, P. 1965. A Mexican cacicazgo. *Ethnology* 4: 190-209.

_____. 1969. The legitimacy of a cacique. In M J Swartz (ed.) *Local level Politics.* London: University of London Press.

Gillespie, N., Lovett, T. and Garner, W. 1992. *Youth Work and Working Class Youth Culture: Rules and resistance in West Belfast.* Buckingham: Open University Press.

Glassie, H. 1982. *Passing the Time in Ballymenone: Culture and history of an Ulster community.* Philadelphia: University of Pennsylvania Press.

Gulliver, P.H. 1989. Doing anthropological research in rural Ireland: Methods and sources for linking the past and the present. In C. Curtin and T. M. Wilson (eds.) *Ireland From Below: Social change and local communities.* Galway: Galway University Press.

Hamilton, A., McCartney, C., Anderson, T. and Finn, A. 1990. *Violence and communities.* Coleraine: Centre for the Study of Conflict.

Hannerz, U. 1980. *Exploring the City: Inquiries toward an urban anthropology.* New York: Columbia University Press.

Harris, R. 1972. *Prejudice and Tolerance in Ulster.* Manchester: Manchester University Press.

_____. 1974. Religious Change on Rathlin Island. *PACE* 6: 11-16.

Holy, L. 1984. Theory, methodology and the research process. In R F Ellen (ed.) *Ethnographic Research: A guide for general conduct.* London: Academic Press.

Howe, L. E. A. 1990. *Being Unemployed in Northern Ireland.* Cambridge: Cambridge University Press.

Howitt, D. 1992. *Child Abuse Errors: When good intentions go wrong.* Hemel Hempstead: Harvester Wheatsheaf

Jenkins, P. 1992. *Intimate Enemies: Moral panics in contemporary Great Britain.* New York: Aldine de Gruyter.

Jenkins, R. 1977. Witches and fairies: supernatural aggression and deviance among the Irish peasantry. *Ulster Folklife* 23, 33-56.

_____. 1982. *Hightown Rules: Growing up in a Belfast housing estate.* Leicester: National Youth Bureau.

_____. 1983. *Lads, Citizens and Ordinary Kids: Working-class youth lifestyles in Belfast.* London: Routledge and Kegan Paul.

_____. 1984. Bringing it all back home: an anthropologist in Belfast. In C Bell and H Roberts (eds.) *Social Researching* London: Routledge and Kegan Paul.

_____. 1991. Review of J Sluka *Hearts and Minds, Water and Fish. Man* 26: 576-7.

_____. 1992. Doing Violence to the Subject. *Current Anthropology* 33: 233-235.

La Fontaine, J. 1990. *Child Sexual Abuse.* Cambridge: Polity Press.

Larsen, S. S. 1982a. The two sides of the house: identity and social organisation in Kilbroney, Northern Ireland. In A. P. Cohen (ed.) *Belonging.* Manchester: Manchester University Press.

_____. 1982b. The Glorious Twelfth: the politics of legitimation in Kilbroney. In A. P. Cohen (ed.) *Belonging.* Manchester: Manchester University Press.

Leyton, E. 1975. *The One Blood: Kinship and class in an Irish village.* St John's: Institute of Social and Economic Research.

Luhrmann, T. 1989. *Persuasions of the Witch's Craft: Ritual magic in contemporary England.* Oxford: Basil Blackwell.

Marwick, M. 1982. The Bwanali-Mpulumutsi anti-witchcraft movement. In M. Marwick (ed.) *Witchcraft and Sorcery: Selected readings.* 2nd ed. Harmondsworth: Penguin.

Moody, E J. 1974. Magical therapy: an anthropological investigation of contemporary satanism. In I. I. Zaretsky and M. P. Leone (eds.) *Religious Movements in Contemporary America.* Princeton: Princeton University Press.

Nelson, S. 1984. *Ulster's Uncertain Defenders: Loyalists and the Northern Ireland conflict.* Belfast: Appletree Press.

Pelto, P. J. and Pelto G. H. 1978. *Anthropological Research: The structure of inquiry.* 2nd ed., Cambridge: Cambridge University Press.

Polsky, N. 1971. *Hustlers, Beats and Others* Harmondsworth: Pelican.

Richards, A. 1982. A modern movement of witch finders. In M. Marwick (ed.) *Witchcraft and Sorcery: Selected readings.* 2nd ed. Harmondsworth: Penguin.

Ryan, T. and Kirakowski, J. 1985. *Ballinspittle: Moving statues and faith.* Cork: Mercier.

Sachs, L. 1983. Evil eye or bacteria: Turkish migrant women and Swedish health care. *Stockholm Studies in Social Anthropology 12.* Stockholm: University of Stockholm.

Schneider, J. and Schneider P. 1986. *Culture and Political Economy in Western Sicily*. New York: Academic Press.

Silverman, M. M. and Gulliver, P.H. 1986. *In the valley of the Nore: a social history of Thomastown, County Kilkenny, 1840-1983*. Dublin: Geography Publications.

_____. (eds.) 1992. *Approaching the Past: Historical anthropology through Irish case studies*. New York, Columbia University Press.

Sluka, J. A. 1989. *Hearts and Minds, Water and Fish: Support for the IRA and INLA in a Northern Irish ghetto*. Greenwich: JAI Press.

_____. 1990. Participant observation in violent social contexts. *Human Organization* 49: 114-26.

Swartz, M. J. (ed) 1969. *Local Level Politics*. London: University of London Press.

Thompson, P. 1978. *The Voice of the Past: Oral history*. Oxford: Oxford University Press.

Tóibín, C. (ed) 1985. *Seeing is Believing: Moving statues in Ireland*. Swords: Ward River Press.

Vansina, J. 1965. *Oral Tradition: A study in historical methodology*. London: Routledge and Kegan Paul.

Vincent, J. 1989. Local knowledge and political violence in County Fermanagh. In C. Curtin and T. M. Wilson (eds.), *Ireland From Below: Social change and local communities*. Galway: Galway University Press.

Willis, R. G. 1982. The Kamcape movement. In M. Marwick (ed.) *Witchcraft and Sorcery: Selected readings*. 2nd ed. Harmondsworth: Penguin.

Index